THE PLAY MOVEMENT AND ITS SIGNIFICANCE

NRPA Recreation and Park Perspective Collection

edited by Dr. Diana R. Dunn
Director of Research
National Recreation and Park Association

Education through Play	Curtis, H.	$19.00
Education through Recreation	Jacks, L.	$13.00
Education by Plays and Games	Johnson, G.	$15.00
The New Leisure Challenges for the Schools	Lies, E.	$17.00
Play in Education	Lee, J.	$25.00
Play and Mental Health	Davis, J.	$15.00
Education through Recreation	Johnson, G.	$10.00
The Practical Conduct of Play	Curtis, H.	$19.00
The Play Movement	Rainwater, C.	$21.00
The Play Movement and its Significance	Curtis, H.	$19.00
Playground Technique and Playcraft	Leland, A. & L.	$17.00
American Playgrounds	Mero, E.	$17.00
Leisure in the Modern World	Burns, C.	$15.00
The Threat of Leisure	Cutten, G.	$12.00
The Normal Course of Play	NRA	$16.00
The Education of the Whole Man	Jacks, L.	$12.00
The Challenge of Leisure	Pack, A.	$14.00
Off the Job Living	Romney, G.	$15.00
A Philosophy of Play	Gulick, L.	$16.00
Europe at Play	Weir, L.	$45.00
Music in American Life	Zanzig, A.	$28.00
Music in Institutions	Van de Wall, W.	$35.00
The First County Park System	Kelsey, F.	$15.00
County Parks	NRA	$14.00
Central Park—First Annual Report	New York	$14.00
The Spirit of Youth and the City Streets	Addams, J.	$12.00
Annals March 1910	AAP&SS	$16.00
Municipalization of Play and Recreation	Fulk, J.	$10.00
Luther Halsey Gulick	Dorgan, E.	$14.00
Constructive and Preventive Philanthropy	Lee, J.	$15.00

order from:

MCGRATH PUBLISHING COMPANY
821 Fifteenth Street N.W.
Washington, D.C.

THE PLAY MOVEMENT AND ITS SIGNIFICANCE

BY

HENRY S. CURTIS, Ph.D.

FORMER SECRETARY OF THE PLAYGROUND ASSOCIATION OF AMERICA, AND SUPERVISOR OF THE PLAYGROUNDS OF THE DISTRICT OF COLUMBIA

AUTHOR OF "PLAY AND RECREATION IN THE OPEN COUNTRY" "EDUCATION THROUGH PLAY" AND "THE PRACTICAL CONDUCT OF PLAY"

McGrath Publishing Company

&

NATIONAL RECREATION AND PARK ASSOCIATION

WASHINGTON, D.C.

Copyright, 1917,
By THE MACMILLAN COMPANY.

LC#77-143052
ISBN 0-8434-0431-0

PREFACE

THE author's aim in this volume has been to give a concrete picture of the extent of the development of play in this country, the sources from which the movement has sprung, and the direction in which it is going.

The word "play" has been used in its broadest sense, as the effort has been to give a general picture of those movements which mean a better utilization of leisure time and an increase in the joy of life. Its main emphasis has been upon the play of children, but it deals also to a less degree with recreation for adults. It aims to show the place of school playgrounds, of the municipal playground, the park, and various commercial forms of recreation in a general scheme for a city.

The contention is that with the proper development of play and social guidance in connection with various institutions, especially for children, these need not be dreary prisons, suppressing all the joy in life and slaying the future by their routine, but that organized play can do more to correct the evils of institutional life than any other single agency. The facts brought forward seem to demonstrate that the providing of adequate facilities for the play of children and the recreation of adults does not necessarily make the city more expensive as a place of residence, but may often have the opposite effect, and may also be the chief cause of the growth of the city.

This volume is intended primarily for those who are seeking a general view of the play movement, and its significance in modern life, and it is hoped that it may furnish to superintendents of schools, to social workers, to mothers' clubs, and to playground commissions that information which will be most helpful to them. This, along with "Education through Play" and the "Practical Conduct of Play," is intended to cover the play situation so far as city children of school age are concerned. It will be followed by works on the "Little Children at Home" and "Recreation for Teachers."

Portions of certain chapters of this volume have appeared before in the *Educational Review*, in the *American Journal of Sociology*, in *The Playground*, and in *The American City*. All of these chapters have, however, been revised and amplified since the previous publication. The thanks of the author are extended to these magazines for the privilege of reprinting.

The author wishes also to acknowledge with thanks the many photographs which have been generously loaned him for the illustration of this volume.

CONTENTS

CHAPTER I

	PAGES
THE SOURCES OF THE PLAY MOVEMENT	1–10
THE NEW NEED	3
Disappearance of Child Work	3
Increasing Congestion	6
RESULTS	6
REAL CAUSES	7
The New Psychology	8
The New Social Spirit	9

CHAPTER II

THE PLAY MOVEMENT IN THE UNITED STATES	11–29
NATURE AND EXTENT OF PLAY DEVELOPMENTS	11
THE PLAYGROUND AND RECREATION ASSOCIATION OF AMERICA	15
FIVE PLAY MOVEMENTS	18
THE NEEDS OF THE MOVEMENT	21
OUTLINE FOR PLAYGROUND LAW	23

CHAPTER III

PLAY AT THE SCHOOL	30–61
THREE PRINCIPLES OF PLAY EFFICIENCY	30
CRITICISM OF EXISTING PLAYGROUNDS	31

Contents

	PAGES
MUST SECURE THE MAXIMUM USE OF THE GROUND	33
THE NEED OF BETTER GAMES	36
CLASS ATHLETICS	39
TWO RECENT EXPERIMENTS IN ORGANIZED PLAY	39
THE PLAYGROUNDS OF GARY	40
HIGH SCHOOLS AND COLLEGES	43
THE AGE OF PHYSICAL TRAINING	44
Need of the Girls	45
IMPROVING THE SCHOOL GROUNDS	45
Supplies	47
Equipment	47
PLAY AFTER SCHOOL	50
SATURDAYS AND SUNDAYS	51
ORGANIZED TOURNAMENTS	51
DURING THE SUMMER VACATION	51
WALKING TRIPS	52
THE SCHOOL CAMP	54
THE SOCIAL CENTER	54
Who is to Have Charge	55
TRAINING COURSES FOR THE WORKERS	56

CHAPTER IV

MUNICIPAL PLAYGROUNDS . . . 62–90

THE SOUTH PARK PLAYGROUNDS OF CHICAGO	63
The Children's Playground	64
The Field Houses	64
The Library	66
The West Parks of Chicago	66
Lessons from Chicago	66
THE SYSTEM OF PHILADELPHIA	69
Organized Play	69
The Field Houses	71

Contents

	PAGES
SYSTEM OF LOS ANGELES	71
The Field Houses	72
The Director's House	72
The Summer Camp	73
THE SYSTEM OF OAKLAND	75
The Playgrounds Themselves	75
The Play Directors	76
Work with the Women's Clubs	76
Football	77
Track	77
Rowing on Lake Merritt	78
IS THE MUNICIPAL PLAYGROUND NECESSARY?	79
The Organization of Play	81
Politics	84
The Race Problem	84
Games	85
COLOR SCHEME	85
THE ADMINISTRATION OF THE MUNICIPAL SYSTEM	86
PLAY OUTSIDE THE PLAYGROUNDS	87
An Ideal Organization	88

CHAPTER V
PUBLIC RECREATION . . . 91–116

FACILITIES	92
Location of the City	93
THE PUBLIC PARKS	95
The Park Lawns	97
The Park Waters	102
THE VACANT SPACES	105
THE ROADS AND BOULEVARDS	105
A PICNIC OR CAMP GROUND	105
SOCIAL CENTERS	106
Swimming Pools	107
Skating Rinks	108

x Contents

	PAGES
Dance Halls	108
The Moving Picture	109
The Theater	110
The Beginning	111
CELEBRATIONS	112
Band Concerts and Musical Festivals	112
National Holidays	112
Special City Celebrations	113
City Pageants	114
THE STADIUM	115
THE DIRECTOR OF RECREATION	115

CHAPTER VI

OTHER PLACES TO PLAY . . . 117–145

CITY STREETS AS PLAYGROUNDS	117
The Street and Nerve Strain	118
Street Games	119
Street Dancing	120
Street Germs	121
Street Education	122
Street Surfaces	124
The Automobile	125
The Planting of Trees	126
Closing Streets for Play	127
THE RECREATION PIER	129
A SKYSCRAPER PLAYGROUND	130
THE DOORYARD AND COURT PLAYGROUND	131
VACANT LOTS	136
PLAYGROUNDS ON THE ROOFS	138
The School Roofs	139
Other Public Buildings	140
Apartment Houses and Tenements	141
The City Wall or Promenade	144

CHAPTER VII

PLAY FOR INSTITUTIONS . . . 146–177

ORPHAN ASYLUMS	146
PLAY FOR THE BLIND	153
The Games of the Little Children	154
Play Equipment for the Little Children	154
A Concrete Playground	155
Games of the Older Children	156
Field Events	157
Gymnastics	158
Social Recreation	159
The Graduates of the Schools for the Blind	160
SCHOOLS FOR THE DEAF	161
The Graduates	162
INSTITUTIONS FOR THE FEEBLE-MINDED	162
Colonies for Defectives	165
INDUSTRIAL SCHOOLS	166
Physical Directors	169
Reformatories for Girls	170
PENITENTIARIES	171
A Penal Colony	172
SANITARIUMS AND HOSPITALS	173
INSTITUTIONS FOR THE INSANE	174
CONCLUSION	177

CHAPTER VIII

PLAY IN THE COUNTRY . . . 178–225

WHY ARE THE FARMERS LEAVING THE FARMS?	180
Spiritual Starvation	180
Too Long Hours	182
The Farmer Does Not Enjoy His Work or the Country . .	184
The Lack of Social Life and Recreation	184

	PAGES
WHY ARE THE FARM WOMEN DISSATISFIED?	185
Too Long Hours	185
Lack of Labor-saving Devices	188
Have Not Been Trained for Their Life Work	188
The Decreasing Size of the Families Is Making the Country Less Attractive	189
WHY DO THE BOYS AND GIRLS GO TO THE CITY?	191
MUST MAKE THE HOME LIFE FULLER	192
REORGANIZE THE RURAL SCHOOL	194
THE GROUNDS OF RURAL SCHOOLS	195
PLAY IN THE CURRICULUM	200
THE NEED OF BETTER GAMES	201
THE CONSOLIDATED SCHOOL	202
THE PLAY FESTIVAL AND PAGEANT	203
THE SCHOOL EXCURSION	204
CREATE A SOCIAL COMMUNITY	207
The Rural Church	207
The Social Center	208
WHO IS TO ORGANIZE PLAY AND SOCIAL LIFE IN THE COUNTRY?	214
The County Secretaries of the Y. M. and Y. W. C. A.'s	215
The County Director of Boys' and Girls' Achievement Clubs	216
The County Agricultural Secretary	217
A Paid Organizer of Play	218
THE AUTO	219
THE ORGANIZATION OF THE COUNTY	223
THE NEED OF A SURVEY	224

CHAPTER IX

EQUIPMENT AND SUPPLIES . . 226–244

NEED OF STUDY	228
STEEL OR WOODEN EQUIPMENT	230
THE PLAYGROUND WITHOUT EQUIPMENT	231

Contents

	PAGES
WHO SHOULD MAKE THE EQUIPMENT AND SUPPLIES AND ERECT THE EQUIPMENT?	232
Local People	232
The Machine Companies	232
A Special Foundation	233
The Steel Companies	234
The School Children	235
The State Penitentiaries	237
OUTLINE OF LAW GOVERNING THE MAKING OF PLAY EQUIPMENT BY THE STATE PENITENTIARY	243

CHAPTER X
THE BOY SCOUTS . . . 245–268

THE ORIGIN OF THE ORDER	245
Organizing the Scouts	247
IDEALS OF THE ORDER	247
WHY HAS THE ORDER GROWN AS IT HAS?	250
SCOUTING AS A FUNDAMENTAL EDUCATION	252
Courage	252
Truthfulness	254
Friendship	255
Kindness	256
Democracy	257
Thrift	257
THE SCOUT MASTER	258
WHAT SHALL WE DO WITH THE SCOUT MOVEMENT?	259
THE BOY SCOUT AS AN APPRENTICE CITIZEN	261

CHAPTER XI
THE CAMP FIRE GIRLS . . . 269–284

THE ORIGIN OF THE ORDER	271
THE PURPOSE OF THE CAMP FIRE GIRLS	272
THE THREE DEGREES	274

Contents

	PAGES
THE BLUE BIRDS	277
The Guardians	278
ORGANIZING CAMP FIRES	278
THE SCOPE OF THE MOVEMENT	279
THE TRAINING OF THE CAMP FIRE	279
A CIVIC ENLISTMENT	282
The Girl Scouts	284

CHAPTER XII

THE RECREATION SURVEY . . . 285–310

THE SURVEY A NEW BUSINESS AND SOCIAL METHOD	286
WHAT THE SURVEY SHOULD DISCOVER	286
The Ages of the Children and Young People	287
How the Young People Are Spending Their Leisure Time	288
The Need of the Evening Playground	290
The Need of the Sunday Playground	290
What Are the Young People Doing in the Summer Vacations?	291
Results of the Lack of Proper Play Facilities	291
THE STUDY OF THE EXISTING PLAY FACILITIES	295
Size and Condition of the Dooryards	295
Size and Condition of the School Grounds	297
Vacant Lots	299
Condition of the Streets	300
Parks and their Facilities for Baseball and Tennis	300
Swimming Facilities	301
Dance Halls, Poolrooms, and Saloons	302
THE LOCATION OF POSSIBLE PLAYGROUND SITES	302
Cemeteries	303
Reservoirs	304
Ponds and Marshes	305
Vacant Property	305
Slum Sites	306
Outlying Sites	306
WHAT SORT OF SITES SHOULD BE CHOSEN?	307

Contents

	PAGES
WHERE SHOULD A PLAYGROUND BE LOCATED?	308
WHAT SORT OF PLAYGROUNDS?	309
THE MAKING OF SURVEYS A PROPER FUNCTION OF A PLAYGROUND ASSOCIATION	309

CHAPTER XIII
WHAT IS THE COST?   311–339

COST TO THE CITY	311
Prevention of Accidents	314
The Value of the Land	316
Social Insurance	317
City Advertising	317
Keeping the People in the City	319
The Cost of Crime	323
The Cost of Preparedness	325
COST TO THE INDIVIDUAL	326
Saving from the Tuberculosis Bill	329
Increasing Strength and Efficiency of Life	331
The Rival of the Saloon	332
Saving from the Tobacco Bill	334
The Value of the Summer Vacation	334
INDEX	341

PLAY MOVEMENT AND ITS SIGNIFICANCE

CHAPTER I

THE SOURCES OF THE PLAY MOVEMENT

EVERYWHERE among the lower forms of life the animal goes forward without stumbling unfalteringly toward the goal which nature has pointed out, and from its very first day accomplishes with surprising skill the tasks which its life requires. But in all the higher forms, there are many conflicting instincts pointing in opposite directions and leaving many lines of development to chance or opportunity. It is here that play has come in through biological evolution and taken up its task of training.

As Groos has shown us, it is through its practice in springing upon rolling balls and flying leaves that the kitten has always trained itself to catch mice. The puppy, in his games of tag and playful fighting, has got the practice which enables him later to be a successful hunter. The little girl plays with her doll. She dresses it; she undresses it and puts it to bed; she administers first aid; she gives it all sorts of wonderful medicines, and who shall say that this training is not as good a preparation for her life as housewife and mother as the rules of syntax or the history of Greece. But not only have the animal and the child spontaneously pursued instinctive activities of this sort, but anyone who will observe carefully will notice that the mother cat and dog really organize many of the playful activities of their offspring. Among all primitive peoples also there has been considerable of such organization. There are many who seem to think of the play movement as something that has been recently invented by the great cities of the United States; but in actual fact organized play is much older than organized education and has its roots in the most distant past. In Persia, Greece, and Rome a system of athletics and games was the center of the educational system. It has been through play that children have always acquired their motor coördinations, trained their judgments, and formed social habits. The little actor constantly rehearses his performances for the adult stage and dramatizes all the activities of his elders. In this way he gets the best of practice in the things that he has to do and gains a realization of their social significance.

All methods of education seem originally to have been founded rather closely upon some system of play, but the ideals of asceticism which came in with Christianity tended to make this life and all of its activities seem unworthy, and the whole thought of education was preparation for the next world; the body was regarded as evil, and the flesh and the devil were held to be everywhere in partnership. Coming in with the Renaissance, the body was once more glorified, but with it also came the scholastic learning, and the feeling that all that was worth knowing was stored up in these recovered classics. The cultured man was the one who read and spoke Latin and perhaps also Greek. Education was not expected to prepare for daily life, but to set a man apart as a scholar, as one superior to the common herd who spoke only the provincial dialects.

The New Need

However, we must remember the old time classic learning was for the few and for those who had an abundance of leisure time in general in which to lead a satisfying life outside. The public school is only about a hundred years old, and even twenty-five years ago the school term was usually only four or five months of the year, but now it has become universal in civilized countries, and children are required to attend. Instead of a school year of four or five months, we have a year of nine or ten months. Instead of the three R's, we have a program of fifteen or twenty subjects. The school has taken the time during which the children of all previous ages have played. It has taken the energy with which they have played, and in our cities we have built up the vacant places until there has been little room for play. Play has probably reached the lowest ebb during the last half century that it has ever reached during the history of the world.

DISAPPEARANCE OF CHILD WORK

A second great change which has brought with it a great new need has been the disappearance of the work which children in all previous ages have done. It was from the work with the mother in the home and with the father in the shop and on the farm and elsewhere that the child formerly learned to coöperate and become a member of a social group. It was from this work that children heretofore have always acquired the most of their physical development. At the present time, for the most part, the unions do not allow the father to use his own son as a helper, and our child labor laws forbid children to work before they are fourteen or sixteen years of age. These laws have been made necessary by modern conditions, but it is not so much that work in moderate amounts is harmful to children, but that the work which is available for them is work of a monotonous, uninteresting kind which is destructive both to soul and body for man and child alike. Probably the domestic economy which the girl learned from helping an efficient mother in the home was a better training than it is possible to give her in the school; and similarly, the real work which the boy did with his father was probably better than any that the manual training school can furnish. But these things have gone. We must understand that the physical needs of a boy or girl who has grown up to fourteen or fifteen without any work during the previous years are very different from those of the child who from the time he was eight or nine had much to do about the home, the shop, or the farm.

Responsible citizens often say that they do not believe in play and that the child ought to work, but these people fail to realize, apparently, that the work of children has disappeared, and the choice is not between work and play, but between play and idleness. The process of learning any form of work is nearly as interesting to the child as play. But after the activity has been learned and some skill acquired, it ceases to be either educative or interesting; and the great difficulty with the jobs that are open to children is that they consist for the most part in monotonous repetition of the same process, in which full skill is acquired in a short time. The adult may continue such work and find a sort of pleasure in it, because he realizes how his other wants are to be satisfied from the financial returns of his labor.

But the child who is normally supported at home, does not have this motive.

Work in general can never be as educative as play for children, but the greatest misfortune with the disappearance of children's duties is that nothing has come to take their place, and the child has consequently had much time on his hands for which he had no legitimate use.

The work which the child takes up after he has finished his school is also very different from the occupations of our fathers and mothers, which were so largely in the open air or in the home. Fifty years ago, nearly all occupations outside of the professions, which claimed only a small proportion of the people, demanded much physical exercise. But to-day nearly everywhere the heavy work is done by machines, and the worker becomes an operative. The farmer rides the reaper instead of swinging the cradle, and the spinner watches the power loom instead of manipulating the shuttle and beam himself. The excess in efficiency of the machine over the individual is so great that it makes this result almost certain. A little child in the cotton mills of the South at a power loom may do the work of fifty weavers of the olden time, and a single man with a steam shovel at Panama does every day the work of a thousand men with pick and shovel. Mr. Edison says we are only at the beginning, and that the time is not far hence when we shall put the wool and cotton into one end of the machine and the ready-made garment with the buttons all sewed on will come out at the other end. The work is indoors, often in air overheated and filled with dust, amidst whirling wheels and sundry noises. All the operations are proceeding at a speed which imposes an undue strain upon the nervous system, while the muscles are little exercised.

Many of the positions, for women especially, are injurious to the health and to the welfare both of themselves and of the coming generation.

INCREASING CONGESTION

A third profound change that has come over the world during the last half century has been the rapid migration from the country to the city. Where only three per cent of our population were city dwellers a century ago, nearly fifty per cent is now urban. The work is becoming more and more indoors, and the workers are subject to the nervous strain of the modern city and the modern machine. A large proportion of the children are no longer brought up in the open air in the country, but in tenements where there is no yard to play in, or even place where they can be out of doors without danger. Their nervous systems are being constantly overstimulated by the noises, excitement, and dangers of the streets. Out of these conditions there has grown a need of physical training in the open air such as has never existed in the world before.

RESULTS

The conditions which I have enumerated have been recorded nearly everywhere in a great increase in nervous disorders and in the rapid increase of insanity and the growing instability of the nervous system which is often a forerunner of racial decay. Where no systematic effort has been made to counteract the effect of these conditions, the physique of the boys is not as good as the physique of their fathers.[1] Nearly

---

[1] "During the year 1915-1916, there were 41,168 applications for admission to the United States Marine Corps. Of these only 9.31% were accepted

The Sources of the Play Movement

everywhere that physical examinations are given for army entrance, three or four times as many men are rejected as are accepted. At the time of the Boer war, only about three per cent of the men of the manufacturing districts of England were able to pass the lowest test for admission to the English Army. The same conditions are recorded no less surely in the physique of the girls and women. Nearly everywhere the birth rate is going backward. Motherhood is becoming more difficult and more feared. Women are less and less able to nurse their children. Woman is handicapped by her sex to-day as nature never intended she should be, and as primitive woman never has been. If the tendencies which were ushered in with the coming of the public school, the age of machines, and the concentration of people in great cities, were to go on for a generation or two more, it would mean the elimination of the race. It is absolutely essential that we should surround our children by more wholesome conditions, that we should give to them a more stable nervous system and a more robust physique than the average school child of to-day possesses.

Real Causes

While the conditions that I have enumerated have made necessary a system of play and physical training for the children, it has not been these reasons that have weighed

as fit," and the statistics indicate that this percentage of rejections is increasing from year to year.

While the average span of human life has been largely lengthened during the last two decades by the reduction of infant mortality, better control of sanitary conditions in our cities, and the avoidance of contagious diseases, the death rate at every age above twenty has increased, which seems to indicate that conditions have tended to a lower vitality than was found in earlier decades.

most strongly with the people that have promoted the movement, because these changes have been too dimly realized to be effective. But what nearly every parent and observer of children has seen is that there has been little for the children to do in the cities, and that in this time of idleness the devil has found much for idle hands to do; that the children are an annoyance to their parents and the neighborhood and that they acquire many vicious habits during this unused time. The boys often learn to smoke and gamble and tell and hear many obscene and otherwise dangerous stories. There are many accidents to the children playing in the streets, and their parents are constantly worried about them. In the evenings the pool rooms and dance halls are crowded by young people in the early teens who are in quest of a good time, and find no opportunities except those offered for gain where drinking and the sex lure are the main enticements to the spending of money. The home seems to be disappearing, and crime, despite an increasingly effective police and probation system, is increasing everywhere. Through all of these means there has come a general though dim realization that if we would stem this tide, we must surround the children with a different environment.

THE NEW PSYCHOLOGY

There are many sources from which the modern play movement has sprung, but certainly one of the most important ones is the new psychology. As soon as the attention was turned from the course of study to the child, it was discovered that play was the form of education which nature had devised during the long period of biological evolution, and that the child deprived of play was cut off from those stimuli to which his mind most readily reacted. The new psychology has made the child the center of educational effort and has come to realize that no study can be educative that does not stimulate his mind and arouse it to action.

THE NEW SOCIAL SPIRIT

The conditions described reveal a need which demands the best effort of public-spirited citizens everywhere. In response to this and many similar calls there has arisen during the last two or three decades a new social spirit and sense of responsibility. Probably more money has been given in philanthropy in the United States during the past decade than the entire world has given in all the centuries that have gone before, and there is springing up everywhere a new sense of responsibility for the weak and dependent. Playground and child welfare movements, and movements for the prevention of tuberculosis and of a hundred other evils, have arisen before us as at the wave of the magician's wand, and every year they are doubling in volume. Schools of Social Service and social courses in the universities are becoming common; church organizations are establishing social service departments. The settlements are preaching social democracy, and the socialists are preaching industrial democracy. For every person who was interested in the common welfare twenty years ago, there are probably ten persons today. We no longer expect that the teacher will teach arithmetic or geography alone; but every teacher is becoming a social worker, and the child rather than the course of study has become the center of educational interest. Of this new feeling of social responsibility the play movement is one expression.

During the last three decades there has developed throughout the world such a profound new interest in this situation, and so strong an endeavor to remedy these evils has ensued, that we may well speak of the movement as the Renaissance of Play. The limits of this volume do not permit of a review of the movement in all countries, and I shall content myself with the statement that the play movement is found in all civilized countries on pretty much the level of the educational system and the general social progress of the people.

It is now fairly well developed in every country of Europe. There is a good beginning in Japan and a few sporadic attempts in Korea, China, and India. It seems likely that one of the largest developments of the immediate future will be in South America.

CHAPTER II

THE PLAY MOVEMENT IN THE UNITED STATES

THE play movement in Germany was primarily a physical movement. It is plainly to be seen through the deliberations and discussions of play congresses and play courses that the thing that looms largest in the minds of the promoters is the fitness of the men for military service and of the women to be the mothers of a vigorous race. To this end, also, the sickness of school children must be reduced. One reads very little in German magazines about the effect of play upon the training of character or its effect upon social conditions. In England the play movement has been largely the spontaneous expression of the life of the people and has been for its own sake, though the effect of play on the development of habits and character is always held in view. In this country it has been primarily a social movement from the beginning. We have not been thinking so much of health or physical development, as we have of the social environment. We have been trying to keep the children away from temptations and off from the physically and socially dangerous streets. Each of these points of view is fundamental, and an adequate play movement must form its ideal through the union of them all.

NATURE AND EXTENT OF PLAY DEVELOPMENTS

In a movement of this kind, which is a vital expression of the spirit of a civilization, it does not matter much which city or individual took the initiative, because in the nature of things it was to be. The city of Boston, however, seems to have been the pioneer, as an organized playground was opened in one of its school yards in 1868. But this was a mere sporadic attempt, and the real beginning in Boston came in 1886 and was inspired by the play developments in Germany. The Charles Bank Outdoor Gymnasium was opened the same year. However, there is nothing to show that these beginnings in Boston had any effect upon the action in other cities. The next important date was 1898, when New York City opened some thirty-one playgrounds under the Board of Education. These received abundant notice in the New York dailies, and a number of cities took up the movement immediately afterwards. At the time the Playground Association of America was started in 1906, there were some twenty cities that were maintaining playgrounds. That was ten years ago, and there are now something over five hundred cities, showing that the number of cities has increased twenty-five times during these ten years.

The beginnings have been made in nearly every case by private organizations, usually by the Playground Committee of a Woman's Club or some civic club, but as time has gone on the tendency has been to organize a Playground and Recreation Association, which establishes one or more playgrounds and maintains them until the city is ready to take up the movement. In many cities, even after the city begins to make appropriations, a portion of the funds still comes from private sources.

In the majority of the cities the movement splits into two parts, one being essentially a movement for school children and for the maintaining of playgrounds in school yards.

These are usually under the Board of Education and are carried on during the summer time, and more and more after school and on Saturdays during the school year. These grounds are usually equipped with swings, seesaws, slides, sand bins, and the like, but they are as a rule too small for baseball or the more vigorous games.

The other movement is the movement for municipal or park playgrounds, and these usually come under the Park Board or a special Recreation Commission. The municipal playground, so-called, is usually a rather small and bare plot of ground from two to five or six acres in extent, located in a congested part of the city. It is generally in charge of physical directors. The ones recently constructed in Philadelphia are good examples. These are from two to seven or eight acres in size, surrounded with high picket fences, and have very large and well-equipped community field houses where the work is carried on during the winter and stormy weather. These grounds are amply manned, and the attendance is probably larger than it is at any other municipal playgrounds anywhere. The municipal playgrounds of New York City have been enormously expensive, costing some sixteen or seventeen millions of dollars during the last fifteen years, but they have never secured more than a minimum use or effectiveness in child training. The park playgrounds of Chicago are really a type by themselves, being a combination of a park and a playground rather than specific playgrounds. The playgrounds in the Chicago parks and the municipal playgrounds in Philadelphia and New York have cost much more than any playgrounds outside of the United States.

This new interest in play is finding expression, also, in many other ways besides the establishing of specific playgrounds, and we have the organization of public school athletic leagues under the Boards of Education in nearly all of our large cities; we have a great new interest in athletics in high schools and colleges and a far greater participation in athletic events than there has ever been before. In the vast majority of towns of 5000 or more in population, there is now some attempt at the organization of play. In not a few of these smaller towns there will be found a good sized municipal playground fairly well equipped, and in nearly all there will be some attempt to maintain the playground during the summer months. In many places play is getting into the curriculum of the schools, and certain periods for the small children at least are set aside for the purpose of play. Teachers, more and more, are being expected to organize and supervise the play of the children in the yards, and school buildings are being used more and more for recreation at night as well as by day. Rural schools are securing much larger grounds than they did a few years ago, and in many counties an annual play picnic is now being held. It is becoming the accepted custom with the more progressive industrial plants, and especially many steel companies throughout the country, to furnish a playground for their employees and for the children of their employees. Many of those connected with the cotton mills of the South, and with the steel mills of Pennsylvania, Gary, and elsewhere, have been notable in extent and in equipment. Some of the concerns have also furnished competent supervisors of play. The Playground and Recreation Association of America has been largely responsible for this great development. No history of the play movement in this country would be complete without an account of its activities.

The Playground and Recreation Association of America

The Association was organized in Washington on April 12th, 1906, through the coöperation of Dr. Gulick, and the writer of this volume.

The latter undertook the organization of the Association, saw nearly all of the people to be invited, wrote the constitution, raised the money for the expenses of the meeting, and arranged for the banquet and speakers.

In the election of officers, President Roosevelt was chosen Honorary President, Jacob Riis Honorary Vice-President, Dr. Gulick President, and the writer Secretary and acting Treasurer.

The next day the organizers were received by President Roosevelt at the White House, and met later as a committee to consider and approve a recreation plan for the city of Washington.

The Association was without funds or an office, and it became the duty of the Secretary-Treasurer to raise the funds to put the Association before the public. He had charge also of the general arrangements for the congress in Chicago, and of securing all the speakers and publishing the papers.

At its second meeting the local committee on arrangements in Chicago resolved itself into the Playground Association of Chicago and as such it has continued since that time. The organization of the play festival was a feature of the congress and the first large festival of this kind in America. It has resulted in such a festival being held nearly every year in connection with all of the larger play systems in the country.

The Chicago meeting came just after the meeting of The National Conference of Charities of Minneapolis and was attended by many of their delegates. At the business meeting a Committee on State Laws and the Normal Course in Play were appointed on the recommendation of the secretary.

In June 1906, Superintendent Seth T. Stewart, Chairman of the Executive Committee, undertook the publication of the *Playground Magazine*, having received advertisements sufficient to cover the necessary expense.

In November 1907, the office was moved from Washington to New York and the Secretary was asked to give one-half of his time until the next annual meeting on salary. In the work assigned to the Secretary he was to have charge of making a study of playground sites or a recreation survey of the City of Washington, of the committee on Equipment, of the committee on Play in Institutions, of preparing a historical account of the play movement, and to supervise the work of the committee on State Laws and a Normal Course in play. The report of the recreation survey appeared in the Survey Magazine the next spring. Mr. Lee with the assistance of Ralph Davol of Taunton, Massachusetts, was enabled to secure a law requiring every city of ten thousand inhabitants in the state to vote whether or not it would maintain playgrounds. The normal course in play has been the inspiration of most of the courses that have since been given in the normal schools and universities throughout the country and has probably done more for the movement than any other one thing thus far.

The various machine companies objected strenuously to the committee on play equipment and it was impossible to have a meeting of this committee.

At the fourth meeting of the Playground Association, which was held in Pittsburgh in the summer of 1909, the Secretary was elected Second Vice President, and Mr. Howard S. Braucher, Secretary. Under his able administration the work of the Association has broadened out rapidly, as it now has two associate and nine Field Secretaries. Just before the annual meeting the office had been moved to 1 Madison Avenue, New York, where it occupies a suite of rooms on the ninth floor of the Metropolitan Life Building, and has a considerable collection of play literature, of photographs, and of lantern slides.

The annual budget has now passed the one hundred thousand-dollar mark.

The main work of the Association during the last seven years has been field work in making surveys and the attempt to furnish expert information and guidance to cities. Especially has the Association sought to have them secure an expert supervisor and maintain their systems for the entire year. In securing these results it has worked largely through Chambers of Commerce and other influential bodies.

At the fourth annual Congress of the Association, Dr. Gulick retired from the presidency, and Joseph Lee, who had formerly been First Vice President, was elected to succeed him.

Dr. Gulick is probably the most original social genius in America. His contributions to the early literature of play, to athletics, to the Boy Scouts and Camp Fire Girls, and to education in general have been significant. But his large contributions have not been in the specific field of playgrounds, except in giving publicity to the movement.

Joseph Lee, the choice of the Association for President, was the first man in America to write a book on the subject, and was one of the first promoters of the movement in Boston. He has given largely to it both of his time and money. He has always been, also, the one philosopher of the movement, who had the gift of adequate expression and has said, in his inimitable, epigrammatic style some of the deepest and most significant things that have ever been said about play. If there is any one man who may claim to be the father of the American Playground Movement, it is undoubtedly Joseph Lee.

Through its field secretaries, the Association has tried to keep in touch with developments going on over the country and to stimulate and guide the movement. It seems likely that in the future much of this work is to be done by the extension departments of the state universities.

The extension departments of the Universities of Wisconsin, Iowa, and Indiana, at least, have devoted a considerable time during the last few years to the making of community surveys, and recreation has always been one of the subjects investigated. They have always sought in connection with these surveys to stimulate the development of appropriate facilities. At the University of Kansas, Professor McKeever, at the head of the Child Welfare Department, has carried on campaigns for improving recreation facilities in the cities of Kansas. Especially with the smaller cities, this work under Dr. McKeever has probably been more successful than any work carried on elsewhere.

FIVE PLAY MOVEMENTS

There are really five play movements in America, each of which has its distinct place and is nearly or quite independent of the others. The first of these is what is ordinarily known as the play movement. It seeks to provide a place for play where the children can go during their leisure time, and be off the street and away from the evil influences which they might encounter there, and under the constructive leadership of trained directors. This movement includes the school, the municipal, and the park playgrounds as ordinarily understood, and would be accepted by the majority, probably, as the play movement itself. The inadequacy of this movement is that there are no permanent groupings of the children, that those of different ages and ability are mixed together, and that the anæmic, weakly, and tubercular ones that need the play the most are apt to stay away. Probably playgrounds of this type are not reaching more than ten or fifteen per cent of the children in any of our cities.

The second play movement has been more largely developed abroad than in this country thus far. It is built on the assumption that play is essential to the development of children and that it must be furnished to every child every day. The only way that this has been found possible thus far anywhere is by putting it into the program of the schools. The city of Gary has provided two hours and a half a day of such organized play for the first six grades of its schools, and one hour a day for the next five grades; and probably one hundred or more cities have put a larger or smaller amount of play into their school programs in the last two years.

The third movement, which is quite comparable in significance to either of the other two, has scarcely come to consciousness as yet. It consists in furnishing an adequate opportunity for outdoor life and play to children below the school age. What has been done is only a beginning, and probably not more than five per cent of the little children have been reached. Ultimately this movement must provide a place where all of them can be outdoors and play in safety during most of the time. This must come through the facilities in the yards of the houses, in the interior courts of tenements, and by leaving an open park and playground in the center of all congested blocks.

The fourth movement is the movement for public recreation. There has been more done along this line than there has in the way of providing play for the little children, but this movement is also in a very rudimentary state. This is the more remarkable as public recreation is undoubtedly one of the most powerful lodestones in drawing people to the cities, and keeping them there afterwards. If we were to take all the different recreational features which have been developed in the different cities and put them together, we should get a composite picture of a fairly complete system of public recreation as it may be some time, but such as no one city has thus far realized. This would doubtless seem socialistic to the last degree to most people, but it is unquestionably the direction in which we are moving. Such a development of recreation would mean the providing of social centers in the schools with public gymnasiums, dance halls, and swimming pools either there or elsewhere, the municipalizing of the moving picture and the subsidizing of the drama and the opera, as has been done so generally abroad, the organization of pageants and community celebrations, choral music, and the like, and the development of parks and amusement resorts.

The fifth movement is not a movement for the rebirth of play, but of the spirit of play. We have been overmaterialistic in this country and have constantly forgotten to live.

We must come to see the essential values of life, to work more moderately, and to find more joy in our work. We must find more time to live with our wives and our sons and daughters, to be members of a social community, to do our duty to the state and church and the other organizations which may lay claim to a part of our time. Business must be relegated to its proper sphere and not absorb all the energies of life. That we are beginning to realize this new spirit is shown in the enormous development of pleasure resorts, in the shortening of working days, in the taking of vacations, in the vast increase in attendance at the theater and the opera, and in time spent in travel, automobiling, and in similar ways.

The Needs of the Movement

Any movement is in need of promotion pretty much in proportion as its ideals are unclear or its purposes are out of harmony with public sentiment. The Mazda lamp or the moving picture require little promotion, and probably the greatest need of the play movement at the present time is facts, facts which will show the amount of sickness of school children in cities where play is furnished and in cities where play is not furnished, which will show the physical development of children in such cities; also the amount of delinquency. Statistics such as these have been largely gathered in Germany, but we have few facts of this kind in this country. We need very much an authoritative curriculum of play based on a careful study of games, the child, and the yard, with a view to securing the development of just those qualities which should be trained at the period during which the game is played. We need, no less, authoritative rules for games which are built on careful physiological and sociological studies and which aim at securing the best physical and social results. We need very much a revised and adequate Normal Course in Play which can be recommended to all institutions that wish to establish courses, and through which a practical training for play positions may be given.

Certainly one of our very greatest needs at the present time, for a movement that is rapidly becoming public, is a comprehensive plan for its organization under public control. For it may be taken almost as a corollary that any institution that becomes public must be organized for each political unit in an ascending hierarchy from the township and village to the state and nation. The Child Labor Committee has rendered a great service to the country by drawing up a standard child labor law and seeking to have this adopted by as many states as possible. We have no standard playground law anywhere and no standard form of organization. Probably an adequate organization of play facilities would provide a director of recreation as one of the assistants of the county superintendent of schools in each county; would give such an assistant to the state superintendent of schools, with the proviso that those counties and cities which furnished adequate play facilities should receive a certain extra amount of the primary money over those cities and counties which did not make this provision. And there should also be some one in the office of the National Commissioner of Education whose work it would be to keep in touch with the work over the country and furnish such advice and suggestions and to gather such statistics as would be most helpful. At a meeting in the City of Bakersfield, California, the following outline of a law was recently drawn up. As this seems to embody substantially those features which should be included in any playground law, it is inserted here. If such a law can be passed and enforced in any state, it will probably furnish at once to the children of that state two or three times as much play and physical training as is now being provided by all the playgrounds and gymnasiums within the state.

Outline for Playground Law[1]

BE IT ENACTED IN THE STATE OF . . . . :

FIRST: That hereafter no city or town school shall be built on less than one block of ground or on less than three acres unless a block shall have approximately this area, nor any high school on less than two blocks or six acres of ground, or any rural school on less than three acres without special permission from the State Commissioner of Play and Physical Training as hereafter created in this bill.

SECOND: That no school or schools which already occupy forty per cent or more of the available space of their ground within the building line shall hereafter be enlarged without also enlarging the ground, and that no school shall be enlarged so as to cover more than forty per cent of the space within the building line of its lot.

THIRD: That five hours of play and physical training each week, over and above the fifteen-minute recesses during the morning and afternoon, and the noon intermission, shall become a part of the program for each grade of the elementary and high school.

FOURTH: That wherever any city school system shall provide qualified directors of play and physical training on its

[1] Note this was drawn some time before the New York law appeared.

school grounds after school and on Saturdays, and during the summer, and shall also furnish the equipment, such as balls, bats, and the like, which are essential to play, and such apparatus as swings, slides, and sand bins for less organized play activities, and where a rural school shall furnish a suitable ground of not less than two acres, play apparatus costing not less than twenty-five dollars, with such equipment for play as indoor baseballs, volley balls, tennis nets, and croquet as the conditions warrant, that said schools shall receive one half dollar extra from the state funds for each pupil in average daily attendance, provided, however, that the funds furnished by the State shall not exceed one half of the entire amount expended on play and recreation.

FIFTH: That the office of Commissioner of Recreation in charge of play and physical training is hereby created in the office of the State Board of Education. The incumbent to have charge of promoting the health and physical welfare of the children throughout the schools of the State; to prepare plans and specifications for the laying out and equipping of school grounds and to supervise the conditions of this act. On his recommendation the State Board shall withhold or grant to schools the extra compensation contemplated in this bill, the compensation of this Commissioner to be the same as the other Commissioners of Education.

SIXTH: An appropriation of fifty thousand dollars is hereby set aside to meet the conditions of this law. If, however, a sufficient number of school systems do not meet the conditions to require the entire amount thus appropriated, the balance so accumulated shall be placed to the credit of the appropriation for the following year.

SEVENTH: All other acts or parts of acts inconsistent with

or in conflict with the provisions of this act are hereby repealed.

While the facilities demanded by this bill are somewhat greater than those found anywhere at the present time, they are entirely in harmony with present tendencies. There is no state that demands five hours of physical training throughout the elementary school so far as I am aware; but the law requires three hours a week for all grades in the schools of Germany. About ten hours a week is provided under the Gary system for the first six grades, and five hours a week for the next five grades. A law was passed in the state of Illinois a year ago requiring one hour per week throughout the elementary school, and the new law for the state of New York demands one hour and forty minutes per week for all children of the state eight years of age or older. After September 1st, there are to be three extra hours of organized recreation and physical training.

There has been no state that has offered state aid to work in physical training until this past year, but the law for the state of New York which went into effect September 1st, 1916, provides that one half the salaries of the physical directors required by the law shall be paid from state funds.

So far as I know, there is not at the present time a Superintendent or Commissioner of Education for any state except New York who has as one of his deputies a Commissioner of Physical Training; but in several other states the idea of creating such a position has been considered and a number of state superintendents would welcome such a deputy.

The New York law is probably the most significant advance that has thus far been made in the field of play and physical training in this country.

It is not certain that a law such as the one outlined could be passed in any state. There is no question but that under certain conditions securing the area required would be difficult and perhaps involve a hardship, though the clause permitting the State Commissioner of Recreation to permit of a lesser minimum under certain circumstances should cover most of the difficulties. There may be a question, also, as to how far it is wise to force upon local communities standards for which they are not yet ready, but there can be little doubt but some standard of what is desirable is very much needed at the present time.

School boards are short-lived bodies for the most part, who come and go, and those holding these positions at the present time in any city may have accepted these positions less than a year ago. They came to their new office probably without much knowledge of existing educational movements or requirements, and without any study of the special problem of play. To them, very often a site little larger than the school building seems adequate for school purposes and they hamper educational developments for a generation by securing a ground on which a modern school cannot be operated.

There can be no question but the general tendency at the present time is toward larger and larger control by larger and larger units. The National Government is taking over many of the activities which were formerly held to belong exclusively to the state. The state is taking over functions of the counties, etc.

A law such as the one outlined, if carried out, would provide over two or three times as much organized play as is now provided in any state in the Union, and it does not seem impossible that such a law should be enforced at least as well as many of the other statutes which have recently been enacted. It is certainly much less radical in its nature than the national child labor law which excludes from interstate commerce the products of child labor throughout the United States.

Outside of this development in connection with the schools, there should be some organization and direction, also, looking toward recreation for adults, and this should doubtless be in connection with the city parks, the county parks, state parks, and national parks, in all of which the purpose of public recreation is well-nigh paramount, and where real efficiency can be secured only when this aim is always held in view.

One of the greatest needs of the immediate future is a very careful study of the conditions and possibilities throughout the country. The state of California has led off by making a very definite survey of the recreation facilities of California. Such a survey with a good deal more time and money at its command should be made for every state in the Union, for each county, and for the United States. As every one knows, Switzerland has been supported for a century mainly on its tourist crop, and the tourist crop is undoubtedly worth much more to California than its oranges. In almost every county and township in the United States, there are many spots of beauty which only lack a little initiative and insight for their development as pleasure resorts. These might readily become large financial assets in the districts in which they are placed. A very large proportion of the money of every class of people, especially of those who have most of it, is spent on recreation, and to allow the money to go out of the city, state, or country because the facilities for recreation in the district have not been developed is surely bad business and a poor social policy.

There are great opportunities in connection with our national parks, and also in connection with our national forests, wherever they are located. Within the last few years the government has been pursuing a more enlightened policy in regard to these forests; has been making paths, setting aside particular localities for summer camps and encouraging tourists and campers to make use of the public domain. President Taft recommended that a Bureau of National Parks should be established, and, in the Sixty-third Congress, Representative Kent of California introduced a bill establishing such a Bureau. A special lectureship on national parks has been established in the Department of the Interior, to give free illustrated lectures on the national parks throughout the country so that the people may be encouraged to make a fuller use of them. This is a movement which should be still more encouraged, and booklets should be published showing prospective campers and summer residents how they may reach the described places, secure provisions, and the like. The State of California, in building fine automobile roads into her mountains, and wherever beautiful scenery may be found, has set an example which the rest of the country might well copy.

We are living under absolutely unique conditions so far as play and recreation are concerned at the present time. Some seventeen different states have passed a prohibition bill during the last two years, and there is probability of our securing national prohibition soon. This means that the saloon, which has been the poor man's club in the great city, is soon to close its doors, and that the public must make some provision for this gap in social life which will result. There will be such a demand for social gathering places of the people as has never existed before.

A second tendency which is in the same direction, is the shortening of the hours of labor which is going on apace. More than one hundred thousand workers have secured the eight-hour day within the last six months; and this means that they will have two additional hours for recreation or education. Through our national and state child labor bills we are rapidly taking the children out of industry, and unless we provide for vocational schools and public recreation for these children, it will be a question whether they will be benefited by keeping them from work.

A half a dozen states have recently introduced bills more or less similar to that in the state of New York, calling for a State Commissioner of Physical Training. There is a feeling in every quarter that the people of the United States must be prepared in case of war, and that preparedness lies largely in the ability of the young men of any country to bear the labors and privations and hardships of military life. In other words, preparedness is largely physical preparedness and lies in the physique of its manhood.

CHAPTER III

PLAY AT THE SCHOOL[1]

THREE PRINCIPLES OF PLAY EFFICIENCY

THERE are three ideals of play which are absolutely essential to any large success. None of these ideals are being adequately realized anywhere, but they are no less clear on this account. The first requisite of any adequate system is that it must furnish play to every child every day. This needs no discussion. We all realize that outdoor air and exercise and social relationships are essential to the physical, social, and intellectual welfare of children. They cannot be really well and grow up into vigorous men and women unless they are getting at least an hour or two of such activity every day. The second principle is that the children who are playing together must be of approximately the same age and for most of the time of the same sex. There has been much discussion and a rather general approval of the threefold division of the playgrounds in the parks of Chicago, which puts the boys and girls under ten in one playground, and furnishes another for the older girls, and a third for the older boys. But for real efficiency in play there must be a much

---

[1] For fuller treatment of this subject, consult the author's *Education Through Play*, published by The Macmillan Company.

narrower separation according to age than the Chicago system provides for. Boys of eighteen do not care to play with boys of ten or twelve, nor even with boys of fourteen or fifteen. In order to secure real efficiency in play up to the age of eighteen, there must be not more than two or three years' difference in the ages of the children. Children in all of their natural groupings tend to come together and to form friendships and to carry on enterprises with other children with just about this amount of latitude in regard to age. The third principle is that the same children must play together every day. Friendship is an absolutely essential condition of all good play, and where the children are strangers or indifferent to each other, the activities are always likely to degenerate into horseplay or loafing. If the games that are played are team games, it is impossible to secure a team spirit unless the same children play together frequently.

Criticism of Existing Playgrounds

The existing playgrounds, whether they are municipal, park, or school playgrounds, are not adequately realizing any of these ideals. None of them are securing the daily attendance of much more than ten per cent of the children, as can easily be seen; for a playground that has from four to six thousand children living within a radius of half a mile will seldom have an attendance of more than four or five hundred children a day, and often the attendance is much smaller than this. A study of this attendance will also show that it is the vigorous and capable children who excel in the athletics and games who are coming for the most part, while the weakly, the anæmic, and the tuberculous children who need the outdoor air and exercise the most, but who are least efficient in its activities, are the ones who are staying away. This would indicate that on the ground of attendance alone our present playgrounds are not more than ten per cent efficient.

But the problem of attendance and use efficiency is much more complicated than this. All through the school year the playground is empty during the school day, and during the summer it will have perhaps forty or fifty at nine o'clock, a hundred at eleven o'clock, one hundred twenty-five at two o'clock, three hundred at four o'clock, and five hundred at five or six o'clock. Under these conditions there will not be enough children to utilize the space or the equipment during the forenoon, and during portions of the afternoon the space and equipment will be inadequate. It is impossible to provide either direction or equipment that will not be excessive for fifty and that will be adequate for five hundred. Hence, such a playground must always be over-equipped and over-supervised for a part of the day and under-equipped and under-supervised for another part.

Again, as we are aware, none of our playgrounds are separating the children by those narrow age limits within which children ordinarily associate with each other for purposes of play, and the range of age from ten to twenty-five is far too great to secure efficiency.

But probably the most serious criticism is that the same group of children so seldom get together. Those who are there to-day are different from those who were there yesterday or who will be there to-morrow. The attendance is one of kaleidoscopic change with no usable core or nucleus which is permanent.

Must Secure the Maximum Use of the Ground

Most of our public schools are provided with very inadequate grounds. Many of these are scarcely sufficient for all the children to assemble upon them at once, much less for them to play. Often the other available spaces are also very limited. If any such provision for play as has been indicated is to be furnished, all such grounds must have a maximum use. However, the policy has often been to use these grounds as little as possible, and the children have been forbidden to assemble there before 8 : 45 in the morning and have been required to leave the grounds by 4 : 15 in the afternoon, giving an actual use efficiency of about a half an hour a day. So far as school children are concerned, the municipal playground during the school year can never meet the proposition for a large number of reasons. In the first place, it involves a double trip of a child to go to the school, return home, and afterwards go to the playground, and this extra effort will be sufficient to deter a large proportion of the children from going. But the school day in Europe is nearly everywhere at least an hour longer than it is in America, and educators are very generally talking the longer school day here. If the school day is lengthened, it will be practically impossible for the children during the school year to use the municipal playgrounds at all except at night, which means that they can never be used adequately more than five or ten per cent of the time.

The hours that are available for play are from eight o'clock in the morning to ten o'clock at night, making a total of fourteen hours. Our present grounds, if used to their full extent during all of these hours, would scarcely provide for the play that is needed by the children and adults who surround them. Hence, every system must seek either to greatly enlarge the number and area of its playgrounds, or else to secure some such maximum use of its present grounds. If play is put into the curriculum of the school, it will be possible to furnish play to every child, to use the playgrounds to the maximum extent, to have children of the same age play together, and to have the same children play together every day; and it is not believed that these conditions can be met in any other way.

Play may be put into the curriculum in either of two ways: The time may be taken from the school day as it now is, or the extra time may be added to the school day; and, it would appear, we should be justified in doing either of these things. In the first place, for the younger children at least, our present school day is much too long, if it is to consist as it has in the past of purely scholastic tasks for which the attention of the child is very limited. The efficiency studies that are being made in the cities are showing that the child makes approximately the same progress on fifteen minutes a day that he does on forty-five minutes a day in arithmetic and a number of other subjects. It is also becoming increasingly evident that a considerable portion of all that we have taught children in arithmetic never had any place in a course for children, and pretty much the same thing can be said of geography and most of the other subjects. There is a certain minimum of knowledge and skill in arithmetic, geography, and grammar which is essential, and training beyond this point brings practically no return. At a test which was recently taken by some two thousand teachers in one of our larger cities, it was found that over three per cent of them could not locate accurately the city of New York, and that for the smaller cities the percentage of failures was vastly greater. It is certainly extreme to require of children a definiteness of knowledge in this sphere which their teachers do not possess.

We have been seeking in the past to make children perfect in the arts of adults, but we are coming to see that children are not interested in the arts of adults and that they cannot be trained into interest or mastery of adult points of view or knowledge. We must train children to be more successful children rather than adults; the day must prepare for the morrow and not for the distant future. Success in plays and games has always been the chief accomplishment of childhood, and the skill which gives most distinction and is most coveted is that skill. We must all realize, too, that leisure is increasing very rapidly throughout the world through the great increase of wealth and mechanical power, the efficiency movement, and other things. It is just as necessary to prepare for the leisure time of life as it is for the work time of life, and any person is imperfectly educated who comes up to maturity without having acquired skill and enthusiasm for some form of sport. Wherever the half-day session has been tried under suitable conditions for the younger children, it has been found that they make quite as good progress on the half day as they do on the whole day at the time and that they also acquire better methods of concentration. Our present school day always tends to develop in children a habit of inattention and listless work which make any large accomplishment difficult and tend to train the person to inefficiency. We shall be entirely justified in taking the time that is needed for play out of our present school day, for our younger children at least.

We shall also be justified in adding it to the school day, if this seems to be the best method. Superintendent Wirt of Gary says he has taken "the street and alley time" of the children and devoted it to education. He says that in the early years the children had chores to do or helped in the home, so that it was necessary for them to go home at four or thereabouts and attend to these duties. But these have disappeared and the children are mostly loafing about the streets in the time after school, and often where they are subject to temptations. No one who has observed children carefully in any city during this time between the close of school and supper, has found that any considerable percentage of them were doing anything that was worth while. It will be an advantage for the children to have a longer school day, if they are not thereby overworked.

THE NEED OF BETTER GAMES

Nearly all of our present games have grown up under country conditions, and most of our school sites have been acquired by school boards who did not appreciate the value of play. Country games and city school yards do not go well together. If we are to have anything approaching adequate play in the existing yards, we must have a different type of game. There are four characteristics which any good game for school use should possess: First, it should be a game which provides for a large number of players on a small amount of space; Second, it should be good exercise; Third, it should be reasonably safe; Fourth, it should be a game that will be continued after school days are over. We generally agree in this country that baseball is our national game, but baseball is almost purely a schoolboy game. We begin it at about the age of twelve and discontinue it by the time we are twenty-five. It can never meet the needs of school children at most of our city schools, because it takes too much space, and the hard ball is dangerous in a crowded yard. Pretty much the same criticism may be made of football. Basket ball would seem to meet conditions better, as it does not require a large amount of space. But basket ball is also discontinued in the late teens or early twenties; and, as it is now played, it is undoubtedly our most dangerous game, as the strain of the play is almost continuous. No fellow without a vigorous physique and much preliminary practice undertakes to play football. But young girls who have never taken part in vigorous games before, often get upon the basket ball team and play frequently by boys' rules and for long halves, and nearly all of them are injured. If you play football, you may have a sprained ankle or a broken leg. These will soon mend, but a strained heart is a much more serious thing.

Undoubtedly the best game that we have for school use is the game of volley ball. Volley ball is played by girls nearly as much as by boys, and can be played with pleasure and profit every month of the year. Children will begin to play at eight or nine and will continue until they are sixty or seventy, and every boy and girl can play without danger. It is also the best corrective we have of all the bad postures of the schoolroom, and it is more economical of space than any of our other games. It is adapted to school use because a class of forty can be taken into the yard to play volley ball as a regular exercise, and by having two games going on at the same time all the girls and all the boys may have a perfectly good period of physical training, a good time, fresh air, and a social occasion all at once.

A second good game is the game of indoor baseball, which at the present time is mostly played outdoors on a thirty-five foot diamond. This game is played by the girls nearly as much as by the boys. Children will begin to play it three or four years younger than they will the regular game, and will continue to play it for forty years longer. With the large, soft ball the game can be played without discomfort during two or three months of the spring and fall when the sting of the regular ball would be insufferable. The ball does not break the windows and does not injure the children who are struck by it, and again, any class can be taken into the yard to play indoor baseball, or its variation, long ball, as a regular class exercise. The number of players per acre in the different games is as follows: baseball, nine; football, eleven; hockey, eleven to twenty-eight; basket ball, one hundred eighty; indoor baseball, two hundred forty; volley ball, six hundred.

There are comparatively few schools in this country that have not large enough yards to put volley ball and indoor baseball into the curriculum for the older children, as it takes only a fifteenth of an acre to provide for the play of forty children in volley ball, and only a fifth of an acre to provide for forty in indoor baseball. In other words, a fifteenth of an acre if it were used during a six-hour school day would allow two hundred forty children to play volley ball for an hour every day, or one fifth of an acre would allow two hundred forty children to play indoor baseball or long ball for an hour every day. These are not large areas, and such an amount of ground is already present or can be secured for most schools.

In the small yards that are found at most of the schools, it is almost impossible to have any play that is worth much if all the children are to use the yard at once, because there are too many children, and the children of both sexes and all ages are thrown together. If, on the other hand, the yard is used during every hour of the day and classes play there as classes, one sixth of an acre will be as adequate for the school as an acre would be if all the children were there at once. This arrangement also meets all the conditions that are essential to satisfactory play. It provides time and opportunity for the play of every child every day; it allows the children of approximately the same ages to play together; and the children who are already acquainted and associated in other interests are also brought together in their games. Under city conditions this problem can probably be met in no other way at present.

Class Athletics

Class athletics were first begun in New York City in 1906 when Dr. Gulick was in charge of physical training. Along with the Public School Athletic League they are now organized in most of the larger cities and are being conducted under the physical training authorities. In Oakland, under Mr. Nash, nearly every boy from the fifth grade up is training in the three events required for the standard button, and the records from year to year show a steady increase in the physical achievement of the children. There are few things that have in them greater possibility for the improvement of the physique, grace, and health of school children than activities of this sort.

Two Recent Experiments in Organized Play

During the last three summers, there has been conducted in connection with the summer school of the University of

California, and in 1916 at the University of Wisconsin, an experimental play school, under the direction of Professor Hetherington. This is essentially an attempt to carry out the ideal of Froebel, of education through the self-activity of the child, up through the grades of the elementary schools. The school has sought to develop training along nearly all lines fundamental to education, through the activities in which the children have engaged. It has met with much favorable comment from those who have visited the school.

A second very interesting experiment has been the plan which has been carried on in the first three grades of a number of schools in Oakland, Los Angeles, and Boston. This has been a method whereby the classes of these lower grades have been divided into two sections, and one section has been in the playground while the other has been in the classroom for a part of the day at least. Thus the teacher inside has had small classes to deal with, and all of the children have spent a half of their time in organized play.

THE PLAYGROUNDS OF GARY

But Gary has done these things best. Gary has furnished adequate playgrounds, adequate time for play, and adequate supervision. The first school in Gary was the Jefferson, which has a ground of two acres. The second school was the Emerson, which secured five acres, afterward enlarged to ten. The Froebel school had eleven, enlarged later to twenty-one, and the fourth has had twenty acres from the start. These large areas are not solely playgrounds, as they contain park features for the people and school gardens as well as playgrounds and athletic fields. These playgrounds will be found to contain from one to five classes during practically every period of the day when the weather is pleasant, and during the cold or inclement weather the same classes will be found in the gymnasiums and swimming pools, which are a feature of each of the schools. One quarter of all of the teachers are physical trainers, and all of them have had an excellent preparation. During the first six years at Gary the children have two hours and a half a day, two one-hour periods and one half-hour period, for play and physical training, and during the next five grades they have one hour each day. Gary has put the emphasis in physical training upon the first years, where it obviously belongs. It is also possible by the Gary arrangement of classes to so assign the work of any weakly or anæmic child as to give him two or three more periods in the playground each day, if his health seems to require it.

Since 1914 Superintendent Wirt has spent a week of each month in installing the Gary system in the City of New York. One school was put on the Gary plan in 1914–1915 which proved so successful that twelve more schools were put on this basis in the fall of 1915. It is very difficult to carry this out in New York because the school grounds and shops are so very inadequate for the purpose, but it is planned to extend the system to every school where there is overcrowding and where the facilities make it possible, with the probability of its being put into most of the schools in time.

Probably from a hundred to two hundred cities have put play into their programs during the last two years, or, more correctly, they have put play time in. There has been an extra play recess in the morning, and in the afternoon for the little children, and in many cases at least one extra play period for all; but in general it is to be feared that this has been merely an extra recess which has not been much more effective than was the traditional one.

When any one speaks of the need of play periods for children, there are always many who take the position that these are not needed because the children have abundance of time to play in any case. It is true that children do have time to play, but it is also true that ordinarily they do not play during this time. Any one who will observe the groups of children on the school grounds at almost any recess will surely find that not more than twenty per cent of them are playing, and many of these are playing at games which have little value. The only organization which will meet the need will be one in which all the children, say of the seventh grade, will go out to play volley ball, or indoor baseball, or some other game, for a regular period the same as they would take a lesson in gymnastics. Such a period of gymnastics is now being furnished in nearly all schools having gymnasiums, but a period of play in the yard will have the advantage over the gymnasium period that it is in the open air, that it is recreation as well as exercise, and that it promotes social groupings and the formation of friendships. With such an organization of the play and with a series of tournaments running through the school year, it ought to be possible to give all the children a fairly good physique and to bring them through school in robust health.

While we have no very definite testimony in this regard, what evidence we do have seems to indicate that, where play is organized at the school and fundamental interests are appealed to, the children become more regular in their attendance and do not drop out so early to go to work.

Pushball at the University of Wisconsin

High Schools and Colleges

There is a very general increase in the facilities for gymnastics and athletics that are being furnished at high schools all over the country, and a larger and larger proportion of the young people are taking part. Nearly all of our new high schools have large gymnasiums and many of them good-sized swimming pools. They are also securing much larger grounds than they had a few years ago. It is to be feared that in many cases these are still for the almost exclusive use of the school teams; but a better time is in sight.

In the colleges, also, there is a very rapid increase in the facilities for gymnastics and athletics, and probably twice as many students are taking part this year as did even five years ago. In the University of Pennsylvania every student is required to learn to swim and take part in track athletics along with his gymnastics. The ideal of the college student now is a vigorous, healthy young man or woman such as might be represented by the football man or the tennis girl. It is no longer fashionable to be a semi-invalid. When games are organized on the college campus there is no difficulty in getting college students to take part, and I am beginning to feel that perhaps the playground movement began at the wrong end, and that it should have begun with the university instead of with the elementary school because the universities make the fashions, and whatever becomes popular there soon appears lower down in the educational system.

"Statistics of Harvard for the year 1915–1916 show that 1623 students have engaged in major and minor sports this year, the largest number in the history of the university. The increase was 299 over last year. Football proved the most popular, with 365 names enrolled, while 247 athletes went out for track and 252 played tennis."

The Age of Physical Training

Thus far we seem to have gone on the supposition that the child was born a spiritual being and that the physical side of him developed later. Thus we have made no provision for physical training during the elementary school for the most part and have first made a beginning in the high school or the college. But every one knows that as an actual fact the child is born a little animal, that his physical attributes are the first to develop, and that they come to maturity far earlier than any other of the human qualities. Everything seems to indicate that physical education should be the first education.

There is no later time when physical achievement means so much to the child as it does in the period before twelve, or when skill and prowess along physical lines are so much desired or so easily acquired. The motor restlessness of small children is proverbial, and everything indicates that nature intended that they should be almost incessantly active. It is the inactivity which is demanded by the school which makes it distasteful to many children. Play is the first form of education and it should have its largest place in the early years of life. Probably we should have two or three hours a day of organized games during the first few years of the elementary school, and this should diminish with advancing years to a minimum of one hour a day, which is about as little as adults can get along with and maintain vigorous health.

Upper — South Worcester Gardens
Lower — Volley Ball at the Sargent Camp

NEED OF THE GIRLS

Thus far most of the physical training has been for the boys. But from every point of view the girls are our great problem. Boys have always been encouraged by their parents and the community to play. Skill in running and jumping and throwing and similar activities confer a distinction upon the boy which they do not confer upon the girl. Boys will play whether playgrounds are provided or not, but girls sit about and gossip or play jackstraws if no provision is made for them. Physical development is also more significant for women than it is for men. Man's work has largely fallen to machines, but the same change has not taken place in the work of women. Vigorous health and a good physique are always among the chief charms of women. In a series of studies on the feminine ideals of college men, a good physique appeared more often than any other characteristic.

Woman's work has not changed so much as man's, and childbirth has become more and more difficult with succeeding generations. Sterility is increasing, a larger and larger percentage dread childbirth, and more and more women are unable to nurse their babies. For all of these reasons the school and the community need to put very much greater emphasis on play and physical activities for girls, especially during the period below puberty.

IMPROVING THE SCHOOL GROUNDS

It must be evident that if most schools are to provide for the physical welfare of the children, they must secure more adequate grounds than they now have. A block is normally a minimum amount of space for any school. But a block does not represent any standard amount of ground; it varies from about an acre and a half in some cities to eight or ten acres in others. It may be that in some cities of the ten-acre type a full block cannot be afforded, but it is certain that in any city where a block is not more than two or three acres in size the school should have the entire area. This will not be easy in every case, of course, for many schools have been built into business or residence blocks without grounds. In some cases two or three schools may be combined in such a way as to secure a larger ground and a modern school, and to give up space which will nearly pay for the change. Our whole conception of education has developed greatly during the last two decades, and nearly all of these old schools that have been built without playgrounds are as unsatisfactory inside as outside for the purposes of a modern school, and should be abandoned in any case. A plot of ground can be utilized very much more economically by a large school than it can be by a small school, as a school of eight rooms cannot well get along with less than a block, while a school of thirty rooms where the classes use the ground at different times during the day may well furnish nearly twice as much space per child on the same area as a school of eight rooms, where all the children have their play periods at the same time. In a number of cities bond issues have been voted during the last two or three years for the purpose of enlarging existing school grounds, and a vast number of other cities must do this in the future until an entire block has been secured.

The school building should be placed at one end of the block and not in the middle of it, as has been done in so many cases. The playground is not usually large enough to be divided so as to separate the boys from the girls, and this division should not be necessary in school grounds if the play is adequately supervised. The ground should be fenced unless it is very small.

Most of the school grounds of the country are in poor condition for play. The first requisite is that the ground should be level, and many school grounds are side hills that have never been graded. There are many also in which the dirt from the cellars has been left in heaps, apparently without any thought of adapting the ground to play purposes. There are many grounds also which are surfaced with brick or coarse gravel, both of which are nearly impossible surfaces to play upon. Many grounds have been washed and gullied by rains till the projecting roots of trees constantly trip the runners. Often they are littered with brickbats, paper, and ashes. As a matter of course every school ground should be leveled, surfaced in some suitable manner, and kept in a tidy condition.

SUPPLIES

There has always been opposition to furnishing baseballs and similar equipment to children, and the feeling has generally been that the children should provide these things themselves. But these are the most essential equipment, and, if organized games are to be carried on in the school yard, they must be furnished by the school.

EQUIPMENT

The necessary provision for athletics should be made on every school yard. There should be a running track along the edge, a jumping pit both for the broad and high jump, and a horizontal bar with sand underneath where various stunts can be done. The interest in athletics of this type probably reaches its climax before the age of puberty and not during college days, as we have seemed to think. There should also be in every school yard a little simple equipment, a few low swings in some secluded part and parallel to the fence, a good-sized sand bin in some retired corner under a tree or around a tree, a slide, and perhaps a giant stride.

During the fall of 1915 a boy was injured in falling from a swing in Tacoma, Washington. The parents sued the school board and secured a verdict against them which required the school board to pay damages for the injury received. This case resulted in the removal of play equipment from the yards of many schools in the state of Washington.

A similar case occurred in the city of Milwaukee where the judgment was against the claimant on the basis that the school in maintaining playgrounds was performing a government function and was not liable.

On the surface neither decision seems to correspond with accepted practice in such matters. It is reasonably evident that if a boy climbs on a swing frame and falls off, the school board is no more responsible for his action than if he had climbed into a tree or upon the school building and fallen. There can be no more reason for taking out play equipment on account of such an accident than there would for the removal of the trees or the school building.

If, on the other hand, a boy is struck by a swing which another child is using and it would appear that the swing had been improperly placed, subjecting the children to undue risk, the school board should be responsible.

If, again, the boy while swinging properly in a swing is injured by the swing frame or rope breaking because the frame had been improperly constructed or the rope improperly spliced, it would seem that the school board should be responsible just as a city is responsible if a pedestrian falls through a hole in the sidewalk or walks into an open culvert.

If, on the other hand, the court claims that play equipment is inherently dangerous and that the school board is responsible for all accidents resulting from its use, the court is certainly assuming an amount of knowledge on the subject which it does not possess. During the last few years throughout the country industrial concerns have generally been required to pay for accidents suffered by their workmen whether the workman himself was directly responsible or not, but there has been no attempt thus far to apply this principle in the educational field. This would require the school board to pay damages if a student was injured in football or baseball, or in pole vaulting, no less than if he were injured on the play equipment.

There has been a general tendency also, to hold industrial concerns liable for diseases contracted through the conditions of their work. If this principle should be applied to the school, the school would be liable for most of the measles, diphtheria, scarlet fever, and whooping cough which occurs in the community and also for a large part of the anæmia and tuberculosis. On this basis the school board would be compelled to demolish its school buildings at once and erect play equipment and public playgrounds everywhere.

Handball is coming in all over the country, and in California especially handball courts are now being put on nearly all school playgrounds. In the city of Tulare they have made a unique utilization of their school building as a piece of play equipment, as they have put screens over all the windows flush with the building itself so that the children now use the entire periphery of the school for handball courts. The building is of red brick, and the marks of the balls are scarcely discernible.

Another piece of apparatus that might well be added to most school yards, especially yards where there are sheds, is a horizontal ladder. Children of all ages love to walk on their hands along a horizontal ladder. Where there is a shed or similar framework that serves as a basis of attachment, the cost of a horizontal ladder is negligible, and there are very few pieces of apparatus that give so much good exercise at so little cost.

PLAY AFTER SCHOOL

Wherever school playgrounds have been kept open after school, as they are coming to be in a large number of cities, the attendance has probably been as great as it has been during the summer vacation when they were maintained as summer playgrounds, and this use is certainly justified by conditions. There is also every reason for lighting the school grounds at night. The cost of this will be only a trifle in most cases, and the working boys and girls will thus be enabled to play volley ball or basket ball or indoor baseball or any such game after their day's work is over. This provision for the sports of these young people is one of the burning problems in all our cities. To this end grounds for baseball, indoor baseball, and tennis should be provided in the most accessible locations.

SATURDAYS AND SUNDAYS

The school playgrounds should be open as a matter of course on Saturdays so that the children during their leisure time may have the facilities for play. It seems possible that in the near future we shall also open them on Sunday afternoons and evenings as well. The school grounds in Gary are open Sunday afternoons and evenings at the present time. In Oakland and Los Angeles they are or have been open Sunday afternoons, and the tendency is everywhere for a freer use of Sunday for play purposes.

ORGANIZED TOURNAMENTS

In order to secure effective organization of play for the summer vacation, it seems to be almost necessary that tournaments should be organized in the schools during the spring, and that a regular series of games in indoor baseball, volley ball, tennis, and any other activities in which there is especial interest at the time, should be arranged for. These games should be supervised during the summer by the Director of Physical Training. It is not usually difficult to secure medals or pennants for the winners of such tournaments. It would be an admirable thing if the city would offer a pin or button to each of the boys or girls who made a certain record.

THE SUMMER VACATION

The weak point in the play situation so far as the schools were concerned has been until recently with the school organization. It went out of existence in June at just the time when playgrounds were most needed; but, at the present time, in nearly all the larger cities at least, the domestic science, manual training, gardening, and certain classes for backward students are maintained during the summer. It is now a very simple matter to add to these activities the organization of the children's play, and in fact there are many things which seem to point to a four-term school as a probability. If this fourth term should consist almost entirely of nonscholastic outdoor activities such as athletics, play, boy scouts and camp fire girls, gardening, manual training, domestic economy, school excursions, and camping, and the attendance of the children was required for the fourth term, the same as for the others, it would furnish to every child a training that might be very nearly ideal.

WALKING TRIPS

When we consider the number of children who go out under the Wandervogel, and the school journeys, and the various private organizations for promoting walking trips that there are in Germany, it seems likely that the amount of recreation and physical exercise in the open air which is offered through these trips is very nearly equal to that offered by the playgrounds themselves. We have not thus far promoted walking in this country to such an extent as has been done abroad, but recently through the boy scouts and camp fire girls, and many private schools and playground departments in the different cities, we are developing a real interest in walking such as we have not had before. Such trips into the environs of Boston, Chicago, and Philadelphia have been planned with much care, and have been a regular feature of the athletic life of these cities for several years. There are also many smaller cities where walking trips are taken under

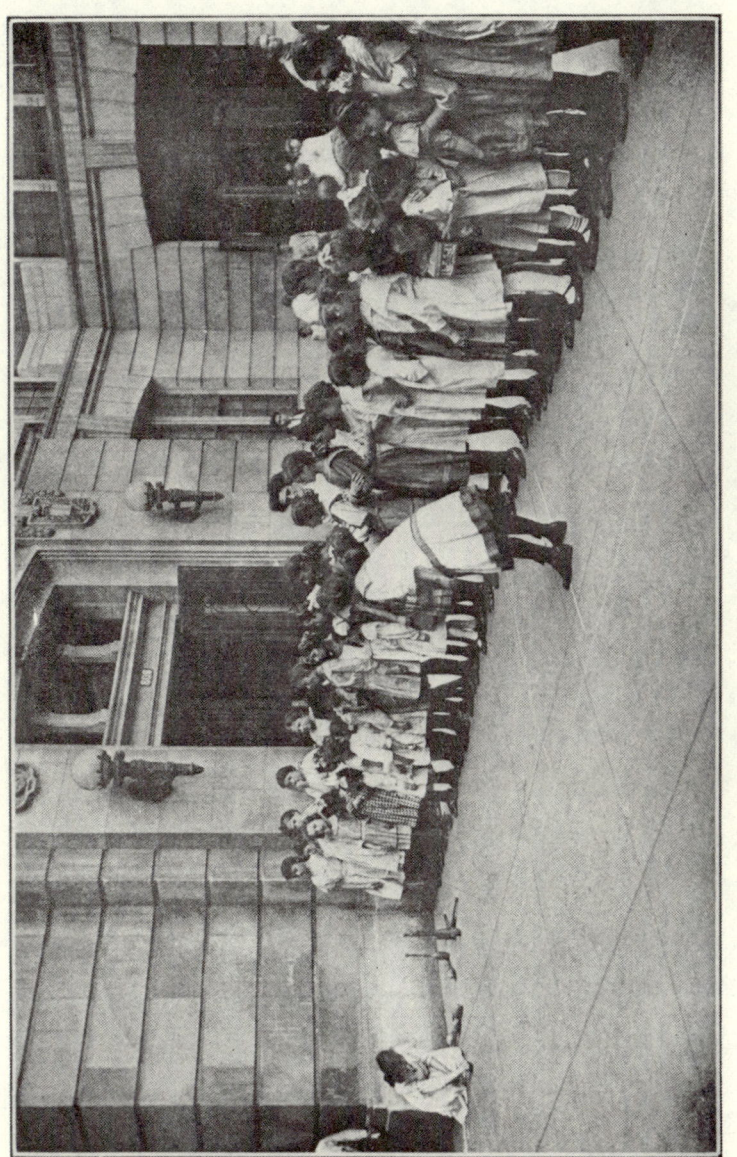

Girls' Games, School Playground, New York City

the direction of the play authorities, but in nearly all cases, these are for only one day or at the most two days' duration, as we have not thus far undertaken any of the long trips such as are so common abroad.

The one organization which has done this on a rather large scale is the Columbia Park Boys' Club of San Francisco. Under the leadership of Mr. Peixotto the boys from this club have gone on walks of from three to six hundred miles each summer. Fifty-two boys walked from San Francisco to the San Diego Exposition, six hundred and fifteen miles, during the summer of 1915. They were followed by wagons which contained camping and cooking utensils and the necessary blankets, though in California during the summer tents are not strictly necessary. The boys are mostly boys from poor families, and they are accustomed to paying their way on these trips by holding matched baseball and basket ball games, or giving amateur dramatics, and entertainments in the cities through which they pass. During certain summers they have picked fruit or worked on the farms or done other work for half of each day. In this way they have not only made their expenses, but have often gone back with a considerable sum of money which they have saved from the work of the summer.

Such long trips as those taken by the San Francisco boys would seem to most people overambitious, but these boys have a splendid time, they grow sturdy and strong under the outdoor life, they have many opportunities of meeting people, and seeing sights that are worth while, of making collections, and getting a really valuable experience. It is doubtful if any boy could spend his summer vacation in a way which would bring larger returns in health and experience than is to be derived from such a trip. The one thing, however, that is absolutely essential is that they should have a competent adult in charge who is a real leader of boys, and who can secure their coöperation in the enterprises determined upon.

The School Camp

More and more we are coming to feel that the city is not a good place for children during the summer, and that so far as possible they ought to be taken outside where they can be brought into closer contact with nature. More than thirty per cent of the children in Copenhagen are sent out every year to farm colonies, and over fifty thousand children were sent out by German municipalities in this way during the summer of 1914. The best possible arrangement for children during the summer would be that each city should have in its neighborhood a good-sized farm where the older children could be sent about the middle of June and remain until about the first of September. Here they should have an opportunity for gardening, for the raising of chickens, pigs, and the like, and also abundant opportunities for athletics, games, nature study, and other recreations, and for the activities of the Boy Scouts and Camp Fire Girls. Such a brief separation would also tend to develop self-reliance and would often be a great and much needed relief to the parents.

The Social Center

One of the principles of the efficiency movement is that the plant must be utilized for as many hours per day and week as possible. We are coming to feel that it is almost criminal to allow our great city buildings to lie idle for nearly twenty

Folk Dancing, Community Center, Roxbury

hours each day while the young people are thronging the streets, the pool rooms, and the dance halls for the lack of a better place to go. Throughout the country there is a rapid development of the use of school buildings during the evenings for public lectures, exhibitions, moving picture shows, gymnastics, dances, and various civic and social meetings. This is one of our most hopeful movements for a better democracy. Our great difficulty has been that there has been no place where the people could get together to discuss their problems, and there has been little opportunity for the developing of community life. In a large number of cities during the last three years, school buildings have been used for polling places, and, in some places, the principal of the school has been employed as the civic secretary for the district. There have been few social movements which hold in themselves greater possibilities for the public welfare than this socializing of the community by finding it a common meeting place.

WHO IS TO HAVE CHARGE

In the German and English schools the play, for the most part, is conducted by the regular teachers, while the tendency in this country is to employ special playground teachers or physical directors. It seems likely that there will be the same line of development here that there has been in drawing, music, etc., and that all teachers will have a certain amount of play with their children, but that there will also be certain play or physical training specialists attached to each school system. The first requisite to any successful play system in any city is that there shall be some competent person in charge who can outline and supervise the work for the city and see that all the children secure the training which they need. The second requisite is that there shall be one or more competent people who can have charge of the work at each school.

Training Courses for the Workers

The great weakness of the play movement thus far has been that there have been no workers adequately trained to take charge. Wherever there is an attempt to organize play for the student body in the college, the normal school, or the high school, it is often the physical director who is least interested and most apt to be absent. Many of these men have never had any special training and merely came from winning teams at the colleges and universities. The weakly student has not interested them. One great trouble on the playgrounds, also, has been the weakness of the conscience of the director. It is hard to supervise playgrounds closely, and it is to be feared that most of them do not open on time, and that the directors do more loafing than is good for the cause. Any one who will observe a playground for a considerable period will be convinced that the qualities which make a good director are more largely social than physical, and that it needs leadership much more than muscle, though of course muscle and technical knowledge of games are desirable. The courses thus far given for playground directors have not realized adequately this social side of their problem, and the directors have often failed to get the proper viewpoint, or to receive any considerable training along the lines of organization and leadership.

Probably the most hopeful single thing in the whole field at the present time is the very rapid increase of courses for the training of play workers throughout the country. In the spring of 1914 the Russell Sage Foundation enumerated fifty schools which were giving such courses. In 1916 there are probably nearly a hundred such schools. These courses are increasing rapidly in popularity. At the teachers' institutes, also, the subject of play has very often been presented. From all of these sources many of the teaching body are getting at least an elementary knowledge in games and the organization of play.

There are four different types of schools which are now giving courses for the training of playground workers. The first of these are the schools of physical training which are multiplying very rapidly throughout the United States at the present time in order to meet the new demands which are coming in from playgrounds, schools, camps, Y. M. C. A's, and other sources. Practically all of these schools now give longer or shorter courses for playground workers. They are, however, nearly all handicapped by the fact that they have no model or training school for elementary children so that their students do not have adequate opportunities to play games or organize athletics under conditions such as prevail upon playgrounds. Too often, also, those who have taken these courses have come to the school because their interests were predominantly physical and they have not had quite the viewpoint which is desirable in a profession which is so largely social as the organization of play. Then, too, there can be but little doubt that in the long run the special schools of physical education themselves will disappear before the physical training departments in various public normal schools and universities. Just as the private academies have largely disappeared before the public high school, the business colleges are giving place to the commercial departments of the high schools; and the private normal schools are being supplanted by the public normal schools.

There are now probably forty or fifty normal schools in the United States that are giving a normal course in play, though it must be confessed that many of these courses are of a very attenuated nature and consist almost entirely in the teaching of games. The increase in number has been so rapid during the last two years, and the feeling for it seems to be so general among normal schools everywhere, that it seems likely that all the larger normals will soon have such a course. The normal school has peculiar advantages for this work such as is not possessed by the schools of physical education, for the reason that it usually has a good-sized model or training school with several hundred children. This makes it possible to have a model playground, and for the teachers actually to play games with the children. A model playground is necessary to the normal school in any case.

In many ways the model school of the normal corresponds to the experimental farm of the Agricultural College. It is the place where educational theories and experiments can be tried out. It furnishes the best opportunity there is anywhere at present for the evolving of new games, modifying the rules of play, and, in general, securing a higher type of educational result from play activities.

The summer school is just now the crux of the whole play situation because the summer schools throughout the country are attended by teachers from all quarters. Most of them need play and the open air as much or more than they do study and scholarship. If, at the summer schools, they can get something of the spirit of play and take part in play activities adapted to their schools, they are likely to carry these back to the children. The sympathetic coöperation of the teachers would nearly double the effectiveness of the play movement at the present time. Practically all of our larger universities also now have summer courses in play. These are strengthening each year, and the one at the University of California has registered as high as 1300 students during certain summers.

In connection with the Departments of Education, there are also developing at most of the larger universities special courses in play activities which run during the entire year. Harvard has recently called Mr. Geo. Johnson from the School of Philanthropy in New York to have charge of a play course, and the University of Pittsburgh has maintained such a course for the last eight or ten years. At California, Wisconsin, and Wellesley such courses are maintained in connection with the department of physical education. The probabilities are that there will soon be graduate courses for specialists in physical training which will prepare for the Ph. D. degree and fit men to take charge of city systems and university departments of physical training. In these higher courses, the study of play and of social conditions will both have a prominent place.

One of the most interesting developments in the field is in connection with the extension departments of the universities. At the University of Indiana, Professor Pettijohn has been holding each year a series of community institutes in which communities have been aroused to their need of public recreation. As the result of these institutes, many requests have come for men to take charge of recreation positions, and the University is now starting a training school in order to prepare the workers. During this past year it held a state conference on recreation at Indianapolis that brought together a number of the prominent leaders and secured considerable publicity. It gave a three weeks' training course at Indianapolis in the summer and it has recently started an all-the-year training course at Bloomington where the physical training in the public schools has been turned over to the university department for practice. Such a course should be popular with undergraduates because, while giving them just the type of physical exercise which they would enjoy most, it also offers a training which will enable them to earn enough during their summer vacations to very nearly pay their expenses during the college year.

At the University of Kansas, Professor McKeever has reached and stimulated nearly all the cities throughout the state, and forty-two of the smaller towns of seven hundred to two thousand population are now employing a paid director of play during the summer time at least, and in some cases both a man and woman are employed.

The municipal universities at Toledo and Cincinnati are giving courses of training for playground positions in these cities. In many ways a municipal university might be an almost model school for the training of playground workers because of the opportunities for practice and because of its knowledge of the conditions and aims of the city.

One of the most interesting recent developments in the field of training is the work started in Gary where the girls and boys in the high school are put into the gymnasiums and playgrounds to do apprentice work on the same basis that boys and girls have done apprentice work in the shops. When these young people get this practice during the high school period they will probably have more of the spirit of play and will be more proficient than they could be if they waited until three or four years later before making a beginning. They receive advanced standing in the School of Physical Education in Chicago on account of their practice in the Gary schools.

CHAPTER IV

MUNICIPAL PLAYGROUNDS

The municipal playground is a largely unorganized and anomalous institution at the present time in our American cities. The name does not describe the playground, as park and school grounds which are under city authority are municipal no less than the one so called. In most cases this name is used to describe a ground from two to ten acres in size, located largely in congested sections of the great cities. It is usually surrounded with a fence of some sort, and bare of grass and ofttimes of trees. Although its use is mostly by school children, it is usually entirely independent of the public schools. In most cities it is either under the Park Department, or a Recreation or Playground Commission. As it is almost impossible to give a discussion of the municipal playground as an institution and find things which are true of one also true of the others, I shall content myself in the main in this chapter in discussing the systems of the four cities of Chicago, Philadelphia, Los Angeles, and Oakland. These four cities are selected, not necessarily because they are more successful than other systems in the country, but because each of them has certain distinctive features which seem worthy of being copied, and which represent the newer developments in the play movement.

UPPER — HAMILTON SQUARE PLAYGROUND
LOWER — ARMOUR SQUARE PLAYGROUND, SOUTH PARK SYSTEM

The South Park Playgrounds of Chicago

Probably more has been said and written about the park playgrounds of Chicago than any other play system in the world. It is doubtful if in any other American city there has been another municipal improvement that has been so splendidly conceived and supported. Every day of the year the system has been the end of pilgrimages from every corner of the world. Not infrequently an entire park board or a company of business men has come from our eastern or western seaboard to investigate, and usually they have carried back the concept of the South Parks as the ideal that they would seek to follow. The whole country has justly taken pride in what Chicago has done. It has given us through its expenditures a new conception of the value of public recreation.

The first thing to be said about the Park playgrounds of South Chicago is that properly speaking they are not playgrounds, but parks with special playground features. They are from ten to sixty acres in area, of which not more than three or four acres are devoted to the so-called playground. The park is surrounded by a high steel picket fence, with shrubbery from one to three rods in depth banked about it on the inside. In all the larger parks there are lagoons for rowing and fields for tennis and romping. In all there are ball fields, flooded for skating in winter, outdoor swimming pools, a playground for the small children, a playground for the older boys, a playground for the older girls, and a field house or recreation center building. Each of the playgrounds is separated from the others by its own picket fence.

THE CHILDREN'S PLAYGROUND

The children's playground is usually about half an acre in area, with a good-sized wading pool in the center, and sand bins around the sides. It has probably the best combination framework of climbing and sliding poles, swings, etc., that is to be found in any playground in America. This ground is unsupervised except during a part of the time in the summer.

The girls' playground is usually not more than a quarter of an acre in size, with a good-sized gymnasium frame in the middle.

The boys' playground is usually about an acre in size, has a gymnasium frame in the center, and a fine cinder track around the edge. Of late handball courts and tennis courts have also been installed in most of these playgrounds.

The ball field is just outside the enclosed playgrounds and is used for baseball in the spring and football in the fall. It is flooded in the winter for skating. Its use is the same as that of any other park ball field.

The swimming pools of the South Park System are very fine and costly. They are open from ten o'clock in the morning until ten o'clock at night, two days a week for girls, and four days a week for boys.

THE FIELD HOUSES

The field houses of the Chicago system are magnificent buildings. Designed by Daniel Burnham, placed in a beautiful park setting, they are among the most attractive public buildings in Chicago. It would be difficult anywhere to find structures more wholly in harmony with their surroundings, and seemingly better adapted for the purpose for which they were erected. The cheapest of these buildings cost $70,000. The latest one, the field house in Fuller Park at 45th Street, cost $318,000, and is a people's palace on a scale that Walter Besant never dreamed of. Each of the older field houses contained two gymnasiums, one for girls and one for boys, two small plunge pools, three or four clubrooms, a branch library, an auditorium and dance hall combined, and a small restaurant, where everything was formerly sold at cost. Recently the restaurant has been closed because it did'not pay.

The first gymnasiums were rather small and had no galleries; the new ones are larger and are so provided. These gymnasiums are operated from about the first of November to the first of May. The work is outside after that. They are used by the school children in the afternoons and by the young men and women in the evening. The afternoon work in the gymnasiums is usually better attended than the evening.

The club rooms are probably the most beautifully appointed rooms that have ever been offered free to the public for social purposes. The aggregate attendance at the club rooms of the eleven small parks in 1914 was 99,000, or an average of 9000 to each. This represents twelve months' use, or an average attendance of 750 per month of thirty days. This is 25 per day for four club rooms, open both afternoon and evening.

The auditoriums are splendid halls. There are no better anywhere. Sixty per cent of their use, according to the report of the superintendent, is for dancing. The average attendance is about seventy per day. The dances are not organized by the playground authorities, but the hall is furnished free and lighted for any group that may wish to use it. Dancing is also taught by the various instructors, when the young people wish to learn. These auditoriums are also used for public lectures, for exhibitions, and dramatic and other entertainments.

THE LIBRARY

The library is probably the best patronized feature in the field house. It is practically a branch of the Chicago public library. Mr. Hild, the previous librarian of Chicago, said that the only criticism that he had to offer was that the rooms were not large enough to accommodate the readers. In actual fact nearly every seat in the reading room is apt to be full much of the time.

THE WEST PARKS OF CHICAGO

Under the West Park Board of Chicago, there have been maintained for the last three or four years three parks similar to those on the South Side. These parks have been less advertised than those to the south. The grounds are smaller, from two to eight acres in area, and the maintenance is much less, but the annual attendance is considerably greater. Regular courses of lectures are carried on in the auditoriums of some of the field houses. There are many organized celebrations, athletic contests, etc. In Eckhart Park there are extensive and well conducted children's gardens. In Stanford Park there is a corps of twenty-four volunteer helpers, which looks as though this park were securing the coöperation of the community.

LESSONS FROM CHICAGO

Chicago has shown that the evening playground is the cheapest and most efficient playground. If the use of any piece of property can be doubled through an expenditure for lighting that is less than the interest and sinking fund of the original cost, it will be a good investment, as it virtually gives the city another playground of the same dimensions as the previous one. Chicago has also given us the conception of winter sports as a part of the legitimate field of playground authorities, and it has made the outdoor swimming pool a part of our general concept of a playground. She has also given the whole country an entirely new sense of the value of public recreation through her expenditures.

On the whole, however, it does not seem that the form of development which has taken place in the South Park System of Chicago is a form that should be recommended to the balance of the country. The field houses, although magnificent and admirably adapted to the purposes for which they were designed, have not proven superior to the public schools as community centers. The attendance has not been as good as it has at the school centers in a number of cities, and they have not secured the same kind of coöperation as the schools have secured. It has not been possible to give at the same time domestic economy and manual training and evening classes which the school can furnish.

Conduct, both in regard to rowdyism, smoking, and bad language, is more difficult to control in a public park than it is in a public school.

During most of the school year school children can scarcely use them at all except at night, and if the school day should be lengthened, as it has been in Gary and in a number of other cities, the use by day would be almost entirely eliminated. But there is a possibility of our getting the four-term school, and with a seven-hour day and a four-term school, any park system is necessarily almost useless for children, unless there can be some arrangement for the schools to use them during school hours.

The attendance at the park playgrounds by school children, according to the reports of various boards, cannot well exceed 14,000 per day. The average time spent on playgrounds is probably not more than an hour. An hour a day for 14,000 children would be equal to six minutes a day for 140,000 children, or three minutes a day for the 280,000 children or more who are in the public schools of Chicago. It would appear, therefore, that the park playgrounds of the city are furnishing to the children opportunity for play which is about equivalent to a three-minute recess, or one tenth of the amount of the two fifteen-minute recesses offered by the public schools. But there is every indication that within a very few years we shall have at least an hour devoted to recesses organized for the children in the elementary schools, and in that case the present opportunities for play offered by the park systems of Chicago would be equal to one twentieth of that which would be furnished by the public schools. No one who realizes that every child needs an adequate opportunity for outdoor play and exercise for the sake of his health and development, can think that any park system will ever solve this problem. Not only are very many of the children not reached by it, but it is those who are not reached who need the play and exercise the most, for it is always the anemic, tubercular, and weakly children who do not excel in games and athletics, and who are likely to be imposed upon by stronger children who absent themselves from such playgrounds.

The System of Philadelphia

The city of Philadelphia was the first city in this country to make appropriations for playgrounds connected with its schools. This was in 1896. The municipal system of Philadelphia is of much later growth, and the features which are especially valuable have been developed since 1912.

This municipal system is separate from the playgrounds connected with the schools, but is nevertheless in very sympathetic and close relationship with it, as Dr. Brumbaugh, until recently Superintendent of Schools of Philadelphia, was also President of the Recreation Commission. Hence the two have been operated with the closest coöperation throughout. There are maintained under this municipal system, twenty swimming pools, eleven all-the-year-round playgrounds, and twenty-six summer playgrounds. Six of these playgrounds at the present time contain splendid modern field houses of the latest type, and four more field houses are now under construction. Of the playgrounds operated, eight or nine belong to the city, and the land for two or three of them is loaned to the city by private parties. Nearly all of these playgrounds are in congested quarters of the city, and the attendance is probably larger than that of any other playgrounds in the country.

ORGANIZED PLAY

While the South Park System of Chicago was undoubtedly the inspiration of the play development in Philadelphia, Philadelphia's system contains several radical departures and improvements over the South Park System. The most radical difference is that while there are not more than one fourth or one fifth as many attendants in these playgrounds and field houses, there are two or three times as many paid workers, and the play shows the evidence of much closer organization, as does also the increased attendance. Visiting the grounds at Hallowe'en in the Fall of 1916, I found organized soccer games being played on practically every ground, as well as matched games in hockey in many of which there were both girls and boys playing on the same teams, and evidence that volley ball and basket ball and many other games were being constantly played.

The extensive playing of two games, more or less distinctive, is perhaps worthy of mention. On most of the grounds there was a plot worn entirely smooth of grass and kept in excellent condition, which was used almost entirely for playing dodge ball. Mr. Mason, the athletic director, has invented a modification of tether ball which is played with a volley ball attached to a strong cord. There are five players on a side, and the ball is batted with the hand. This is a very popular and excellent exercise.

Most of the smaller grounds where grass cannot be maintained have a special surfacing which is made by excavating the ground to a depth of about ten inches, rolling down with a heavy roller, and grading so as to drain into the sewer. This is then filled with seven inches of coarse cinders, covered with three inches of broken stone, and surfaced with the finest of stone grits. This is afterwards sprinkled with glutrin and appears to be both dust and rain-proof. It is probably the best surfacing to be found in the country, for small playgrounds where a large number of children play.

THE FIELD HOUSES

The field houses are very fine. While not as costly, and lacking in some of the artistic effects of the Chicago Field Houses, they are quite as large as, and some of them considerably larger than, the average Chicago field house. They have some six to ten paid social and physical directors in each building. There are facilities for gymnastics, dramatics, club meetings, and various social gatherings. The buildings and grounds both are used to a considerable extent by organizations from the neighborhood that come in as organizations and hold their meetings there. This is probably one explanation of the large attendance.

System of Los Angeles

The play system of Los Angeles is under a Playground Commission of five members, of whom Miss Bessie Stoddard, one of the leading exponents of play throughout the West, is a prominent member; for a number of years the secretary and afterwards the president. There are seven playgrounds under the Commission, which conducts also, during the summer, play in the yards of a number of the schools. There are several notable deficiencies in this system, and there are also several notable features which are worthy of imitation by other cities. The unfortunate part is that most of its grounds are small, that they are not lighted at night, that there are no swimming pools, and no facilities for water sports. Its great advantage is that the system is situated in a climate where outdoor play can be maintained for the entire year, and where it is seldom too hot and never too cold for vigorous exercise.

THE FIELD HOUSES

Each of the grounds in Los Angeles contains a small bungalow-like field house or social hall. These field houses are very inexpensive, costing only six to eight thousand dollars apiece, with a single exception. They contain a branch of the public library, a stage and hall used for dancing, dramatics, meetings of neighborhood clubs, and the like. There are also club rooms, and, while there is no refectory, there is a range where light repasts may be prepared. These field houses are of a kind that could be afforded by almost any community, and their use has been an ample justification of them.

THE DIRECTOR'S HOUSE

The most distinctive feature of the system in Los Angeles, is that a house is furnished to the director and his family on each playground. This makes the director a real member of the community in which he works, keeps him in closer touch with its problems, and enables him to supervise the playground both by night and day. It is the fundamental idea of the settlement brought over to the playground. These bungalows probably do not cost on an average over twenty-five hundred dollars each. While located on the playground, they are separated from it by a picket or wire fence. The grounds are usually full of flowers, and often beautiful. There are a number of cities that have put rooms for the director and his family into their recent field houses; this is an idea that is worthy of imitation. The one danger in connection with it is the temptation of the director to putter about the house, instead of being out on the ground, if the attendance there is not large.

THE SUMMER CAMP

Los Angeles probably has the most notable playground camp that there is in this country. It is located in the mountains above San Bernardino in the National Forest Reserve. This is seventy-five miles from Los Angeles, and the parties were taken there during the first year or two, in large motor busses, but for the last year they have been taken to San Bernardino by trolley, and from there up in motor stages. The camp provides for about one hundred and fifty at a time, and it is used by girls, boys, and families at different periods, each set being taken for two weeks at a time. This ground is amply directed, is always full from June to October, and there is usually a waiting list. Each individual is charged seven dollars and fifty cents for the two weeks. Three dollars of this is for transportation, and four dollars and fifty cents covers the board and lodging at the camp. The profits for the Summer of 1915 on this basis were nine hundred dollars. During the Fall and Winter of 1915–1916, twenty-five new cabins were erected on these grounds. These are built like the cabins for the tuberculous patients, the lower part being of wood, and the upper part of canvas; and it was hoped that they might be enabled to take care of twice as many during the coming summer as was possible previously. Indeed, since there is an actual profit from maintaining the camp, there seems to be no reason why the system should not be extended, to provide for all who wish to come. A competent man and his wife live at this camp during the entire year, and it is planned to throw it open for week-end excursions and holiday trips for teachers and others who wish to go at that time. There is an open-air swimming pool at the camp and also a number of mountain brooks which are full of trout. The camp booklet has the following list of activities and trips.

> The activities are unlimited, there being opportunity for:
> Hiking, swimming, fishing.
> Baseball, tennis, volley ball, croquet.
> Camp fires.
> Camp-fire stories, songs, and entertainments.
> Talks by Forest Rangers.
> Books, magazines, and daily papers to read.
> Burros to ride.
> Quiet games.
>
> **INTERESTING TRIPS**
>
> To the giant pine tree (1 mile).
> To the wonderful heart rock (¾ of a mile).
> To lumber mills in operation (1 and 2 miles).
> To Mojave River (three miles).
> To Mojave Desert (five miles).
> Evening hike to the summit to see twinkling lights of San Bernardino Valley.
> Overnight hike to Little Bear Valley.

It is to be regretted that this camp is so far from the city, in one way, as it nearly doubles the expense, but this is an advantage to the country at large, as an object lesson, for it shows that a city may maintain a summer camp even at a distance from the city itself, where both supplies and children have to be transported for long distances, and that such a camp need not be unduly expensive for the children. What Los Angeles has done, hundreds of other cities might do throughout the county, and thus furnish a much-needed outing to both the children and the families who might not otherwise be able to afford such a vacation in the country.

The System of Oakland

Probably the City of Oakland has the most complete organization of facilities of any city in this country with the exception of Gary. It is also reaching a larger proportion of its children than any of the other cities, with the exception of Gary, and possibly Washington, D.C. The Recreation Commission of Oakland is an unpaid commission of five members. It has charge of eight municipal playgrounds, ten all-the-year-round school grounds, and twenty grounds supervised by school teachers after school hours only, thus making thirty-eight grounds in all. The director of Physical Training in the public schools is an assistant in the office of the Supervisor of Recreation, and there is also a very able supervisor of boys, and another supervisor of girls' work. Thus all the physical training and recreation work for the city is under the Director of Recreation. This is, I believe, the only city in this country where this is true.

THE PLAYGROUNDS THEMSELVES

The playgrounds which have been created under the Recreation Commission of Oakland are probably the most beautiful in the world, or at any rate in the United States. They are surrounded with woven wire fences which are covered with rambler roses, honeysuckle, or English ivy. Many of them have magnificent live oak and eucalyptus trees which give abundant shade, and borders of flowers add a touch of color which makes them really beautiful.

The grounds, from two to ten acres in size, are not as large as would be desirable, and there are no swimming pools, which is a serious handicap; but there is a generous use of the grounds, which bespeaks a real appreciation. In two cases these grounds have been acquired by buying a fine residence with a private park around it. By this means the Recreation Commission has secured a fine old mansion, which it has taken for a social center, and used for clubs, classes, and a refectory. There are usually some splendid trees already grown. This is an opportunity which might well be seized upon by other cities, for in most cases there are old mansions of this character belonging, as a rule, to one of the first settlers, and containing all the facilities that are needed for a playground and social center.

THE PLAY DIRECTORS

All the play directors both in Los Angeles and Oakland are trained people. They are well paid. Most of those in Oakland have taken special courses in the University of California, and a large proportion of them are University graduates. In Oakland they receive from ninety to one hundred and ten dollars a month, and in Los Angeles the women receive from ninety-five to one hundred and five dollars, and the men one hundred and twenty dollars a month and a house.

WORK WITH THE WOMEN'S CLUBS

One of the notable features in Oakland is that a large number of the women's clubs come to the playgrounds one or two afternoons a week to play volley ball, or to have folk dancing, or other exercise. This is one of the most significant recent developments in the organization of play. The women of the country at the present time are not getting nearly as much exercise as they should, and every woman who is confined during the week by home duties should come out at least one afternoon a week to exercise in the open air. In the small cities and towns where there are not enough children to make adequate use of a playground, the solution of the problem of attendance must be in organizing the work with the adults as well, and the country should take notice.

FOOTBALL

In Oakland they play three kinds of football, the American game, Rugby, and Soccer, and there are tournaments in all of these games. Rugby is played with fifteen on a side. There is much more passing than in the American game, and often they play that the person who is touched is "down." There are four seasons, the Spring, the Summer, the Fall, and the Winter season, each with its own tournament in the various games. The work is well organized; in part very likely because Mr. Dickey has charge of the play and physical training in the public schools as well as on the playgrounds themselves.

TRACK

The Report on the Track Season for 1917 contains the following significant paragraphs:

In 1915 the average Oakland boy in the eighth grade could jump 11 feet $7\frac{3}{10}$ inches. In 1916 he leaped 12 feet $3\frac{3}{10}$ inches. In many other events progress was also made.

Behind that eight inches which have been added to the distance over which he soars from take-off to soft earth; the two inches which he gained in the high jump; the gain in time in the dashes, and the increased number of boys taking part — is the story of coöperation between the Oakland School Department, the Oakland Recreation Department, the Parent and Teachers' Associations, the Mothers' Clubs, and the enthusiasm of the boy himself. It is a story that recognizes the value of athletics for educational purposes — a story of health, achievement, and supervised play on a large scale.

At the main track meet of the Oakland school boys held in Bushrod Park, April 8, 1916, 1600 boys participated. In the training season, which culminated in the meet, 2160 boys took part.

No individual medals were given at the meet, nor were individual prizes of any sort given. A large cup was given to the school making the largest number of points.

ROWING ON LAKE MERRITT

Perhaps the most interesting and successful feature is the rowing. Lake Merritt is a small lake about one mile long and one half mile wide, situated within the city. Some two years ago when a number of the whale boats of the Mare Island Navy Yard were offered for sale at public auction, the City of Oakland bought them and turned them over to the Recreation Commission. These boats are twenty-eight or thirty feet long and are used in the Navy for rowing practice, and for racing. They contain air tanks of copper which make them practically unsinkable, and their width makes it very difficult to upset them. These boats are furnished without charge to crews organized in the public schools. The crews consist of from ten to sixteen rowers for each boat. An adult must accompany each crew, and the crew must furnish its own oars. There are now some twenty of these upon the lake, and the demand for them exceeds the supply. This also is a feature which might well be copied by other cities. A large boat which might be enlarged a little, so as to provide for twenty to thirty rowers, gives an opportunity for many young people to learn how to row. There is little danger in rowing in a boat of this size and character. It is perhaps the best exercise that can be offered. In connection with rowing parties of this kind, it is possible to have picnics, and all sorts of excursions and good times; and the social features are not to be despised. There are about an equal number of girls and boys in the crews upon Lake Merritt, and a regatta is held on the last Saturday of each month. The one danger in connection with such rowing facilities is that there may be an attempt at long races so as to strain the hearts of the contestants, but there has been no such tendency thus far in Oakland.

Besides the rowing in whale boats, the Recreation Commission has also canoes and rowboats, and furnishes storage for private boats on Lake Merritt, and there is also a small refectory. Boats are rented out at twenty-five cents an hour, and the profit from these not only defrays all the running expenses, but returns a small surplus for a sinking fund on the investment.

Is the Municipal Playground Necessary?

As was said in the beginning of the chapter, the municipal playground holds an anomalous position in our municipal life. This kind of play development is not attempted in any other country to any considerable extent. While its purpose is essentially educational and social, in most cases it has no connection with the educational authorities, and it seems in idea to be a useless duplication.

It is quite apparent to any one who has studied a play system such as that of Gary, Indiana, that there is in connection with the schools of that city the facilities for the carrying on of nearly every kind of play and athletic exercise which is required by the young people. In Gary a municipal playground would be an unnecessary duplication of effort.

It is equally evident, however, to any one who is familiar with American cities, that very many of the schools are located in residence blocks with only a little more ground than that required for the building itself, and on these grounds it is impossible to have any considerable amount of organized play, and that the games of baseball, football, tennis, hockey, and the like cannot be played upon them. In these cities it is therefore necessary that either the school grounds shall be greatly enlarged, or that other grounds shall be secured on which children and others may play.

It would seem that so far as school children are concerned, the purpose of the municipal playground should be to supplement the work of the school playground, and to supply to children those facilities which the school is unable to furnish. So far as it is in this way a supplement to the educational activities of the school, it would appear that the municipal playground should be under the school authorities, but it is also reasonably evident that there are two kinds of activities for which the playground must provide. One of these is essentially educational. It aims to give to every boy and girl health, and a good physique, and social habits through its sportsmanship, and a general training in games. These activities are essentially educational and belong by their very nature to the public school, but children do not wish to go to school all the time. They have leisure time besides their school time, and there should be some place where children and adults can go at any time that they have leisure in order to have recreation or physical exercise. The purpose of this second type of activity is not largely educational, but recreational and social. The municipal playground embraces activities of both these types.

THE ORGANIZATION OF PLAY

In general the activities are not as closely organized as those on the grounds of the public schools, but they are considerably more closely organized than those in the public parks. In this respect municipal playgrounds hold a halfway position.

The organization of play on the municipal ground is exceedingly difficult for the reason that the children come and go, and that the group is changing from moment to moment. The children are of different ages and different sexes, and those who are there to-day are different from those who were there yesterday, or will be there to-morrow. It is nearly impossible to have organized play with a group of this character. For this reason, in nearly all of our municipal playgrounds, at least nine tenths of all the play is scrub play, which the children make up for themselves on coming in. Many of the children loaf. Play of this kind can never give that training either of body or conduct, which organized play should give; for in order to develop the body, it must be vigorous, to train the intellect, it must be exciting, to train the social conscience, it must be socially organized. None of these results come from the scrub play.

The municipal playground in most cities has not thus far secured the attendance of a large proportion of the children, and in most cases those who attend are the strong children, who already excel in the games and athletics, and the ones who stay away are the weak ones who need the training the most. During a recent school vacation the writer kept careful account for a week of the attendance in one of the largest municipal grounds of one of our cities. There was on this playground an average attendance of twenty-five children during two hours in the morning, and from seventy-five to one hundred during three hours in the afternoon. This would mean a total number of hours of attendance of about three hundred and fifty a day. If the other six playgrounds in the city had an equal attendance, it would mean a total of two thousand four hundred and fifty hours of attendance at the municipal playgrounds. There are in the public schools of this city approximately one hundred thousand children, and these figures would represent an attendance of one hour by two and four tenths per cent of the children. It is equal to a recess for the school children of that city of a minute and one half. It would thus appear that a fifteen-minute recess in the morning would furnish to the children in the city about ten times as much play as the municipal playground system is at present furnishing, and that two recesses each day would offer twenty times as much. An hour for each child in the program, which is becoming the slogan, would mean forty times the facilities offered by the present system. On this basis, — and these figures are typical of attendance in the municipal grounds, — it must be evident that so far as securing physical training and social training for the children of the city is concerned the municipal play-

UPPER — NEIGHBORHOOD DAY, WORCESTER PLAYGROUNDS
LOWER — DOLL AND BABY CARRIAGE PARADE, WORCESTER PLAYGROUNDS

grounds, as at present conducted, are an almost negligible factor.

Probably one of the leading reasons for the establishing of playgrounds has been that the little children were constantly bullied by the big children on the streets and the vacant lots, and never had a fair chance in the games. Very much the same condition will be seen on many of the municipal playgrounds that is seen on the streets, and it is evident that so far as a social and educational result is being sought, these playgrounds are not doing their job, as they have failed to give the required training. It is doubtful if it is possible to organize such groups of ever-changing elements efficiently. Certainly if an organization is to be effected, it must be through directors of quite a different type from those found in the average municipal playground, and the qualities required are much more largely spiritual than physical. The playground of this type needs a director of a dominating personality who can impress his ideals upon those that come. His ability in baseball or basket ball may count for very little in his effectiveness.

In the cities where the organization of play on the municipal playgrounds has been most successful, it has always been because there has been some opportunity for organization other than that of the open ground itself. Groups already organized in the neighborhood have been brought in to take part, or there have been groups from schools or churches, or classes in connection with the field house or gymnasium.

A series of tournaments in the different games and athletic events is also essential, both to the securing of training, and to the securing of permanent groupings on the grounds, but it is evident that this would be much simpler if the organization might be effected in the school, and the playground be merely a place where the activities were carried on.

POLITICS

Another great danger of the municipal playground is politics, and it is hard to say whether civil service where it is found is doing harm or good. In some cases where there is no civil service, political retainers with no fitness whatever for playground positions have been appointed, and there is always a possibility of playgrounds and especially field houses and social centers becoming the political headquarters in the worse sense, unless they are kept out of politics. On the other hand, civil service commissions are not usually well enough informed on public recreation to give satisfactory examinations, and a written examination for a job where so much depends upon personality and energy and social spirit is a very poor means of obtaining the best workers. The securing of efficiency in playground management, as in city management, depends very largely in giving much authority to the person in charge and in holding him responsible for results.

THE RACE PROBLEM

There is nearly always a problem of cliques on the municipal playground, and ofttimes a division along the line of races. In some places this makes a serious problem, as the children of one race or nation are apt to annoy those of another, or even keep them away from the playground altogether. In a good many sections the question of the attendance of negro children upon white playgrounds is a vital one. While the writer is a believer in the negro and in democracy, he is of the opinion that in nearly all sections where it is possible to have separate grounds for colored and white children, it is better to do so, for the reason that there is often prejudice on the part of white parents against having their children, especially the girls, play with colored children, and because the colored children are very apt to form a clique by themselves, and be an unassimilable element within the playground. As such they tend to break up the harmony of the ground, and cause quarrels and friction. This is not true in all grounds, but it is true in many.

GAMES

The municipal playground should make provision for those games and sports for which the schools do not offer an opportunity. There should be as good facilities for baseball and football as it is possible to furnish, with the ideal that there be one acre of baseball ground for each five hundred of the inhabitants, with the same ground used for football in the Fall. There should be one acre of tennis for each twenty-five hundred people, and a swimming pool, and a bowling green, for each five thousand. It should be the policy to maintain tournaments in all of these events throughout the year, and always to give the preference in the use of courts, and fields, to organized teams rather than scrub teams.

COLOR SCHEME

A large proportion of the municipal grounds are in charge of the park authorities, and the park authorities have taken it for granted that any color scheme which has been worked out for a park will be suitable for a municipal playground also; but in general in the parks the ground is covered with grass, while in the municipal grounds it is usually bare, and the green benches, and black or galvanized equipment, do not harmonize in color with the ground. Probably in nearly all playgrounds, except those surfaced with fine broken stone, the best color for equipment of all kinds would be either tan or brown. The brown pavilions in the playgrounds of Los Angeles, with their dry palm thatch, really harmonize better with the ground than any other equipment.

The Administration of the Municipal System

In most of our cities municipal grounds are either under the Park Board or the Recreation Commission. The writer is of the opinion, however, that, so far as these are for organized play, they should be either directly under the school authorities or at any rate should be used by organized groups from the schools. Often this is not feasible in practice for the reason that the grounds belong to the parks or to some special commission, and also because the school board is either out of sympathy with the play movement or has not the funds to maintain the play activities. Perhaps as good an arrangement as there is anywhere found at the present time is that found in the cities of Milwaukee, Detroit, Oakland, and San Francisco. In the city of Detroit there is a Recreation Commission of three members, consisting of the Superintendent of Schools, the Superintendent of Parks, and one other person chosen by the Mayor. The Supervisor has charge of the municipal and settlement playgrounds, of the school grounds after school, and, during the summer, of play on the streets, of the public swimming pools and gardens, and has also the regulation of private entertainments and dances. Mr. Jayne is thus in charge of the play and physical training in the city of Detroit, outside of the regular physical training exercises in the public schools, and the school recesses and play periods.

In Oakland, Mr. Dickey has a yet larger control, as the director of physical training in the public schools is also one of his assistants, and there is thus a practical unification of all the physical training and play exercises in the city under a single director; but one who is familiar with the work in the public schools cannot but feel that there is always a possibility of friction in any situation where an outside person, not directly under the school board, undertakes to control the policies of a large part of the school program, such as is involved in the organization of recesses, play periods, class athletics, and general physical training.

In San Francisco under the new arrangement, Mr. DeGroot is employed jointly by the School Board and the Recreation Commission, though his work is primarily with the School Board, and it would seem as though the situation there might work out into a rather ideal organization of play.

Play Outside the Playgrounds

As was pointed out in another chapter, play on the playgrounds is only a small part of the play movement in Germany, and it becomes increasingly evident that in any adequate system this must everywhere be true. Walking trips which the children take from the German schools and cities, in themselves represent an amount of activity and social opportunity that is very nearly or quite equal to that offered by the playgrounds. Very likely this may soon be true here. We need everywhere a summer camp to which children can go for longer or shorter periods; we need the organizations of the boy scouts and the camp fire girls; we need to have all the facilities which are offered by vacant lots and other unused places, for playing baseball, croquet, bowls, and tennis, and a full development of every facility which the city has for water sports, in the nature of rowing, swimming, and skating. The opportunities for coasting, snowshoeing, and skiing in the northern cities should also be developed. Besides these activities for children, there is also the management or regulation of dance halls, moving picture shows, and pool rooms, the organization of pageants, and civic festivals of various kinds, the development of city choruses, municipal bands, and even the possibility of our having in our American cities, as they have in so many foreign cities, our own municipal troupe of actors.

AN IDEAL ORGANIZATION

It would appear that our municipal playground as organized at present is a loose cog in the wheel. If it has been successful, it has been successful largely on account of some organization in connection with the schools, or in the community outside. While there is a real demand in most of our cities for playgrounds that are not connected with the schools, so far as the purpose is to furnish play aiming at definite physical and social results, this organization belongs to the public schools. It does not matter whether the play attempted be on the school yards or on grounds outside, it should be under the control of the school authorities. But it is equally evident that outside this province there is also the problem of public recreation, and the question of leisure time and what is to be done with it, and there should always be in every city places where young and old, especially the older young people, may go whenever they have the time, to play such games as they may choose. These grounds should be open from early morning until ten o'clock at night. They should furnish facilities for all the games and the athletics in which people wish to take part; but it is doubtful if there should be any attempt at the educational organization of these grounds, though a person of refinement, with a dominating personality, should always be in charge. The person in charge of this larger department of recreation would be apt to be the most determining element in making a city attractive as a place of residence, and his success in the organization of the activities under his control would largely determine the value of all the property within the city.

It is realized that there are many seeming inconsistencies in this chapter. While three systems have been discussed in which certain features, at least, have been conspicuously successful, it has nevertheless been urged that the municipal playground is an inefficient method of furnishing organized play to school children. It is believed, however, that this conclusion is warranted by the facts. There are very few, if any, municipal systems in the United States that are furnishing an average of five minutes' attendance a day to all the children of the city, and of this five minutes, probably pretty nearly a half is given to loafing, or activities of little value; consequently, it would appear that there are few municipal systems that are furnishing more than one sixth of the play which is offered through the regular recesses of the schools.

It has been urged that organized play in general, and certainly organized play for school children, belongs to the public schools, but it is recognized that there are many places where this cannot occur on the school ground. It is also recognized that there are many school boards that are not favorable to play, and that there are many cases in which all the funds granted for school purposes by law are needed for the present school activities. Under such circumstances, it is impossible to have a proper organization of play under the school board, and it will be necessary in such cases to adapt the method of organization to the actual conditions in the city.

CHAPTER V

PUBLIC RECREATION

In the common literature of play, the words play and recreation are often used interchangeably, but in origin, of course, recreation means re-creation, and is used to describe the rebuilding process which follows toil. As such it might be called the play of the adult, but it is a very different sort of activity from the play of the child.

Recreation is necessary for the individual very much in proportion as the work he is engaged in fails to yield him the normal satisfaction which should everywhere attend it. Perhaps the greatest tragedy of modern times and a capitalistic organization of society is that we have so minutely specialized our industries that the person does not make the whole of anything, but repeats endlessly a single operation, with the result that the finished work is never wholly his own, and that he cannot take the same pride in it that the old-time shoemaker might take in a shoe. It was from this feeling that modern industrialism destroys the worker in its processes, that Ruskin withdrew into his sheltered valley and there started arts and crafts industries in which the individual might be independent of the machine, and each an artist in the work that he did. Whether it is possible that our great factory system should be so reorganized that the individual should, at his machine, find joy in the work that he does, is a problem which we have scarcely tried to solve, inasmuch as we have sought to produce shoes and fabrics rather than human happiness. And we have not realized that out of these conditions of work has grown so much of our industrial unrest, strikes, and other social evils. It may be that in time we shall solve this problem by eliminating the unskilled labor till every man becomes a mechanic operating a machine, or a series of very complicated machines; but, whatever the future may hold in store, the greatest need of recreation at the present is for the people who find no normal satisfaction in their work.

For them at any rate society must demand the right to leisure. They must have the eight-hour day and a half-holiday on Saturdays, if they are to have a chance to live at all. It does not require an exhaustive review of existing conditions, or a report of the number of unions in the different cities that have gained the eight-hour day during the last decade, to show that this is the present tendency of our civilization, and it seems a fairly safe prediction that the eight-hour day will be general in all of our principal trades within the next decade, or, at the farthest, two decades. With a larger amount of leisure, it is necessary that the city should provide places where this leisure time may be profitably spent, that it may not lead to dissipation, or the social undoing of the laborer.

FACILITIES

Under this head I shall speak of the physical outdoor facilities which the city may and should furnish for the recreation of its people. There is probably no city that at the present time furnishes all mentioned in this chapter,

Bowling in Franklin Park, Boston

but probably if we could take a composite picture of the facilities furnished in all American cities, we should find all of them. They represent in general the tendency of American municipal development.

LOCATION OF THE CITY

The first great problem in regard to recreation for any city is what are the opportunities available for recreation. These are practically determined by the location of the city itself. The location, to be ideal, should furnish for recreation three kinds of facilities: water, either of a lake or a river, hills or mountains, and forests. A fourth, which is really as important, though purely a negative feature, is the absence of flies, mosquitoes, dust, fog, excessive rain or wind.

In the olden days the larger cities were usually located on rivers or harbors for commercial reasons. During the last three or four decades the river commerce of most of our inland towns has been strangled by the railways, but the facilities for pleasure which come from the location upon some body of water are far more important to-day than they ever were before. Wherever any suitable body of water is found adjacent to a good-sized city, its banks usually become the chief pleasure resort. The water furnishes an opportunity for rowing, sailing, motor boating, for swimming, skating, and pleasant walks by the waterside, — features which add much to the attractiveness of the city possessing them. It is the contention of this chapter that these waters with their shores should, so far as possible, be under the control of a Department of Recreation in each city, which should develop the facilities for swimming, boating, and any other forms of recreation which the climate warrants. These resorts should be under public control, not only to insure public safety and a reasonable rate to the public for their use, but also to safeguard public morals.

Wherever a city is near to high hills or mountains, it is usually possible to get some of these for an outlying park system and observatory, at a very reasonable rate. The advantage of such facilities to a city has not always been appreciated, but they give an opportunity for mountain and hill climbing, for many interesting excursions, and a general view of the city which is sure to give its people a better understanding of it and loyalty to it than they would have without this opportunity. There are at present many cities in the United States overlooked by magnificent hills of little industrial value, which are used purely for grazing purposes. There are also hillsides covered with scraggly trees where the public may not go without trespassing, and which yet give views of the city and the surrounding country which are worth a climb to obtain.

Likewise every city should own a municipal forest as a part of its outlying park system. Such a forest will yield opportunity for shady walks and drives and picnics, and camping out, and in time, the feeling which comes from being among great trees. This might seem to the American, who is not familiar with the forest preserves of European cities, to be a decided innovation, but in actual fact city forests such as the Bois de Boulogne of Paris, or the Epping Forest of London are amongst the oldest of municipal possessions, and very many of the cities of Germany are very nearly supported by the proceeds from them. The city of Boston acquired the Blue Hills, a forest preserve of ten thousand acres, some fifteen or twenty years ago, and a law was passed in Massachusetts in 1913 to facilitate the acquiring of municipal forests by all the cities of Massachusetts. The city of San Diego, California, is planting a forest of seven thousand acres of eucalyptus, putting out several hundred acres each year.

In regard to the suppression of nuisances in the city, such as flies and mosquitoes, many of our Eastern cities have had very effective campaigns during the last few years, and both the fly and the mosquito are much less in evidence than they were ten years ago. The dust also is being kept down to an increasing extent by oiling, and by a more thorough cleaning of the streets. As to the rain and the wind and fog, we shall probably have to take what the Lord sends us, as no city can determine what its condition shall be in regard to them.

The Public Parks

The park is the dooryard of the city, which has come largely to replace the private yard. There are two originals from which it has developed, the hunting forest of medieval times and the private garden. The idea of sport is thus inherent in the idea of the park. The commons and greens of the New England towns were common cow pastures, parade grounds for the soldiers, and playgrounds of the children.

We are moving away from the ideal of the park as something to be seen and are coming to regard it more and more as something to be used. There is not a feature of the park that does not lend itself to recreation.

Very often the people living around the parks object to their being used as playgrounds, saying that it injures the value of the property and they wish the peace and quiet of open lawns and flower beds. Any attempt to put play of any kind into interior parks always meets with opposition. In nearly every case these parks were bought by the city and furnished to these people as a semi-private dooryard. They paid no more than any one else and received nine tenths of the benefit, both on the financial side from the increase in the value of the property, and on the scenic side from the opportunities of nearness. They now seem to feel that they own the parks. Having been made a present in actual value of an unearned increment often equal to the original value of their property, they want to put a fence around the park and keep the public off.

Childhood is usually divided into three divisions. The first of these is the period before the entrance to school when their chief playground is normally the yard of the house. The second period is approximately the period of the elementary school from six to fourteen, where their natural playground is at the school. The third period is the period of adolescence and in fact the remainder of life. During this time the games played by the boys are largely baseball and football. Often the park must furnish the place.

The park has several legitimate relationships to the play of the little children also. It should always furnish a safe and attractive place where mothers or nurse girls with little babies can get the air amidst pleasing surroundings. When the children are two or three years of age, the park walks and lawns furnish the best place to try out little legs. It is a safe and wholesome place to run and romp. Such an opportunity is necessary to the health and robustness of these little people.

As the children grow a little larger, perhaps four or five years old, the pile of sand, such as is so generously scattered about the German parks, is appropriate. I am inclined to think that these bins should be small, for only a few children, and that they should have seats for parents and nurse girls as the German sand bins do. Near this should be a few low chair swings. These should not be over seven feet high, and the chairs should be so small that they would be no inducement to children more than six years old to use them. It would be well, also, if there might be a small wading pool, not over fifteen or twenty feet across with the water not over eight inches deep. These facilities should be for small children only. No supervision outside that of the mothers and nurse girls should be required. But a watchman and caretaker should be in the neighborhood to see that things are kept sanitary and that the facilities are not appropriated by the larger children.

THE PARK LAWNS

One of the largest park discoveries in recent years is that it is not necessary to "keep off the grass." Fifteen years ago these signs were found everywhere, but they have almost entirely disappeared from the modern park. It is necessary to prevent paths being made, but moderate romping over the grass does no injury. Games that involve running and especially sliding with heavy shoes will wear it off in places, as the base line and the pitchers' box on a baseball diamond, but grass will stand a great deal more play than has been supposed. The Bermuda grass that is used in the South seems to flourish under almost any kind of play in almost unlimited quantities. The grass used in Northern parks will not stand as much, and there should be an attempt, at least, to find a grass that will thrive in the North and stand the same intensive use. We seem, however, to have been under several delusions in regard to grass. When the playground was installed in Tompkins Square, New York, the authorities turned the benches around, so that the spectators might not have to face the ugly bare ground where the children were playing, but the next day the benches were found to be all turned around again, and they have remained so ever since. People seem to be fully as much interested in the activities of children as they are in grass.

The free play on the park lawns has not, as a rule, injured them, and, as Mr. Lee has said, "After all, the children are fully as important as the grass" when it comes to a question of blighting one or the other. As Walter Vrooman has said, the old attitude was, "It is better for the grass to grow green over the children's graves than yellow under their feet."

There have been as many as fifty thousand children in Central Park, New York, at District and other picnics, in a single day. There are sometimes as many as 30,000 at May Pole parties. These parties leave an immense amount of litter behind them, but while they are there, they are one of the most attractive features of the park. Such occasional use does not injure the grass.

The park should furnish facilities for baseball, because it is almost impossible, in most cities, to get areas large enough outside the park. The game requires as a minimum space two acres of ground, and for league games at least five acres. Permits are usually required. Back stops are sometimes furnished. In Central Park, one may often see two or three games going on in practically the same space, the one being played across the other. As Joseph Lee has said, such games are actually played "with a surprisingly small number of fatalities." In Philadelphia they furnish separate fields for the schoolboys. This seems like a good idea, as they do not require so large a field and the boys are always likely to be driven off from the large diamonds, unless they are closely protected by the police. The facilities for baseball are very inadequate in all our cities at present. Still it is possible to furnish adequate facilities in many cities. The baseball age is from twelve to twenty-five, though there are very few who begin to play on regular teams so young or continue to play so long. The fever is at its height from fourteen to twenty-one. Approximately twenty per cent of the male population or ten per cent of the entire population are of baseball age. The baseball diamond contains 8100 square feet; an acre contains 43,560. In other words, the diamond covers a little more than one fifth of an acre. Of course the game overflows the diamond on every side, but two acres are ample for amateur games in general, and an acre will do fairly well for the younger boys. Suppose each team has one substitute, this would make twenty players to each game and would permit of an average, allowing for rainy days, of perhaps five matched games a week for each diamond, as games will have to be played after school or work hours. This would make one baseball diamond do for one hundred players or a population of one thousand. This would require for the city of New York, with a population of something over 5,000,000, a little over 10,000 acres for baseball. There are probably not more than one hundred acres of park ball fields in New York City. Chicago has a population of approximately 2,200,000 and would require 4400 acres of ball fields if all were to play. Chicago probably has more than two hundred acres of ball fields. The fields used for baseball in the spring will be more than ample for football in the fall.

It may not be possible to furnish adequate baseball diamonds to the people of New York City, but it should be possible for the smaller towns and cities to do so. The main use of the baseball diamonds is on Saturday afternoons and Sundays, if Sunday use is permitted. The rule of one baseball diamond and football field for a thousand people or one acre for five hundred people is an ideal which the smaller cities might well work for. Baseball and football require more space than any other of our games. The small towns are losing in population in many places, while the large cities nearly everywhere are growing. The people are going to the large cities, largely on account of the recreational facilities furnished there. It would be good business policy for the small cities to furnish the parks and facilities for play and to seek to develop the habit.

An acre of baseball field for each five hundred of the population may seem to be an excessive amount. Of course not every one of baseball age will play baseball, but this entire calculation is based on the supposition that those who play will wish to play only once a week and on different days, which is contrary to the facts. Boys want to play baseball from two to seven days a week in May and June.

The facilities for football are not as good as for baseball, but there are not nearly as many who wish to play, so that they probably come as near to meeting the actual need.

The tennis court as laid out for doubles with backstop is usually 36 feet by 90 to 110. This would allow twelve courts to the acre. Ten would probably be safe. This would permit forty people to play at once on an acre of ground. Many of the courts will be used two or three times during the day, but many of them will also be used for singles. It would probably be safe to say that an acre of tennis grounds would provide in the park for the daily play of fifty people, or of two hundred and fifty during five days. If ten per cent of the people wish to play, this would mean that the city should furnish one acre of tennis grounds to 2500 people. This would require approximately 1000 acres of tennis for the people of Chicago or 2000 acres for New York.

The maximum for tennis, however, is at least five times that, as the age range of tennis is about fifty years, from twelve to more than sixty and for both sexes. About fifty per cent of the people are of tennis age.

It is the custom to change the courts about, especially in the dry weather, in order to save the grass. Tennis grounds are usually used by permit in New York, and tennis rackets and nets are stored. In many places the park furnishes the net, and, in some places, rents the rackets and balls. All school children ought to be required to learn to play tennis, because it furnishes such admirable exercise for later years. As the schools do not, as a rule, furnish the ground, this should be provided in the park.

Park lawns have no other considerable use, except for play. There is no great landscape effect from a broad and empty meadow. The introduction of a few sheep or cows always adds greatly to the scenic charm, but there is nothing else that has quite the landscape value on an open lawn that children have. Groups of playing children in bright-colored attire are the ideal decoration for any lawn or meadow. If a field is to be used as a ball field, the park authorities might suggest uniforms to the various clubs that would lend harmony and charm to the general scene.

One of the live questions is whether or not play shall be allowed in the parks on Sunday. The present tendency is toward a more liberal use. On the continent of Europe, most of the great athletic events take place on Sunday afternoon. If the play is limited to Sunday afternoon, it will not interfere with church. Sunday is the only time that working people have to play, and the arguments that are advanced for playgrounds as a means of getting the people away from the temptations of the streets apply better to Sunday than to any other day, because on Sunday there are many idle, and it is just after pay day. The police courts usually show a much larger number of arrests on Sunday than on other days. There can be little doubt, but it is better for those who play that the grounds be open to them on Sunday afternoon.

The basis of the objection, however, is not, as a rule, that these "wicked" people are going to be harmed, but that their play will detract from the church attendance and will lead to a general disregard for the Sabbath.

There is another class of people who object to baseball on Sunday because it is noisy and they wish the Sabbath quiet. Baseball certainly ought not to be played on Sunday in a congested portion of the city.

THE PARK WATERS

It is believed that the park waters, thus far, have not been well utilized. St. Louis has just created a stir by making a cement swimming pool four hundred fifty feet long by three hundred feet broad. This is more than three acres and a

The New Swimming Pool, St. Louis

good-sized park lake as such lakes go. This pool has had the immense use of nearly twelve thousand bathers per day during the summer of 1914. Cement pools of this size, however, are very costly, and we may well question if the cement is really essential. Certainly most people would rather step on sand than on cement, and sand at least is necessary in order to keep down the mud in the lakes as they now exist. The pool with a sand bottom cannot be scrubbed down, of course, but it is not certain that this is necessary in a pool with a sand bottom. Such pools will consume a large amount of water, if it is to be changed often. But there is not the same danger of infection from a pool that is open to the wind and the rain and the sunlight that there is from an indoor pool. If the waters, or a part of them, were available for swimming, it would probably double the use of nearly all of the parks during the summer.

In London men are allowed to swim in the open-air pool in Victoria Park all day and, in the park lakes, sans garments, up to eight o'clock in the morning.

There is also a minimum use for skating under the existing arrangement. The ice has to be six or eight inches thick before it will hold the skaters on Central Park Lake. This means that the weather will have to stay around zero for some time and be too cold for comfort before the lakes can be used. When the ice breaks under the army of skaters, the results may be serious. If the lakes could be provided with a flat bottom, the water might be allowed to run off when the cold weather came on, till there was only an inch or two left. This would freeze solid at a comparatively high temperature, and thus give probably twice as many days of skating as are now possible in most park lakes. It would remove all danger of drowning or serious chilling, and it would permit of skating when the weather was not very cold. If the swimming pool is not cemented, the same pool may be used also as a skating pond in the winter, though the difference in the depth of the water in the swimming pool might be hard to correct. If there is a considerable area of ice for the number of skaters, there should be provision for ice hockey and curling.

The commonest use of the park waters is for rowing. In nearly all parks, the privilege of renting boats is let to the highest bidder, and consequently the boats are often too expensive to be used by most people. In Chicago the park authorities own the boats and let them out at a nominal rental, just sufficient to pay expenses. This method would cause the small lakes in our great cities to be overcrowded, perhaps, but it is certainly to be commended where this would not be the case.

The same things are true of water sports as of lawn games. Water used for swimming is much more interesting than water used for fish and swans, as everybody knows. There are probably one hundred times as many spectators along any beach where bathing is allowed, as there are around the swan pond. Bathing in the North is practically confined to three months a year, and skating to two months in most places. One thousand people will swim in a small lake or pond, properly provided with booths, where ten would row, and where swimming is confined to the summer months, the waters are most desired for boating in the spring and fall and in the evenings. Any one who has ever seen, from the top of East Rock, New Haven, Lake Whitney full of skaters will not soon forget the sight. The use of the water and the ice does not detract from but greatly adds to its scenic value while it is in use, and it adds to these features a variety that they would not otherwise have.

The Vacant Spaces

The Department of Recreation should seek to make adequate provision for baseball, football, tennis, bowls, swimming, and similar activities, by taking possession of and developing such facilities about the city on any vacant land that can be obtained, up to the actual demand for them. As this matter is treated in detail in another chapter, I shall not consider it here.

The Roads and Boulevards

The street is commonly thought of as an avenue of commerce, but, in actual fact, many streets are far more playgrounds than they are thoroughfares. The business streets of any city represent only a small proportion of the total. The avenues and residence streets are used constantly by the children for their games, for roller skating, bicycle riding, and pleasure driving, and their significance in the business world is very slight. These residential streets as well as the drives in the parks and avenues leading to any pleasure resorts outside the city should be under the control of the Department of Recreation, and its director should determine the sort of surfacing and the nature of highway that will yield the greatest pleasure to the people using it.

A Picnic or Camp Ground

It has not been counted in general that cities should acquire outlying sites for camping or picnicking, but there can be little doubt of the advantage of it. The city of Los Angeles with its camp seventy-five miles distant in the mountains above San Bernardino, which has been so abundantly used, has demonstrated the advantage of such a camp ground. Wherever there is a fine body of water, or a pleasant mountain side within a distance of twenty-five or fifty miles, which a city might secure, it should be done, and the necessary drives to such a spot should be developed.

Social Centers

Another feature in the large scheme for the Department of Recreation should consist in the series of facilities which are now handled by private enterprises almost altogether, and are often spoken of as commercial amusements. They include the skating rink, the bowling alley, the swimming pool, the dance hall, the pool rooms, moving pictures, and the theater. Many of these facilities are being taken over by the public school at the present time, to some extent at least, through its social center development, and many others are sure to be as the years go by. So far as this is done, they will supposedly come under the Board of Education, and not under the Department of Recreation. However, there are many cities where schools have been built without auditoriums, where there are no gymnasiums or swimming pools, or playgrounds, and little possibility of the development of a social center in connection with the school. In such cities the social center must be developed outside the schools.

In some cities most of these features are handled well, or ill, by commercial interests which conduct them as business enterprises; but many of these become demoralizing to the community. As drink and the looseness of morals lead primarily to freedom in the use of money, these are often encouraged by commercial forms of recreation.

Not only are these facilities badly managed by private interests, often leading to the demoralization of the youth, but they are nearly always over-expensive, and a considerable number of them are not found in many cities.

Sooner or later our Chambers of Commerce will discover that it is just these features which constitute the lure of the city, and which draw the boys and girls from the farms and the smaller places to the larger towns, and that no city, which wishes to grow, can afford to be without these attractions, nor can it afford to have them over-expensive or demoralizing. In order to make the city attractive, it must either regulate or else take over and manage them.

SWIMMING POOLS

Very many of our smaller cities at present are entirely without facilities for swimming, unless these are furnished naturally by some stream or lake. Where some one puts in a swimming pool as a private venture, it often takes considerable time to build up the patronage. During this time it is not profitable, and private parties do not always furnish adequate safeguards against drowning or immoral conditions at the baths. The city can do these things cheaper and better than the private individual. It can build a pool and wait, if necessary, for eight or ten years before its patronage makes it a source of profit, and all this time the city can be sure that there is adequate protection against drowning, and that moral conditions are as they should be. There is no reason why the city should furnish swimming to its people for nothing, any more than it should give them free lunches in its park refectories, or free boats at its beaches; but it seems probable that, under city control, bathing could be furnished at a lower fee than is demanded by private pools, and still be self-supporting. It is always possible also to use such a city pool for the teaching of swimming to the school children.

SKATING RINKS

Skating rinks are not found in all cities, but probably most towns of two thousand inhabitants have one or more of them. On the outskirts of many of our eastern cities skating pavilions are erected in outlying parks, by street railways. These pavilions are often patronized until late hours, and as the surrounding woods are entirely unsupervised, the conditions are seldom as they should be.

DANCE HALLS

Dancing has been almost entirely under the control of commercial agencies until the last five years. The conditions which these agencies have furnished of their own accord have been most demoralizing. In the investigation of the dance halls both of New York and Chicago, about ninety per cent of them were found to be connected with saloons, and in every case the hall was maintained for the selling of intoxicants. A dance hall of this kind always leads to freedom of speech and freedom of conduct and it usually becomes the hunting ground of the prostitute and the procurer. For the last four or five years nearly all of our large cities have undertaken to control or operate their dance halls, and regulations have been passed forbidding the use of these halls by girls under sixteen or eighteen, the admission of prostitutes, the sale of intoxicants, and making certain requirements in regard to exits and safety from fire. This regulation has not proven altogether satisfactory, and dances are now being held in connection with the social centers of the public schools of most large cities. Dances represent sixty per cent of the use of the field houses in the parks of Chicago, and special dance halls are also being operated with city chaperons in charge in the tenement sections. A number of pavilions have been erected for this purpose in the parks of Cleveland, and Philadelphia has started three such centers in residence sections. Apparently our cities will soon either regulate or conduct public dances on a large scale.

THE MOVING PICTURE

Sooner or later our cities must also take over the moving picture. The process is already well under way, for we have the moving picture in most of our new high schools, and in a good share of our new grammar schools; it is a feature in nearly all social centers, and, in not a few cases, picture exhibitions are given in the open playgrounds themselves. There are many reasons why the moving picture should be under public control. At the present time the films are censored by the National Board, and also by a local board in many cities, but, as every one knows, the quality of pictures seen in the ordinary picture show is still low. The majority of the stories are merely dime novels in picture form, which are false to life, to history, to literature, and everything else they represent. The charge for the common reel, even at five cents, is excessive, as a fair profit can be made from a public auditorium that seats five hundred or a thousand people at a charge of one cent for admission. Just now the moving picture is the chief attraction at night in most of our cities, and a satisfactory moving picture theater which furnishes good films at a reasonable price is no less an asset to any town than a new factory. Even if the city should furnish moving picture exhibitions of high order to the public for nothing, they would still be much cheaper than the band concerts which have been given under the park authorities for many years.

THE THEATER

In Greece and Rome the theater was the great public gathering place of the people. The actors were city employees, and the plays might be said to be a part of the school curriculum. At the present time in the larger cities of Europe, the theater is at least a semi-public institution, and the troupes of players are either paid directly from the city funds, or receive city subsidies. The theater in this country, on the other hand, has been almost entirely a private enterprise, and has been conducted for the making of money. Under the European system it is possible to give high type plays, which may not secure a large audience for a fee, but which do give valuable training. The city of Northampton in Massachusetts has recently organized a troupe of municipal players, and this troupe has probably given the best repertoire of classical drama that has anywhere been played in America. This experience of Northampton has been so much and so favorably spoken of in all municipal publications, that it seems inevitable that other cities will soon follow suit and that we shall soon have many theatrical companies on much the same plane as those of Europe.

THE BEGINNING

If now a city desires to make a beginning on this large problem of social recreation, its municipal auditorium or convention hall very likely offers the right starting point. This auditorium was probably built to house conventions, chautauquas, and similar large public meetings. It can be used also, if its floor is level, and the seats are not fastened permanently to it, for play festivals, for gymnastic or calisthenic exhibitions, for public balls, for roller skating, for band concerts, and for moving pictures. If such a hall were used three evenings a week for moving pictures, two evenings a week for roller skating or gymnastics, one evening a week for a public dance, and Sunday afternoon for a band concert or choral singing, a very slight admission fee would make the auditorium a source of profit, and it would be sure to add much to the social life of the city. If now the city were one of five thousand population, or more, next to this auditorium might well be located a municipal swimming pool. The use would probably warrant also a separate moving picture theater, and one or two gymnasiums. As a part of this equipment there should be bowling alleys, and perhaps pool rooms. There should be rooms for the meeting of the Mothers' Club, and the Civic Association of the neighborhood, and a large-sized restaurant, a part of which should preferably be in the open air. This set of buildings in the average city would probably cover an entire block. It should be centrally located, and under the direction of the Department of Public Recreation. It is believed that all of these facilities could be offered to the public much more cheaply than they are now offered, that they would promote the social life, and the formation of friendships, that they would add much to the attractiveness of the city, and that they could be controlled so as to safeguard the public morals.

CELEBRATIONS

BAND CONCERTS AND MUSICAL FESTIVALS

In connection with our Park Departments, there are now being held concerts on Saturday and Sunday afternoons, throughout the year, in most of our larger cities; and in Denver and Houston, and a number of other cities, there is a municipal band paid by the city, which gives programs on Sunday afternoons and certain evenings, in the City Auditorium. Similarly in a considerable number of our larger cities there is now an attempt to hold a period of choral singing, in which, with the assistance of certain distinguished prima donnas and oratorical singers from the great cities, local talent of hundreds or even thousands of voices will render the great oratorios and cantatas. This is a feature which might well be developed in every city, and should offer an opportunity for musical training to all of those who cared either to sing or to listen. On the financial side, there is no reason why it should not at least pay expenses. The University of Wisconsin has had for several years a chair of Community Music, which has been held by Professor Deikema. The University of Indiana established such a chair in 1915.

NATIONAL HOLIDAYS

A Department of Celebrations was created for the City of Boston some four years ago, for the organization of the celebration of all the national holidays. This movement is, of course, in its infancy at the present time, but Boston made a notable beginning in its celebration of Columbus day, in which she got out all of her foreign races, each with its own parade and pageant, to represent what the Irish, the Jews, the Italians, the Chinese, and others had done for this great country of their adoption. A safe and sane Fourth is now organized in a good share of our larger cities, and during the last two or three years a very large percentage of them have had a community Christmas, with a great Christmas tree brilliantly lighted, upon some public square, with choral singing, and often some great prima donna to take a special part in the evening's program. Hallowe'en in Philadelphia and Harrisburg, at least, in 1915 was a scene of parades and color, and masquerading, such as I have never witnessed anywhere before. Already we have a fairly good program for the organization of all of our national and other holidays.

SPECIAL CITY CELEBRATIONS

Besides these celebrations of our public holidays, there has been a decided tendency during the last decade for the different cities to develop their own special frolic or carnival of some kind. These are a sort of ebullition of the spirit of youth for the city, in which, with many pageants, and much masquerading, everybody throws off all inhibitions, and does pretty much as he chooses. Some of these have been so dignified and worthy as to be counted as really great works of art, and some of them have been on a very low plane indeed. Of course, the classic celebration of this kind has been the Mardi Gras in New Orleans, which has every year brought many thousands of people from all parts of the North and East to the southern metropolis to view the gorgeous floats, attend the great balls, and revel for a time in the spirit of freedom. Kansas City had a somewhat similar celebration, though far less famed, under the direction of the Knights of Pallas. Then there is the Rodeo in Los Angeles, and the very notable Rose Carnival in Pasadena. This carnival on January first, 1916, was a parade some three miles in length, in which there were hundreds of floats, which represented cities, schools, business concerns, and private individuals. In color scheme, in the form of the floats, in the trappings of horses and attendants, many of these were works of art, which one might well go far to see. This carnival brought more than a hundred thousand people to the city, and more than a hundred thousand dollars. The carnival is one of the delightful bits of color which shows the possibilities of California, not to Pasadena alone, but to the tourist throughout the southern part of the State.

CITY PAGEANTS

Of far more significance, however, than these special city celebrations, are the pageants which have been organized during the last few years to represent to the people the history and the future of many of our great cities. The pageant in Philadelphia and in St. Louis each cost many thousands of dollars to produce, and had thousands of people in special costumes upon the stage, either as actors or singers in special choirs, yet they have practically all paid expenses, and have created a feeling for the city, such as the people did not have before, and have given a vision of what its future might be, which will be sure to have an industrial, as well as a social, significance.

The Stadium

In order that a city may have a real outdoor life and develop a civic spirit, there should be some place where the city can really assemble. There are many cities of England that have held a municipal play-holiday for the last twenty years. This holiday is given over to the playing of games and taking part in athletics by the school children. The City of St. Louis established a municipal play-holiday in the Fall of 1915. In nearly all of our cities there is now an annual play festival or picnic, in which the children from the playgrounds give exhibitions of various play activities. All of these along with the band concerts, pageants, and the choral singing, demand that every city should sooner or later acquire a great outdoor theater, or stadium, where its great city festivals can be staged, with the whole city to sit as audience, and see presented the activities which represent its city life. Such stadiums were built for San Diego and Redlands, California, in 1915, and a much larger one is projected in Griffith Park, Los Angeles, for the near future.

The Director of Recreation

As the Department of Recreation has been outlined in this chapter, it has little to do with the play of school children, or with educational or organized play of any sort. The department might take charge of the municipal playgrounds, and it should have charge of all recreation features which might be said to be unorganized, or where the initiative in organization comes primarily from the participants, rather than from paid directors. The person in charge of this great department would be a far more important official than the present City Mayor. He and his department would probably determine for the most part, whether or not the city were to grow, and what the social morality should be. All of these facilities can be offered to the public more cheaply through the city than they can by private enterprise, and they can be made more attractive and much more wholesome socially than they are likely to be where the making of money is the aim. Where politics are very corrupt, such a social center as has been described might become a Tammany Hall headquarters of the most dangerous kind, but in general any movement which brings the people together to discuss their problems, will lead powerfully to their solution, and will tend to prevent every kind of municipal corruption and inefficiency.

There is nowhere found, at the present time, a Department of Public Recreation such as is herein outlined. However, some two years ago a Department very similar to this was created in the City of Boston, but was afterwards abolished by the Mayor. Such a department is certainly in line with the tendency of present development in the recreation field.

CHAPTER VI

OTHER PLACES TO PLAY

THERE is no solution of the child problem of a section such as lower New York by providing playgrounds. There are too many children and the land is too expensive. Where the child population is four or five hundred to the block, they need the entire area for their play. This can be at the street level only by abolishing both the street and the block, which would abolish the children as well. There are five possible solutions: The setting aside of certain streets for play; the clearing out and improving the interior courts; the utilizing of all vacant spaces; the larger use of the roofs; the building of more recreation piers or skyscraper playgrounds; or in all of these means together.

CITY STREETS AS PLAYGROUNDS

In 1903 a communication was addressed to a number of street commissioners in our largest cities, asking them if the function of the street as a playground was recognized in their respective cities, and if they had made any provision for it. The answers of the various commissioners are well illustrated in the following from New Orleans:

"Sir:—We have not contemplated putting our streets to any such use."

That may well be, but whether such use is contemplated or not, the streets always have been and always will be the playgrounds of the children for a large part of the time. Usually it is scarcely possible to provide a sufficient number of playgrounds, and always the street is the most accessible place. A playground which ministers to four thousand children will seldom have an attendance of more than four hundred, even while it is in operation, which means that not more than one tenth of the children are at the playground at any one time during the day, and probably the average number present is not over one twentieth. Then, too, in most cities, the playgrounds are probably not open more than two thirds of the daylight hours, so that seven eighths or nine tenths of the children's free time will still be spent in the house or on the roof, on the street or in the dooryard or court of the house. Inasmuch as the street is at present practically the only playground of a large proportion of city children, and as it is to remain the playground for a large part of the time of all city children, it is quite time that our city fathers and especially our street commissioners took notice of the fact, and endeavored to make it a more decent place for them.

THE STREET AND NERVE STRAIN

The greatest density of population in our Eastern cities is generally found in the oldest parts, where the streets are narrowest. They are so full of the ordinary traffic that there is no room for the children. If posts were planted at intervals along a street, it would be possible to avoid them, because posts are not frolicsome. But it is not so easy to avoid a playing child. He is likely to make the most unexpected movements at any time. The motormen, the drivers, the chauffeurs, and the bicyclists are all put under strain when the children are abroad. All sorts of vehicles have to slow down, and the street loses nearly half its efficiency as a thoroughfare. On the other hand, all these children are in danger much of the time and their parents are kept under constant strain from worrying over their safety.

STREET GAMES

It is interesting to observe the play that has developed under such conditions. There is no room for organized games, and almost every sort of play that the child cares for is against the law. He must not play ball, he must not throw stones or snowballs, he must not build fires, he must not utilize vacant lots. The policeman becomes his natural enemy, and one of his chief sources of amusement. Every game undertaken is subject to constant interruptions from the ordinary traffic of the street, so that the child comes to play with a listlessness which is indicative of his feeling that it is hardly worth while. These games inevitably tend toward loafing, for after they have been broken up by half a dozen carriages and cars, the children are apt to sit down on the curb or the sidewalk and seek to amuse themselves in some other way. Joseph Lee has said, "The child without a playground is father to the man without a job." He might have said with equal truth, "The girl without a playground is the mother to the scandal-monger of the future." It is not the play but the idleness of the street that is morally dangerous. It is then that the children watch the drunken people, listen to the leader of the gang, hear the shady story, smoke cigarettes, and acquire those vicious habits, knowledge, and vocabulary which are characteristic. When they are thus driven from the street to play upon the sidewalk or the doorstep, the only common games left which they can pursue are tops, marbles, jackstones, war, craps, and pitching pennies. Of these, craps and pitching pennies are the most interesting.

What seems very curious and is quite unexplained, is that each of the street games reappears at about the same time every year, runs its course of a week or two, and is in turn displaced by something else.

The politeness and ethics of a game played on the streets are on a lower plane than those of the same game played elsewhere.

STREET DANCING

During the last few years in a number of the cities of southern California public dances have been held on the asphalted streets in the evening. The street has been waxed and amply lighted and has served the purpose apparently very well. One of the Tacoma papers for Friday, July 21, 1916, contains the following account of a dance for the berry pickers at Puyallup:

"In accordance with the suggestion of some of the leading citizens of the valley to provide recreation and amusement for the berry pickers, a street dance will be staged to-morrow night immediately following the band concert. Street dancing was the cause of a spirited debate at a special meeting of the Commercial Club last night. The votes of the meeting were evenly divided, but the committee finally decided to stage a dance under strict censorship. The dance will be held on the street pavement at the corner of 4th Avenue and 2d Street northwest. Every one is welcome, but the dance is especially for the entertainment of the berry pickers.

"Bandmaster Cramer has arranged a good concert for Friday night, and with ideal weather and the great horde of berry pickers at hand a record crowd is anticipated."

There seems no reason why dances such as this should not be staged in any of our cities during the summer. From every point of view, it would probably be more wholesome dancing than if it were carried on in a hotel ballroom.

STREET GERMS

On the physical side the street means degeneracy. It stands for an overstimulation of nerves, for heat that is almost past endurance at times, for air that is charged with noxious dust and germs, among which the germs of consumption find a prominent place. The analysis made in 1907 showed more than 100,000 germs to the cubic centimeter of air taken from near the curb on some of the down-town streets of New York. In the examination which Commissioner Woodbury made into the condition of the street cleaning force, he found that five years' work on the street rendered the average individual a consumptive, and he sent hundreds to sanitariums in the country to be treated.

Dr. S. A. Knoff in the *New York Medical Journal* says: "It is not the tubercle bacillus alone that makes our street cleaners consumptive, but it is the constant inhalation of all kinds of dust and the constant irritation of the pulmonary surfaces, which make the invasion of the germ of tuberculosis more easy. It is not the air, but the dust in the air, which renders New York such a dangerous place, particularly in summer, to people predisposed to pulmonary troubles. While as a natural consequence of being in closer proximity to the dust, the street cleaners are the first to suffer, the citizens at large who are obliged to remain in New York during the summer months suffer also to a considerable degree."

As the children have been in the streets almost as much as the street cleaners, and their lungs are nearer to its surface, in proportion as their legs are shorter, if they have not suffered as much it must be due to their greater vitality.

The bacillus of tetanus is also found in larger numbers in the air near the gutter, and any wound inflicted there is peculiarly liable to result in lockjaw.

STREET EDUCATION

On the intellectual side, some streets and avenues which are lined with great buildings and along which pass the splendid equipages of wealth have much of educational value. But in the streets of the city slum, the sights are different. There are coal wagons and beer wagons, street cars, and push carts, and the sides are usually lined with saloons and petty shops.

We have a comprehensive picture of the education of the street in the street gamin. He is a graduate who has caught the full spirit of the school. From him, we see that the street gives a boy a sort of sharpness and cunning. It is difficult to fool him. He is suspicious and perennially untruthful. He is self-reliant and can take care of himself anywhere. If we can trust recent statistics, his development stops at about sixteen or seventeen, and his chance of rising to a position of prominence in the world is almost nil.

The manners of the street are proverbial. Its law of success is to push in and grab for the thing you want, and to shout everything you have to say for the reason that it will not otherwise be heard. The boy has to compete with the myriad noises of the street, and his voice is likely to grow harsh and rasping. By force of example he is apt to become profane.

It must not be thought that these conditions apply only to great cities. To my mind the alleys of such a city as Washington, with their connecting stables and outbuildings, are at least as dangerous morally as the worst streets of New York.

Many parents realizing these physical and moral dangers keep their children in the house and forbid them to go on the street to play. They are the most troublesome ones at school. Never having the exercise they need, they are usually restless, and lacking in self-reliance and manliness. The street, despite its dangers, is a better playground for a growing boy than a ten- or twelve-foot room.

Of course the less congested streets up town are not nearly so bad as they are down town. They are cleaner, usually shaded with trees, wider, and are often almost deserted by vehicles during a large part of the time. The traffic is usually with light delivery wagons, and the driving is much less careless, because the drivers realize it will be no small offense to run over one of the children.

The girls suffer more than the boys from these conditions. The boys still play despite the dirt and the traffic, but the girls scarcely play at all, and they are more largely kept in the house, but they have a certain compensation in the housework. If the boys also had something to do, their condition would not be so pitiable.

STREET SURFACES

From the examination which we have given the street thus far, it has not appeared to be a very desirable place for the children's play. Nevertheless, in all our great cities it is, and is to remain, one of their chief playgrounds, and the practical question is, what can be done to make it more suitable for this purpose? The first improvement suggested is that the law should require that every street in a residence section should be paved with asphalt or cement. There are still thousands of miles of cobblestone or block pavement in the poor and densely settled parts of our cities. It seems scarcely necessary to dwell on the disadvantages of such a playground; one risks a sprained ankle at every step in running over it; any ordinary vehicle rattling down it, raises such a din that conversation becomes well-nigh impossible. The filth lodged between the stones cannot be properly removed, and every gust of wind raises a cloud of dust to fill the eyes and lungs of the children. These reasons are conclusive against permitting the use of stone block or cobblestone pavement in any residential section of a city, unless the houses are surrounded with yards, and open playgrounds are provided. The only interesting thing that the children can do on such streets is to build fires, and that is a rather dangerous amusement. Asphalt or cement give a usable surface for play, for roller skating, and when a hurdy-gurdy comes along and the children dance around it, they seem to forget for a while their lost heritage of field and stream. Moreover, an asphalted street can be cleaned. In the past, most of the down-town streets have been so filthy that a child could hardly be recognized by his parents after he had played in them for an hour. We are, however, securing more competent organization of the street departments, and better mechanical devices for cleaning and washing the streets. The horse, which has furnished more than nine tenths of the dirt in the past, is rapidly disappearing, and the streets are becoming cleaner. The asphalted street that is properly cleaned and washed largely does away with the dust and the germs.

THE AUTOMOBILE

In a way the coming of the automobile has improved the streets very much. It has removed more than nine tenths of the filth. It is saving more than half the room, as it is only half as long as the horse-drawn vehicle and not so many vehicles are required to handle the hauling, because the auto trucks are much swifter and more powerful. The drivers of drays and beer wagons may be intoxicated and are often criminally careless. The drivers of motor vehicles must have licenses, and they are undoubtedly a more responsible set of men than many of the old drivers; but still the auto is taking a frightful and increasing toll of lives from our city streets. The driving is too fast and some of the drivers are irresponsible. The railroads refuse to employ an engineer who drinks; and no person who is known to get intoxicated at times should be allowed to drive an automobile. Even a little drinking takes off the inhibitions and makes a man a dangerous driver. The horse will probably nearly disappear from our streets within five years. He is practically gone already from the drives and boulevards. If the auto can be strictly regulated as to speed and the responsibility of the drivers, it will be wholly an advantage to the children.

THE PLANTING OF TREES

A second great improvement which must be made in the streets for the sake of the children is the planting of trees. There may be certain objections to this on the ground of shutting out the light and sunshine from the houses, but the people usually suffer from heat more than they do from anything else, and they can dispense with a large part of the direct sunlight in summer when the trees are in leaf. The shade will cool the air on the streets and prevent the burning reflection from the asphalt. The leaves of the trees will take up a part of the carbonic acid gas and thus improve the quality of the air. With this natural shade, the streets will be vastly improved for the children's purposes. A few years ago the New York Medical Association passed the following resolution: "Resolved that one of the most effective ways of mitigating the intense heat of the summer months and diminishing the death rate among the children is the cultivation of an adequate number of trees on the streets."

John H. Ranch, M. D., in his "Report on Public Parks with Special Reference to the City of Chicago," shows that the infection and diffusion of malaria or noxious emanations are arrested by trees. "This was based on a careful study on the effect of tree shields as a protection from malaria and fevers along the rivers of the South." The tree is the chief element in urban beauty and the one possible relief in slum sections from the monotony of continuous brick walls. The City of Paris has more than 100,000 trees. Washington has more than 80,000 and employs a special forester. The tree is required for its beauty, for its shade, and for the relief it gives to the eyes. The trees would cost comparatively little, yet probably hundreds of children die every summer, who might have been saved, had the streets been better shaded.

CLOSING STREETS FOR PLAY

Another improvement which should be made in the streets for the sake of the children is that certain streets, during the hours when the children are not in school, should be closed to traffic. There are many streets in crowded sections which are but little needed as thoroughfares. Their function as streets is quite subordinate to their function as playgrounds. In this way a safe if not attractive playground might be furnished, which would be accessible to every child. It has many disadvantages, but it would be almost infinitely preferable from the child's point of view to the condition which now obtains. A directed playground with simple apparatus and games has been maintained in Gault Court, Chicago, for the last three summers, and the Parks and Playground Association has furnished play leaders on certain streets in New York and Commissioner Woods has recently closed certain of the down-town streets to traffic from two to six in the afternoon in order that the children might use them as playgrounds. A number of the short streets of Boston are used for coasting in the winter time. In the Year Book of the Playground and Recreation Association of America for 1913 it is stated that organized street play was conducted in fifteen cities during the summer of 1913 and in twenty-six cities in 1915.

Reading, Pennsylvania, has made a very successful use of what is generally waste space, under the outer arches of one of its bridges. Under one space is a roller skating rink, which is flooded in winter for ice skating, another is surfaced with smooth concrete for folk dances and for games, and a third contains swings and similar apparatus. These playgrounds are cool in summer and warm in winter, and are protected from the rain and wind. A similar use, though much less developed, has been made of some of the spans of the bridges between New York and Brooklyn.

The New York terminus or esplanade of the Manhattan Bridge contains a great mall and playground for the children. This space is probably two hundred feet wide and six or eight hundred feet long, so that it is really larger than many of the playgrounds that are located at the surface.

There was recently an interesting proposal from the Deputy Street Commissioner of New York, that elevated parks and playgrounds should be erected over the down-town streets of the City, which are not already occupied by elevated railways. It was pointed out that it would be quite as easy to support parks and playgrounds in the center of the street as a street railway, and that the weight of the park would be much less than that of the elevated trains. The suggestion was that alternate blocks should be used as parks and as playgrounds, and that the public might enter these in the same manner as they now go upon the platforms of the elevated railways.

To summarize, the streets are and will remain one of the chief playgrounds of the children. They are undesirable playgrounds, and we would gladly see the children removed from them, but this seems impossible, and we must try to improve the street for their sakes. If they are paved with asphalt, cleaned for purposes of play as well as for purposes of traffic, planted with trees, and certain streets are set aside for play after school, it will be a great advantage.

The Recreation Pier

The ordinary pier is a place for storing merchandise about to be put on vessels and receiving merchandise as it is unloaded from vessels. For commercial purposes, thus far, it has been made only one story high. The recreation pier is usually a second story added to such a pier. These piers in New York, some seven in number, are painted in bright colors and decorated with the flags of all nations, so that they suggest an excursion boat off for a picnic. Band concerts are given on Saturday afternoons and every evening during the summer. The evening crowds are usually large.

The recreation pier is a delight in the hot weather. To go from the close and sultry East Side on to one of these piers swept by the breezes from the river and harbor is like a trip to the seashore. It brings an immediate change of climate to a section that needs relief from heat at times more than any other city in the country. It is always interesting to watch the boats coming and going and the endless panorama of the river with its varied craft. The piers in New York are in pavilion form and are little more than a roof over another pier. During certain summers, these piers have had kindergarteners in charge and have been used as outdoor kindergartens. During other summers, they have been used for teaching folk dancing to the girls from the playgrounds.

One can but wonder that this idea has not been carried further. The Municipal Art League of New York made a plan several years ago for an elevated drive, an extension of Riverside, that should encircle all the piers on the lower part of the island. With such a drive, the upper stories of the piers would become the most attractive place for the development of all sorts of hotels, restaurants, theaters, etc.

It seems a shame that around such a crowded and shut-in section as the East Side, any pier should be content with one story. Every pier should be a recreation pier. It would be comparatively easy to surface a third story with soil and have a park there, and a second story might be used for a series of different games such as basket ball, indoor baseball, volley ball, tennis, handball, etc. It would cost no more to provide these here than it would elsewhere, and it must be remembered that in most cases the land already belongs to the city. The recreation pier would be the finest sort of a place for a municipal dance hall in summer.

The finest recreation pier in this country, and doubtless in the world, has just been completed in Chicago. This pier is three thousand feet in length and cost nearly four millions of dollars. It has place for the docking of nearly all the pleasure boats and many of the lake boats that come into Chicago; has vast promenades, restaurants, observatories, and an auditorium that will seat three or four thousand people.

A Skyscraper Playground

It has been suggested by various people that the best solution in the most congested sections is to build playgrounds that shall be more than one story high, and in the original plan which Mr. Stover made for Seward Park, it was to have been five stories in height. Dr. Gulick has prepared an elaborate plan for such a playground to be twenty stories in height, the lower five or six stories to be devoted to business purposes, the succeeding stories to be used for swimming pools, basket ball, volley ball, tennis courts, kindergartens, general games, and the like, while the top floors were to be used for a library and training school for playground workers, and the roof for a roof garden and open playground. It was understood that a beginning was to be made on such a playground on East Houston Street two or three years ago, but nothing further has been heard about it.

The Dooryard and Court Playground

When a movement for playgrounds is begun in the smaller cities, there are usually many who say that they are not needed because there are ample dooryards in which the children can play. It will usually be found that the people who present this argument have made no provision for the play of the children in the dooryard. Still the dooryard has a legitimate place in any well-rounded play scheme, and its absence cannot well be compensated. It amounts to little for boys of twelve or thirteen who wish to play organized games, but it is essential to the welfare of the little children below the school age.

This is from many points of view the most important of all of the play periods, and perhaps the dooryard is to remain the most important of our playgrounds. The little child is a little animal. He has a motor restlessness that requires him to be almost ceaselessly active. He cannot sit still for more than a minute at a time even for candy. He has few intellectual interests and no duties. All the energy that he develops is normally expended in or in connection with activity. To keep him still is to repress at once his physical and mental development. This is also the most dangerous period of life when child mortality is the highest. He needs to be in the open air just as much of the time as it is possible for him to be. He cannot go about the town by himself without getting lost, and there is always danger that he will be run over by autos or street cars. Even if the city has abundant playgrounds, this does not help the situation very much in general, because these children cannot go to them, unless they have an older brother or sister that can take them.

Wherever there are houses, there should be dooryards and space where the children can play. It should be recognized that it is possible to build an unsocial block, a block that does not provide for the human needs of the family. A block that is under two hundred and fifty feet wide as a minimum is almost necessarily such a block. It does not furnish room for a dooryard or any space for play. This means that even the little children must play either on the street or the sidewalk. Old blocks cannot well be reconstructed to make them wider, but all new blocks should be at least three hundred feet wide. The blocks are six hundred feet square in Salt Lake City.

In this dooryard there should be a certain minimum equipment. There should be a simple sand bin, made of boards or planks with a seat running around the edge. This bin can be made in an hour by any one who can use a saw and a hammer even a little. It requires no bottom, and the cost should not be much over a dollar. It will be used almost constantly by the little children. There should be a swing hung from a limb if there is a tree or from a framework erected for the purpose. A garden swing will also be used by children in a very social way and will often serve for imaginary railroad trips, etc. There should also be a low trapezium,

Other Places to Play

parallel rings, a horizontal ladder, and some sort of a playhouse or tent, unless the yard is very small. A small slide twelve feet long can be purchased from the mail order houses of Chicago for $15, and it will be used almost constantly by the small children. There should be some animals, either chickens, pigs, rabbits, or a dog or cat. For the children a little older, the dooryard furnishes an opportunity for quoits, croquet, and tether ball, of which the latter is the most vigorous game that can be played anywhere in a very restricted space.

In tenement sections, it is not possible for the families to have a dooryard, but it is possible that there should be a playground in the center of the block for the children of the block. There are few things that are more essential in tenement sections at present. The little children cannot go on the tenement streets with safety. They are too filthy for the small child who often falls down, and we must remember that his eyes and nose are much nearer the street level than the eyes and nose of the adult, who is five or six feet tall. The mothers of these little children are often working during the day, and they are locked in the tenements. It is essential to their health that they should get much open air and exercise, and there is no way that this can be done, except by furnishing them a place within the block itself.

Of course there are objections to such a plan. There are the clotheslines, for instance, which fill so completely this interior space in New York. Such an idea is communistic, of course. It would involve the destruction of existing interior tenements. It would take the private property of the interior and devote it to public uses, but the law in New York does not now allow that this interior space should be used for new buildings. If it were turned into an interior park and playground, it would be sure to increase the attractiveness of the interior apartments and be worth while as a business venture, if the entire block belonged to one owner so that this center could be improved solely for the advantage of his tenants instead of somebody else's. In fact, a number of the fine new apartment houses that cover a block or nearly a block have already this interior park, though not for the children, because children do not grow in apartment houses. In places where there are a number of owners, this would only be possible by requiring it by law or by the tenement house or some other department taking charge of this inner space. It is under the park department in Berlin. These changes would involve expense, but it must be remembered that conditions at present in tenement sections are now dreary almost beyond endurance and the tenement is the residence of the poor not for eight or ten months a year, but for twelve months a year, and it is seldom relieved by excursions or trips of any kind. Present conditions produce degeneration in one or two generations and yield a constant crop of crime, delinquency, and social unrest.

In the better sections of the city there would probably be more objection to the removal of the partition fences by the well-to-do who wish to be exclusive than there would be from the poor who are more democratic. Ideally such a block should be inhabited only by neighbors who were friendly to each other and constitute a sort of social or socialistic community, members of the same club or church or what not. No one should be allowed to come into the block without being voted on, because this would really be a neighborhood club that met in the center of the block.

In such a block three hundred by four hundred feet in

size, it should be possible to have a park one hundred by two hundred feet in dimensions with a few good trees, flower beds, benches, etc. At one end there should be a good-sized playground with sand bins, swings, slides, and a day nursery for the little children during the day. There are probably enough working mothers in nearly every tenement block to keep such a nursery full. There might also be a pavilion for dancing and a place for games. Such an interior park would naturally become the center of sociability during summer evenings. It would create a sense of neighborliness and put a new meaning into life for many. It would be the most wholesome kind of social life that it is possible to have in the city. It would furnish a place where the little children might play out of doors all the year round with absolute safety and greatly reduce the child mortality.

There is a good example of such a playground in connection with the Union Settlement at 104th Street, New York, and in fact nearly all of the settlements have such playgrounds. As has been said, many of the new apartment houses also make this provision.

There is much interest at the present time among reform housing associations in the establishing better facilities for the play of children in connection with new tenements. I have been called into consultation several times during the last two years in making plans of this kind, and in many new tenements [1] both in New York and Philadelphia fairly ample

[1] Three of the new apartment houses constructed in the Bronx during 1915 have plots 120 × 173 feet in size, but will occupy only 110 feet in depth, the remainder of the plot to be used as a playground for the tenants.

The Octavia Hill Association of Philadelphia is planning to construct a number of apartments in the Kensington district. "On a large plot of ground a set of buildings are to be erected in the form of a rectangle. The houses are playgrounds for the children are being furnished in the interior of the tenement block. In most cases these grounds are not supervised, but they contain no interior fences and have fairly ample space and equipment.

Probably the best suggestion for the organization of the work comes from the Houses of Childhood, established under Madam Montessori, in the Lazaretto section of Rome, where the children in this poorest quarter of the City are assembled under teachers, whom Madam Montessori herself calls directresses, and are given an opportunity for play and wholesome life under their guidance. The idea of Madam Montessori, that her directoresses should always observe and seek to understand the children, that they should hold themselves in the background and guide through suggestion and occasional personal talks and helps, rather than by a definite set of tasks, is an admirable suggestion for playground directors everywhere. Such Houses of Childhood ought to be in the center of every tenement block in New York City, and in many other of our most congested sections. There has been much dispute in regard to the significance of the Montessori method in pedagogy, but there has been no unfavorable comment on the Houses of Childhood as a method of dealing with the small children in the tenement sections.

Vacant Lots

In our congested cities it is too bad that any vacant spaces should not be utilized, and there should be a systematic

to be very small, just big enough for a workingman's family, and are to rent for about $9.00 monthly. A new feature is the interior court which all the renters are to share in common. In it will be a very large parklike enclosure, the greater portion of which will be fitted up as a children's playground."

effort to keep an inventory of all of them. These should be secured from the owners, put into condition by removing brickbats, tin cans, and the like, and utilized either for gardens, for the playing of baseball, volley ball, and similar games, or for kindergarten playgrounds for the small children.

Which of these uses should be made of a particular ground would be determined by its location. In certain sections the playing of baseball on a vacant lot would be very annoying to the houses in the neighborhood and might result in many broken windows. In such a section, while ball might be objectionable, the use of such a ground for children's gardens might be entirely feasible and meet with the complete approval of the neighborhood. It is almost impossible for the little children to go to playgrounds that are more than one or two blocks away. While it would be best for them to play in the dooryard or interior courts of the tenements, it is impossible that this should be done at present in many sections, and it is often desirable that vacant lots should be improved and a sand bin, kindergarten tent, and kindergartener furnished for them. The large grounds and grounds in the more open sections, where residences do not abut directly upon them, could be utilized for playing indoor baseball and general games. The complete utilization of such spaces would mean a very great relief for a time in most of our cities. But it must be realized that this use is temporary, and little permanent equipment, and, as a rule, no sanitary conveniences can be afforded, because sooner or later they will be taken for other purposes unless purchased by the city. Wherever vacant spaces are devoted to this use, the police should be asked to furnish such supervision over them as it is possible for them to give. It cannot be thought that these spaces will be playgrounds of a high order, but children need unsupervised as well as supervised play; and as the play is organized on the regular playgrounds of the city, play on all the vacant spaces and in the streets will be improved at the same time through the new games which the children learn and through the new conceptions of sportsmanship which they acquire.

Playgrounds on the Roofs

During my first summer in New York, I had charge of a playground in the lower part of the city, and, in order to be near the children, I took a room in the vicinity. I had always supposed before that the stories which we hear of the sufferings of the people by the heat were overdrawn, but I soon learned from experience that this was well-nigh impossible. There were no shutters to the room and the sun soaked into the carpet and the bedclothes until it was like a furnace until after 12 o'clock at night. I would go out and sit in Tompkins Square or some other of the small parks until the small hours, and then go back to my room, where I was not usually able to sleep much before four o'clock in the morning. The streets, the small parks, and recreation piers were thronged, until after midnight, by thousands, many of them children under ten years of age. Nearly a hundred children and old people were dying of the heat every day. Almost the only place in the whole section where we could have been comfortable was the roof, yet the roofs, for various reasons, were not suitable or accessible to us.

Any one who has lived for any considerable period on the East Side comes to feel in the end that the section itself weighs upon his spirit like a stifling atmosphere. He cannot escape from it. All is hurry and rush. Everything suggests the bitter struggle for the necessities of life. The only place where one can throw off these feelings and conditions, is the roof. The ugliness of the street is unconquerable; the dirt, the brick walls, the noise, the traffic, are all repulsive; there is no blade of grass, there are no trees, there are no flowers. Conditions like these make the saloon seem a paradise and drive people to excesses. The only place where there is any natural beauty is above. Even an ugly slum section may be a fairyland when seen from the roofs by moonlight. The stars and the clouds and the great depth of the summer sky are no less beautiful from the roof of the tenement than they are from the mountains or the seashore. The sun rising over the housetops and sinking behind them in the west repeats again the world-old miracle. To the people of Eastern lands from Bible times to now the housetops have been the place of social gathering in the evening.

THE SCHOOL ROOFS

In London and New York, and to a lesser extent in most of our larger American cities, the newer public schools, in crowded sections, are provided with roof gardens. In New York they are all open at recess times, and some of them in the afternoons and evenings, in summer, when they are lighted by electricity, and used for basket ball and similar games. There are tables for quiet games such as checkers, dominoes, and authors. On some there are given regular concerts. These roofs usually hold about 2500 people; they are opened at 7.30 in the evening and kept open until 9.30 or 10 o'clock. Often the doors have to be closed within half an hour because the full number of people that the roof can accommodate are already present. They are almost the only places in lower New York where a person can be reasonably cool on a hot summer's night. All the school roofs should be open from 3 o'clock when the school closes until 10 o'clock every night, except during the three winter months. The roof of the University Settlement is used practically all the time.

OTHER PUBLIC BUILDINGS

The hospitals, the public library, the fire houses, the police stations, and the public baths and the armories should similarly be provided with roof gardens; the first four, for the use of their occupants, and the last two, for the use of the public. A number of the branch libraries in New York already have roof gardens, and fifteen fire houses were so furnished during the summer of 1914. But the buildings with the greatest possibilities are undoubtedly the armories. They are very large, usually covering an acre or more; they are generally only one or two stories high, are used at night so that it is not necessary for them to be brightly lighted by day, and in every way the roofs seem suitable for playgrounds or public parks. Many of them are quite as large as existing playgrounds in New York. There would be ample room for a hundred yard dash, for a dozen games of basket ball or volley ball, for a dozen or more tennis courts, besides leaving space for seesaws, sand bins, giant strides, and other apparatus for small children. The air there is fresher, and there is an absence of dust which often makes the street level so disagreeable. It is doubtless true that this would involve the reconstruction of many of the armories, perhaps of all of them, but where the ground site is worth half a million or more, considerable can be spent in reconstruction without the cost being excessive. In many sections this would provide the only playground which it would be possible to secure without demolishing blocks of five- or six-story buildings. It does not seem impossible even that an armory should become a sort of hanging garden with trees and shrubbery such as the gardens of Babylon. A draft of such an armory roof, prepared at my suggestion, has been exhibited at some of the congresses of the Playground and Recreation Association of America.

APARTMENT HOUSES AND TENEMENTS

The big new apartment houses which now often cover most of a block offer an excellent opportunity for roof gardens. Perhaps, considering what we hear of the birth rates and rules of these apartments, it may not be necessary to provide a place for the children, but there seems no reason why there should not be flower beds and shrubbery, and a pleasant place for every one to sit in the spring and summer evenings. Many of these are already being provided with roof gardens with certain playground features.

But the tenements themselves are the chief problem. If there were a regulation similar to the Paris regulations, requiring all the buildings in a block to be of the same height, it would be possible for each to have a roof garden two thirds the size of the block. If this space were surrounded with a good fence, it would be reasonably safe, and there would be room for basket ball, volley ball, indoor baseball games, as well as every manner of swing, seesaw, and sand bin for the play of the children. Certain parts might be real gardens with flowers and shrubs. It would be scarcely possible to find a more delightful place for ice cream parlors and dancing in the hot weather. This might make it necessary to strengthen the walls of some of the buildings, but it would be worth while. The chimneys would be an impediment, but not an insuperable one; ideally they should be at the side and taller, but in the summer time, when these roofs would be in most demand, there would not be much smoke. In order for satisfactory results to be obtained, the roof of the entire block would have to be treated as a unit, which would be difficult in existing tenement sections, but might be followed in the future in enterprises of large magnitude.

One of the great obstacles in the way of any attempt to reform a tenement house is the laundry. The inmates hang it on the roof, and the roof becomes useless for other purposes; they hang it in the interior court and the court becomes the dreariest spot in the whole "city wilderness." When the lines are bare, the vista of naked poles is depressing, and, when the lines are being run out over squeaking pulleys, or when several thousands of garments in various states of dilapidation fill the only sky space of several hundreds of people, it is equally so. There are three ways of relieving this state of affairs — by furnishing washhouses in every district, by having a washing and drying room in the basement, or by hanging the clothes on a reel from the back porch, or back window. But even if they are put on the roof, there is no reason why they should occupy the front part of the building. These conditions are best met, of any place, in Phipps House No. 1, at 331 East 31st Street, New York. This tenement has a washing and drying room in the basement, and roof gardens surrounded by a hedge with a shelter in the center for stormy days. There are benches for the people, and the roof is used constantly except in the very coldest weather.

It has always been the plan of tenement builders to secure as much rentable space at as little outlay as possible, and they have not as a rule put in anything new which did not bring an immediate return, except as they have been compelled to do so by law. A roof that would be really suitable for the uses of the people would be regarded by them as an unnecessary frill, which could not be rented as such, and which could not even be surely added to the rent of the other rooms. Reform in this direction, as in other directions, must come not through voluntary improvements by tenement builders, but only as such reforms are compelled or made advantageous by law. But why should not the city make it worth while for such buildings to be erected? When country districts in the West wanted to encourage the use of broad-tired wagons, instead of the narrow tires which cut up the roads, they reduced the road tax to every farmer who owned a broad-tired wagon, with the result that the narrow tires went out of use. The present tenement drives its people to the streets, to the saloons, and more or less into the police courts by its very conditions. Why is it not logical that the man who builds a tenement of a better class, which will save the state from various expenses of this character and which will improve social conditions, should have his tax reduced in a proportionate degree? If such an arrangement were made for the tenements which had roof gardens, they would soon become common. The roof means fresh air to the consumptive, play for the children, relief to the street, healthful amusement and social life for the people, and, in short, an opportunity to lose for a time the occupation in the life of the spirit. We cannot afford to surrender such advantages to clotheslines and landlord indifference.

THE CITY WALL OR PROMENADE

Any one who has been in some walled city in Europe during the summer time and has gone up on to the wall at sunset, knows how delightful is such a stroll in the cool of the evening, and how it seems to bring an elevation of mind from the mere physical elevation. How many people evidently feel as you do is evidenced by their presence. The Board Walk at Atlantic City is crowded for miles on summer evenings. Why should not such a promenade be laid upon the roofs encircling the East Side? The sidewalks below are crowded and dirty, and the air is stifling in the summer. The street with its subway, elevated, and surface lines have become three stories high; the sidewalk space is inadequate even for business purposes, and there is no room for pleasure strollers. Bridges over the streets with glass floors like the subway roofs would not perceptibly darken the street below. Certain stories would have to be taken from buildings, and others built up, and the construction of still others strengthened, but it would cost far less than to make a Riverside Drive extension, and would be used by thousands where Riverside Drive is used by hundreds. With such a promenade the roofs in various places would furnish almost ideal conditions for ice-cream parlors and theaters and for evening restaurants and music and the general recreation of the people. If it were one block in width, it would probably be crowded to nearly its

Other Places to Play 145

full capacity all through the warm summer evenings, and there is probably no other place in the world where such an opportunity for fresh air, a cool breeze, and a view of the stars might give more inspiration and relief.

All the activities and the play spaces, with the exception of the roofs of the public schools, enumerated in this chapter should come under the supervision of the Director of Public Recreation.

CHAPTER VII

PLAY FOR INSTITUTIONS

Orphan Asylums

PROBABLY the place where organized play is needed most of all is in institutions for children. These children live at the school and have abundant time to play. Their activities are greatly restricted by the institution, as they are generally not allowed to go far from the building either into the country or the town, if they are allowed to leave the grounds at all. They are denied the association with father and mother, brothers and sisters, which make so much of the sweetness of life, and their days are mechanized to such an extent that they offer almost no possibilities for personal initiative, as they usually arise, dress, go to school, dine, and go to bed at the stroke of the bell. Scarcely anything could be imagined that is more unnatural for children than such a routine, as the child is utterly unsystematic and wishes to do things when the spirit moves and not in accordance with any prearranged plan. These institutions also have often been in charge of matrons who may have been excellent cooks and seamstresses, but who have had no large appreciation of the problems of childhood or the significance of life. They have often felt that they did their whole duty when they gave to these children good food and comfortable beds. But there are few places where the saying of Jesus, "Man shall not live by bread alone," is more appropriate or where it might be written more properly over the doorway or carved on the corner stone.

These children are usually required to do the common work of the institution. They scrub the floors, wash the windows and the dishes, make the beds and often their own clothes and shoes. While the making of clothes and shoes is an educational task of considerable value for the older children, most of the work that has been given to the younger children can only be described as drudgery. It is indoors, without an adequate social motive, and is essentially uninteresting.

Many of these children have very slight opportunity to play out of doors, and in general, unless there has been some systematic effort to develop their play life, they will be found not to be playing games but to be running aimlessly about or indulging in horse play. Such an institution may nourish the body, but it kills the spirit. Almost any sort of a home is better than an orphanage of this kind. During the last few years there has been such a strong reaction against them that the tendency is to make them merely receiving grounds for children who are later to be found homes in the community.

However, it must be reasonably evident to every one that an orphan asylum need not be an institution of this kind, and perhaps it might be the very best place for a good share of the children. We are all familiar with Plato's idea in his Republic, in which he would have all children brought up by the state in orphanages in order that they might be better educated. The English Preparatory and Public School have always been orphan asylums to all intents and purposes, for they have been schools where the children have remained for nine to ten months of the year. They have turned out a larger per cent of successful men and are probably more loved by the children than any other schools. However, in all of them play is compulsory for about two hours a day, and there is a very intimate relationship between the master and the pupil, so that he comes to take the place of the parent during a large part of the year. We have a dozen or more such schools in this country and all of them are growing rapidly in numbers and popularity. Groton, Lawrenceville, and Tome may be taken as examples. President Roosevelt sent two of his sons to Groton, and there are few schools anywhere that stand higher in the estimation of educators than do these schools. They are successful scholastically, the boys become strong and well, have a good time, and develop a sturdy physique and social habits. It seems reasonably evident that every orphan asylum might be a Groton or a Lawrenceville if it were as well organized. It is undoubtedly true that some of the children would need to stay at the school twelve months of the year instead of ten, but there is also a large proportion of the children at the orphanages who have one parent living and who would be glad to go home for two months of the year the same as the children do from the great private schools. Undoubtedly the state would not be willing to maintain its wards at so great an expense as is required at Groton, but we may well question if large expense is essential to the success of the idea. It is the play and athletics and vigorous social life and good teaching that make these schools successful, and to secure these results in an institution in the country or on the edge of town where the children do a large part of the work, no great expense is necessary. In a school of this type there is an opportunity for every boy to learn a trade as he goes along, to have an abundance of play, intimate social relationships, a thoroughly good time, and perhaps to get the very best education all around that is being anywhere afforded to children. Certainly the training of a school of this type would be far better than that of a considerable portion of the homes.

My interest in the idea of play for institutions grew out of several visits which I made to the orphanage founded by Mr. Corcoran in Washington. This institution is amply endowed and located centrally in the city, with nearly a block of land, most of which was devoted to the raising of potatoes, while the children were loafing or running aimlessly about on the small plot of land assigned to them. In several visits there I never found them playing games. Whenever I or any adult came to the ground a half a dozen children usually held on to our hands or coat tails as we walked about, showing that they had that same sort of hunger for adult society that the gregarious animal feels for the herd, or that the person in solitary confinement feels for his fellows. It was very evident that these children lacked initiative in the organization of games and that what was needed most of all was a sympathetic, capable adult who could be what the English master is to the children in the preparatory schools, or what their parents might have been to them; and that so far as they were to have play, they could have it only through the furnishing of some leadership which would teach the games and get tournaments and contests started.

We called a meeting of representatives of all of the institutions in Washington at which this subject was presented, and a number of institutions decided to put in playgrounds. All over the country at the present time orphanages that are able to do so are putting in apparatus such as swings, slides, seesaws, and the like; but these children do not need equipment so much as play. The swing and the seesaw have comparatively little value in the development of initiative or social habits or courage or any of the other things which these children lack on account of their institutional life. Perhaps we have not sufficiently realized how much the social and religious nature of the child has fed on the love of his parents and how much the social life of the institutional child has been impoverished by this lack. Beyond question the easiest way to develop intimate friendships and personal relationships, either among children or adults, is through social play together, and play for these children probably has a greater value in developing the qualities which might make them successful adults than the school can possibly have. The need of sympathetic physical directors or teachers who will also be capable leaders in play is probably the greatest need of orphan asylums.

There are at the present time few, if any, orphanages in the United States that are making adequate provision for the play of their children, or where efficient leadership is furnished. But there are two institutions that are worthy of mention for what they have done along these lines.

Girard College was founded under the will of Stephen Girard at the beginning of the last century and now has an endowment that amounts to nearly seventy millions of dollars. It has about forty acres of ground which is located in a thickly built-up section in the northern part of Philadelphia. Its buildings are all of white marble. It contains fifteen hundred children from the ages of seven to eighteen. There are at Girard some four or five good-sized playgrounds and an outdoor swimming pool, and there is a fine gymnasium and

The Playfield, Girard College

swimming pool in the new high school. Many things are done exceedingly well at Girard. The teachers in the school are well paid and are high-grade men and women. The health and physical training in the classrooms is carefully looked after. The children have an opportunity to learn a number of trades. They also have considerable time and space for play. The college has recently employed seven physical directors to have charge of the play. Girard is built on the model of the English Public School. It produces some very superior baseball and football teams and there is ample opportunity for the older boys to play tennis. Moving pictures are being shown one or two evenings a week after or just before supper, and phonograph entertainments are given at certain times. The smaller children have a story period right after supper in most of the dormitories. Nearly all of this work is fine, and if Girard succeeds in organizing the play as well as the English Preparatory and Public School has, it will be offering a training nearly or quite equal to the training of Rugby or Harrow.

The New York Orphan Asylum situated at Hastings-on-Hudson is in charge of Dr. R. R. Reeder. This school has been recently moved from a down-town situation to its present site, and the children are located in cottages of twenty with capable house mothers in charge. The grounds are large, and besides their school work the children have ample opportunity for gardening, the raising of chickens, and the keeping of pets. Perhaps the most unique thing about their activities is the building of playhouses in which they indulge to a very unusual extent, as nearly every boy and girl or group of boys and girls have houses, sometimes in the trees, sometimes in the woods, or sometimes on the playgrounds. These houses are fitted up with a great deal of care and pride by the occupants. The children nearly all learn to swim in the river and soon become skillful. There is considerable of the ordinary play apparatus such as swings and seesaws, and the hills are used during the winter for coasting. But perhaps the most unique and suggestive piece of play equipment to be found there is a concrete playground about one hundred feet square. At different times this is used for tennis, basket ball, and general play, and several games may be going on at once. It is popular also during the summer for roller skating and is flooded in the winter for ice skating. Moonlight skating parties are held the year round. This institution, under the capable leadership of Dr. Reeder, is doing much for the children, and its only considerable inferiority to such a school as Harrow or Groton is its failure to organize sufficiently the games and athletics of the children.

It is very nearly self-evident that all orphan children are the natural wards of the state or city and that all orphanages should be state or municipal institutions.

The Playground for January 1916 has the following items on the development of play in orphan asylums:

"Play in Orphan Asylums. — Every few weeks word comes that some institution for children is giving special attention to the play life. Quite a number of institutions are employing a special worker to have charge of the play."

"The Erie, Pennsylvania, Home for the Friendless has just sent a report of their field day. During the summer a young college woman from Radcliffe has been play director for the one hundred children. This was the first time that such an experiment had been tried in the forty-four-year history of the Erie Home, but it worked beautifully."

"The State Board of Administration of state institutions for children of Illinois has announced that playgrounds will be established in four institutions as the beginning of a system which will be extended to all institutions for children."

Play for the Blind

The children in institutions for the blind are under conditions in general similar to those found in orphan asylums, but there is here the added circumstance that the children are unable to see. Many of the children are not totally blind, but the majority of them have so little vision that their activity is greatly restricted thereby. Blind children in general are timid, lacking in initiative, and underdeveloped physically because they cannot run with safety or play vigorous games. They are usually advised by their elders to move about in a very circumspect way, and, until they come to institutions at least, have little physical activity of any kind. We have no adequate physical measurements of blind children, so that we are unable to estimate statistically their physical development with that of normal children; but to all appearances they are not so well developed. They seem to have a smaller chest capacity. From the very conditions of their previous life they must be easy victims to tuberculosis. Miss Henderson in speaking of the physical training for the blind says she finds on the basis of their physical examination at the School for the Blind of Kentucky, that "our twelve-year-old boys who have had no gymnastic work are twenty-five per cent below the normal for that age;" and physical trainers in other schools also bear testimony to a physical development that is far below what it should be.

Blind children are much more nervous, also, than normal children, as can be seen by the twitchings of the face and hands and involuntary muscles of the body.

THE GAMES OF THE LITTLE CHILDREN

Blind children cannot well learn games by themselves, and will know no games unless they are taught. But where their play is directed they are not at any considerable disadvantage with other children in many of the games. Where the children hold hands in ring games, the blind do nearly as well as normal children, and for games such as Jacob and Rachel, Blind Man's Buff, and a number of others, they have a decided advantage. In the singing games of the kindergarten and intermediate grades, on account of the voice training which they usually receive, they will often make a better showing than seeing children.

PLAY EQUIPMENT FOR THE LITTLE CHILDREN

Without any question play equipment has a far greater use for blind children than it has for normal children. While many forms of activity are greatly restricted by their lack of vision, they can use the swing, the seesaw, the slide, the sand bin, or the wading pool as well as seeing children. The only serious danger is that the child may be struck by a swing, and the swings ought always to be in a place by themselves and probably set apart from the surrounding area by a chain or rope so that the children will not walk in front of them without realizing where they are. There ought perhaps to be a signal at which all the children will get out of the swings in order to make room for others. The giant stride is often dangerous for seeing children, as the child dropping off may be struck by the child who is coming just behind, but this is managed very well in some schools for the blind by having all the children get on or off at once. Every school for the blind should have just as abundant equipment as it can afford. The sand bin especially will be appreciated by the little ones, and the slide will be no less popular with them than with seeing children.

A CONCRETE PLAYGROUND

It has seemed to the writer that a concrete playground similar to the one installed by Dr. Reeder at Hastings should be found at every school for the blind. The great difficulty for the blind in playing games is the impossibility of knowing where the other children are and the danger of colliding with each other or with trees or other objects as they run. However, if a playground a hundred feet or more in diameter were made of concrete and the children were provided with steel heel clips such as they often wear, it would seem that they might well play tag, pull-away, prisoners' base, and many other such games guided by the sound of the footsteps of the running children. If a playground of concrete a hundred feet or more square were surrounded by a border of hard dirt eight or ten feet wide, the children could tell as soon as they got off the playground. Even if it should not prove feasible to play a great many different games in this way, the concrete would serve for folk dancing, for roller skating during the warmer time of the year, and, if it were flooded, for ice skating during the winter; so that a playground of this kind could not well fail to be of great value.

We must realize, also, that the blind can see as well by night as by day, and the playground will not need to be lighted except for the director.

GAMES OF THE OLDER CHILDREN

In many institutions for the blind there are regular baseball teams, though this must be a dangerous sport for them. Of course the ones who play have a slight amount of vision, though usually far too little to make the game really safe. It would be far better for them to play indoor baseball, as they would be able to see the ball better and would be less likely to be hurt by it. Volley ball and basket ball are much better adapted to these children with a slight amount of vision, because the ball is larger, it is generally up in the air, and the field is smaller.

It seems strange that there should be any attempt among blind children to play football, but every blind school with which I am familiar has a team. Principal O. H. Burritt of the School for the Blind at Overbrook, Pennsylvania, has this to say about football in his institution: "Our boys get much sport out of an adaptation of football. For two years now we have had a junior and a senior league composed of four teams of five or six boys each. In the organization of the teams the instructor must determine the membership of each team: for, if left to the choice of a captain, the boy with a little sight will inevitably be chosen first. Each team has at least one boy with a little useful sight; the others are usually totally blind, or at least possessed of insufficient sight to aid them in locating the ball. When it has been determined in the usual way which side shall 'kick off' from the center of the field, for two fifteen- or twenty-minute halves, the efforts of each team are directed toward kicking the ball over the goal of the opposing team. To prevent the ball from passing over its goal the team depends chiefly upon the boy who has a little useful vision, whom they have designated, 'the stopper,' although the captain has directed his sightless team mates to stand at possible strategic points with the hope that the opposing player, who, four chances out of five, is unable to see where any member of the rival team is standing, will chance to kick the ball against one of them who thus contributes his share toward the stopping of the ball. But the totally blind player contributes his major share to the team in the kicking which he is very likely to be able to do as well, sometimes better, than his seeing team mate. The number of times each team kicks the ball over the goal of the other, within the time limits, determines the final score. I have seen the sidewalks, which constitute the side lines, well filled with partisans of each team vociferously urging their favorite team on to victory." The School for the Blind at Lansing, Michigan, recently played the second team of the Grand Rapids High School a regular game of football with a score of 14 to 17. In this team the right and left tackles were both totally blind, while all the other members had only enough vision to have a faint perception of moving objects.

FIELD EVENTS

It would seem on first thought that it would be almost impossible for the blind to take part in field athletics, but the dashes have been provided for very satisfactorily by placing a guide wire at about the height of the waist and giving each runner a small trolley with a wheel which runs on this small wire. In this way he is able to run at speed, being guided all the time by the wire as he runs. A short distance before the end of the track a fringe of cord is suspended so that the runner knows when he is to slow up. Blind children are able to do the standing broad jump and the hop, step, and jump as well as seeing children. They also often do very well in the high and broad jump, though in these they are at a considerable disadvantage. Some of the eastern schools for the blind are accustomed to hold contests in which are included also the shot put and the hammer throw. At the School for the Blind at Lansing, Michigan, some fifteen boys took a walk of about twelve miles last year. In this walk they were fastened together with a clothesline much like an Alpine party. They enjoyed the trip very much and have been begging ever since to have another walk of the same kind.

GYMNASTICS

In nearly all forms of gymnastics the blind are at no considerable disadvantage with seeing children. They can use the pulley weights, wands, and dumb bells quite as well; they love to exercise on the horizontal and parallel bars and rings. Wherever swimming is provided it is much appreciated, and the girls especially are fond of dancing. As the musical sense of the blind is usually carefully trained from early years and they are required to move around the hall in the same direction, collisions are not much more frequent than they are with seeing dancers, and their performance is quite as good. Where the gymnasium or hall has a border of cement or some rougher material than the main floor, this serves to prevent their colliding with the wall and no danger is involved. They are also at no great disadvantage in wrestling as compared with other children.

SOCIAL RECREATION

Blind children are always well trained along musical lines, and it is easy at most institutions to get up a choral or glee club, or to have a band that can render very presentable concerts. Probably the phonograph or victrola has a larger place in institutions for the blind than it has anywhere else, and there ought to be time provided for concerts of this kind several times each week, usually just after supper or at such times as the inclement weather keeps the children indoors during the play hours. In this way, if high grade machines are secured, it should be possible to give the blind a familiarity with all of the great operas and oratorios, and in fact with nearly all good music.

Perhaps there is no finer institution for blind children anywhere than the one at Overbrook, Pa. It has a magnificent group of buildings which cost in the neighborhood of a million dollars, and some eleven acres of grounds with a special ten-acre athletic field across the road. There are here a good gymnasium, swimming pool, and much equipment for play. Athletics, field events, and vigorous games are probably more largely developed here than they are at any other institution for the blind.

Blind children are always lacking in initiative and are always timid. Probably play has a larger function in overcoming these disabilities, giving them a sense of resourcefulness and power and energy and courage to undertake the tasks of life than has the school; but for them leadership is absolutely essential, as they cannot organize games by themselves. It is in this regard that nearly all of these institutions for the blind are weak; for while many of them are furnishing a considerable apparatus, I know of none where adequate provision for the organization of play is made. In some schools there is a good beginning, and the authorities feel that it has been very successful, but schools for the blind are usually state schools, and it is not always easy to secure funds for the purpose of organizing play.

THE GRADUATES OF THE SCHOOLS FOR THE BLIND

In Massachusetts there is a very definite effort through the State Commission on Blindness to furnish occupation for the blind which will make them self-supporting. But one cannot but wonder if it would not be better to start at several different places in this country, under state auspices, villages with suitable industries for the blind alone, so that this might be essentially a special reservation for them. They will always be at a disadvantage in living among the seeing, they will feel themselves handicapped and inferior, and most of the occupations in the community will not be suited to them. Would it not be better in every way if many of the blind might live permanently in a colony or caste by themselves where they might have industries adapted to their capacities and for which they might be trained in the various schools for the blind? In such a colony the blind might marry and raise families and live among their equals a life as nearly normal as it is possible for them to live.

Most blind children are not born blind, and of those who are born blind most of the blindness is due to infection of the eyes in the process of birth; so there is no reason to think that many of the children of blind parents would be blind. Everything might be adapted to them in a community of this kind. For instance, moving pictures, dramas, and golf might have very little place in a village or colony of the blind, while operas and oratorios and phonograph concerts and social recreations, such as dancing, skating, and swimming, might be very popular.

SCHOOLS FOR THE DEAF

The play problem of the deaf does not differ greatly from that of normal children, because with their vision and by means of signs they are able to play nearly all games. In most institutions for the deaf there are excellent baseball, football, basket ball, and volley ball teams. Some institutions have abundant equipment for tennis and swimming, and the grounds are frequently supplied with ample apparatus. The provision for the girls is generally not as good as that for the boys, but in this they are only following the custom of other schools.

In the case of the deaf, sight has to take the place of both hearing and seeing, and it seems to be the place for the abundant use of the educational moving picture, which should be used far more than it is at present in any of the schools.

Perhaps the chief specific problem of the deaf is the fact that the main avenue of communication between people is cut off for them, and hence that they tend to become diffident and unsocial, a tendency which is strengthened by the fact that they are away from their parents, through whose loving care the social instincts are mostly developed in normal children. As play is the most social activity of childhood, it has its great function for the deaf in developing this social instinct. In order to do this, however, it is absolutely necessary that there shall be skillful and sympathetic direction of the play. The deaf, also, have less initiative than normal children and hence greater need for the organization of their games and athletics.

THE GRADUATES

It would seem also that the state ought to provide a colony or reservation for the deaf where they could be by themselves, have their own industries for which they have been prepared in the schools, and those forms of social life and recreation which are adapted to them. Deaf people who go out into the community, unless they are in the midst of relatives who keep alive their social instincts, often become crabbed and morose and find the isolation almost unendurable. Everything tends to make them feel the handicap under which they are suffering. It would be far better for them to live in a community by themselves where the whole community was adapted to their special problems, and where they could have a social life and recreations adapted to their capacities. As the majority of the deafness is due to sickness, it is not likely that a large percentage of the children of deaf parents would be deaf.

INSTITUTIONS FOR THE FEEBLE-MINDED

The institutions for the feeble-minded present a very specific problem, arising from the low mentality of the inmates. Children in these institutions are usually divided into three classes or types: the morons, or the ones of the highest grade of intelligence; the imbeciles, or middle class; and the idiots. The idiot is nearly helpless, cannot be taught, and will always be a complete charge. But the moron is frequently so nearly normal that he can only be detected by an expert or by Binet or other tests. From twenty-five to fifty per cent of the prostitutes in the cities are usually found to be morons, and as large a proportion, or larger, of the women in most of our reformatories and poorhouses. For the most part, the morons have not been recognized in the past by the community. In the institutions these higher grade defectives are usually given a considerable education in the old-time scholastic subjects, but rather more emphasis is placed on hand work and trade work than is customary in the public schools. They do most of the work about the buildings, such as sweeping the floors, making the beds, and washing the dishes and clothes. Outside of institutions, during most of their lives at least, these morons are usually nearly self-supporting.

My knowledge of defectives of this type is very limited, but everything that I have seen makes me question the value of a scholastic education for them. I suspect that arithmetic and geography, and even reading and writing, are about the stupidest subjects that could be taught to them and are the easiest way to make their lethargic intellects slumber rather than awake to activity. Not only do I not believe that arithmetic, for instance, is educational, but I am inclined to believe it is positively detrimental to their development and that most of this scholastic material should be banished absolutely from these schools. It is true that a few of the higher grade morons learn to read fairly well and do read by themselves, and there is probably a certain small percentage who ought to be taught, but for the great majority it would be easier and cheaper to furnish a reader to read aloud to those who wish to hear than it would be to teach them to read. As they do not handle money, they have little use for arithmetic, and they have very little need for writing.

Play is the natural stimulus to the mind of the child and makes him alert and resourceful. "All work and no play makes Jack a dull boy." Play has the highest value in arousing the slumbering intellect of defective children, and it should be made just as exciting as possible.

These children are below the normal in height and weight at every age, are underdeveloped physically, and have much more sickness than the normal. Work has not much to offer them, and nature has really emancipated them from many responsibilities in denying to them a normal intelligence. When they are happy, the feeble-minded are docile and obedient and inclined to be helpful about the institution; but if they are discontented, they are difficult to deal with. The line of training which is marked out by conditions is one which comes largely through play. As Alexander Johnson says in his study, "For them, the awakening of both the body and the mind is gained by stimulating and feeding the play instinct; as they begin to play, they begin to live." However, they are almost altogether lacking in initiative, and they will not play unless the games are organized for them. But they have ample time and no serious business in life which should interfere with their having a good time.

The games for feeble-minded children need to be graded according to their intelligence, and the kindergarten games will be about right for the imbeciles of fourteen or fifteen. But there is always a certain percentage who are able to play basket ball, volley ball, and even simplified football; and every child ought to be brought into the highest type of game in which he is capable of participating. They should have two or three hours every day for the playing of these games. So far as there is any attempt to give them general information or ideals in regard to life, this should be given almost entirely through moving pictures, because the picture has a far greater appeal to a lethargic intellect than has the written page, and forms of presentation must be found which are appealing enough to arouse a dormant intellect if they are to leave any impression. The music of a good phonograph would undoubtedly be appreciated in most of these institutions, as many of these defective children have a well-developed sense of rhythm and love music. They are often able to perform nearly or quite as well as the normal on musical instruments, and many of them should have some musical education.

COLONIES FOR DEFECTIVES

Again it seems to the writer that, after a certain amount of training and the teaching of certain simple trades such as farming and of certain simple forms of manufacture, upon reaching the age of sixteen these defectives should be placed in colonies by themselves, and that these colonies should be essentially communities just as near normal as possible; that the higher grade of defectives should be sterilized and allowed to marry if they chose. Under a competent general superintendent these colonies might become nearly or quite self-supporting, and even reach a stage of comparative independence and become essentially a caste by themselves. While in a community of normal people they are often the subject of jeers and taunts and are constantly shamed by their inability to hold their own, the feeble-minded living by themselves may be as happy as normal people. If they are allowed to marry and perhaps to adopt feeble-minded children, their lives would be as nearly normal as it is possible for such lives to be.

Industrial Schools

Forty or fifty years ago, if a boy did not choose to go to school he stayed at home; but now attendance is required. Many children are of an active, energetic type to whom the inaction of the schoolroom is torture. They are not interested in books, and the life of the school and the home studies are both distasteful to them. In the days of the pioneers these boys would have been scouts and explorers, successful Indian fighters, and resourceful members of the new community. But the study of books without manual or trade work, organized play, or athletics, strikes no responsive chord in their natures. They become delinquent from the lack of something better to do. It has been said by a number of our most prominent educators that the best schools for boys that there are in the country are the industrial schools for delinquents. Perhaps the chief advantage is that the boys have an opportunity to work, for in nearly all of these schools from three to four hours every day are devoted to some trade or industry, thus restoring to these boys a life such as was largely the lot of all boys fifty or sixty years ago. Most of these schools are located in the country. Farming is one of the chief occupations, but printing, tailoring, and shoemaking are also taught at many of them.

The old name for these institutions was Reform School, but one must search long for a justification of the name in an institution of the old type. The children are taken away from the bad influences at home and from the vicious associates with whom they have mingled, and from opportunities for delinquency perhaps, but one does not find many positive forces for reform. Of all the reformatory influences, it is probable that the work with the opportunity of learning a trade is the most important.

We have called these institutions Reform Schools, but thus far we have made every effort possible to keep the boys out of them, through the juvenile court and our probation system. The old-time reform school was probably about as bad a place for boys as could be found. The discipline and management were largely along the lines of the workhouse or the penitentiary. Those in charge were essentially policemen or custodians. We are creating to-day a new type of institution with sympathetic discipline, an excellent educational system, and the beginnings of an organization of play and social life which may ultimately make these schools real centers of reform.

There are certain specific problems which the reformatory must meet. One of these problems is self-abuse, which is always common among boys, but is probably more common in institutions of this type than it is elsewhere. In the beginning, it was largely to prevent self-abuse that play was made compulsory in the Preparatory and Public Schools of England. A second problem is that the bad boys from all parts of the state are brought together. The old-time penitentiary and the present jail where the vicious teach each other all that each knows of evil, are probably quite as successful as schools of crime as any of our other schools are in teaching their course of study, and any institution for delinquent boys that leaves much time for idleness and gossip is sure to be a place where each boy learns most of the evil known to the others. It seems to be necessary that the children in these schools should be kept busy. The delinquents in general are the motor-minded type with an excess of physical energy, and in order for them to be contented and amenable to discipline, they must find expression for this energy. In the mental and spiritual side certain social ideals must be developed. The majority of the boys in such institutions are there on account of petty larceny. They must acquire a property sense. It has been found in the Junior Republic at Freeville that just as soon as the boys have gardens their sense of property rights becomes acute and they are likely to inflict severe penalties upon those that commit depredations. Out of this sense of ownership there always grows a feeling antagonistic to stealing. Probably the most fundamental defect in delinquents is that they have never acquired a community sense or become members in a vital way of the social group in which they were placed. They have not developed loyalty to it, and hence commit depredations. The easiest way to develop this sense is through the team game where loyalty is essential to success and where all the traditions of the game tend in that direction.

The boys in reformatories are mostly from ten to eighteen years of age, just the period for team games. The ages correspond to those at the old-time Public Schools of England, and there is no other place probably where there is so great need of that type of compulsory athletics which is found in these schools. All the boys should be members of baseball teams, football teams, basket ball teams, at least, and perhaps of others. All of the older boys should be Scouts because of the ideals of manliness, courage, resourcefulness, courtesy, and honesty which are inculcated, and because they would enjoy and have adequate opportunity for the practice of the

Scout crafts and games. It might well be the easiest way also of developing the morals and sense of responsibility among the boys. In this way the idleness would be largely done away with, they would find expression for their motor energy, and they would be too tired at night to practice self-abuse. On the positive side they would acquire those ideals of honor, honesty, courage, resourcefulness, and fairplay which are easiest trained through athletics and scouting and which are absolutely essential in the training of delinquents. It must be remembered that sportsmanship is essentially primitive ethics, in the form which is most applicable and appealing to boys of this age. It is the easiest way to train in courage, loyalty, honesty, and courtesy. These schools should furnish opportunity for at least two hours of play and scouting every day, and a series of tournaments should be arranged in which every team and every boy would take part.

It goes without saying that every such school should have also an adequate gymnasium and swimming pool and other facilities for play indoors during blustery or rainy weather when exercise cannot be carried on outside.

Probably there is no reformatory that thus far has made adequate use of the moving picture and the phonograph in furnishing entertainment and instruction to its wards. Mr. Fairchild in his teaching of morals to school children uses the moving picture extensively. If they are so presented as not to seem to be prearranged sermons, some social ideals can doubtless be taught in this way more effectively than in any other.

PHYSICAL DIRECTORS

The person who is most needed in all of these institutions for boys, next to the superintendent or principal, is a physical director, and there is probably no other place where the right kind of a man could do so much for the welfare of a group of boys as in an institution of this kind. If he has the proper ideals of sport, he may give all of them a training in just those things which are necessary to make them useful members of the community. A probation officer of social interests and personal popularity can do far more in an institution of this kind for the children than he can for children outside whom he probably sees very infrequently.

So far as the juvenile court and the probation system penalizes adults who are contributing to the delinquency of children, reforms the home, and prevents boys who have been merely unfortunate or badly led temporarily from going to institutions of the old type, it has undoubtedly done a great service. But we may well question whether probation has much reformatory value in the hands of the ordinary probation officer. Perhaps it would be better for most of these boys, where the home is unsatisfactory, to be placed in institutions of the newer type. If they prove to be real reformatories, we should not try to keep delinquents out.

REFORMATORIES FOR GIRLS

Most of the girls in these institutions are there because of home conditions or sex offenses, and pretty nearly everything that has been said of institutions for boys will apply also to them. The Camp Fire Girls is probably our most effective method of teaching the virtues of the home and giving a social viewpoint to the girls, and it would seem that all the girls should be encouraged to become members of the Camp Fire Girls and to turn their thoughts toward the home and service to the community.

Penitentiaries

The orthodox treatment of convicts has always been until lately to give them a very meager and unappetizing diet, to confine them in narrow cells, and in general to make their stay in penitentiaries so uncomfortable that they will not wish to return. But for the last two decades there has been a change of attitude, and more and more there is a persistent attempt to improve sanitary and other conditions in prisons and to make the inmates as contented as possible.

Most of the penitentiaries now have baseball teams, and the baseball game on Saturday afternoon is very likely to be the great event of the week. It has been found in a number of cases that the most effective penalty that can be inflicted upon a prisoner is to deny him access to the baseball or football game at that time. It has been found that baseball has done a great deal in many cases to improve the morals of the prisoners.

There will be objection on the part of many to any attempt to make the life of prisoners more pleasant, but it lies in line with present tendencies. A gymnasium and swimming pool would be a decided asset to any state penitentiary. There are a number of penitentiaries that have weekly entertainments with music, recitations, sleight of hand, juggling, phonograph concerts, or moving pictures, for the more trustworthy members of the penitentiaries at any rate. The denial of the privilege of attending these entertainments is found to be one of the most effective penalties that can be inflicted. It might easily be possible, also, to bring in films which would help to impart a social outlook to the prisoners.

It may be said that this would make the prison too pleasant for the inmates and that it would then have no value in the prevention of crime. But we may well question if prison punishments have ever had much value in the prevention of crime. Many of the inmates have never had a fair chance and were almost predestined by the environment in which they were placed to do the things which brought them there. We may also ask ourselves if the doctrine of rendering good for evil and heaping coals of fire on the head of the prisoner by trying to make him happy in return for his misdeeds may not be quite as effective in the prevention of crime as will be any fear of punishment which is aggravated by illwill towards society.

A PENAL COLONY

Discharged prisoners always have a hard time. They are suspected by every one, and no one wishes to employ them. There have been a number of cases where factories have been started for them, but always from private funds and on a limited scale. Apparently the state has not made a great business success of its penal institutions, as very few of these able-bodied men are self-supporting, but it would seem that the graduates of penitentiaries also ought to have provided for them a special colony or village in which the industries which they have learned while in the institutions might be carried on, and that these ought to be owned by the state and managed by some capable and sympathetic state official. The place where the socialistic principle of state-owned industries might be applied with least criticism, and where it is most demanded at the present time, is for the former members of these various institutions.

SANITARIUMS AND HOSPITALS

There is a growing realization of the need of recreation for the sick and convalescent in our hospitals and sanitariums, but, thus far, comparatively little has been done. There can be no question as to the great therapeutic value of any form of recreation that will divert the mind from thoughts of self and sickness to dwell on more healthful themes. It is well known to every doctor that many of the ills from which their patients are suffering have been largely engendered by this morbid dwelling upon them, and that a new interest is often better than medicine. Every sanitarium and hospital, but especially hospitals for tubercular patients and others that are not confined to their beds, should have adequate provision for moving picture and phonograph entertainments of cheerful nature.[1] Every form of recreation in the open air which the strength of the patients enables them to participate in, such as croquet, bowling on the green, gardening, automobile riding, and a modified form of golf with shorter distances and drives, should be provided. There should be also facilities for the study of birds, and the making of collections of flowers, insects, and the like, wherever the location of the hospital or sanitarium makes this possible. There should be workshops where the patients can make pottery, baskets, and do embroidery and other similar forms of manual work. Of course many of these undertakings cannot be carried on except in connection with large hospitals with reasonably ample grounds.

[1] At the Indiana State Conference of Charities for 1915, Rev. Tillotson in speaking of the hospital for tuberculosis patients at Rockville, says: "We feel that a very important thing for us to consider is some method of amusing our patients. We have purchased two dozen phonographs and are considering the

Institutions for the Insane

Most of the inmates in asylums for the insane are there for one of three reasons: their heredity, alcoholism, or syphilis. Of those in institutions who have a hereditary taint of insanity, many might have escaped the disease if they had followed all of the necessary precautions. For the chief causes which bring on insanity in the predisposed are sickness, overwork, worry, and morbid brooding on wrongs. Probably the best cure for this condition is absorbing play or work which will keep the mind fresh, throw off worries, and give the person each day a fresh point of view. Perhaps the greatest therapeutic agent that could be brought into asylums would be proper organization of the recreational life of the inmates. Their general health is not usually good, and they need to be kept in the open air and given abundant exercise. They need to have their minds diverted from themselves and an opportunity for social intercourse. Most of them have nothing to do, and there is no reason why they should not play.

There cannot be a proper development of recreation, however, unless there is some one to organize it. One half the number of custodians or internes who are now looking after the patients inside could, if properly trained, probably take charge of the recreation outside and secure better results. They should have training with this end in view, or physical directors should be employed.

Naturally the games must be graded according to the intelligence and physical and mental condition of the inmates.

purchase of a moving picture machine." Nothing is more deadly than living with a company of individuals who have nothing to do but think of and talk over their ills. — *Bulletin Indiana State Conference of Charities.*

There are many for whom the kindergarten games would be about right. Such games have been organized during several years for the inmates of the asylum at Kalamazoo, Michigan, and have been much appreciated by them. From these low-grade insane up to those who are able to play baseball and tennis, there will be every grade of ability in the ordinary asylum, and there should be opportunity for all the games which the inmates are able to play. Volley ball, indoor baseball, and bowls on the bowling green, and croquet are admirably adapted for institutions of this kind.

Every evening there should be story telling, light and cheerful music on the phonograph or piano, and moving pictures that would suggest cheerful thoughts and a normal and vigorous outlook upon life. In an institution of this kind the insane might be quite as happy, if not more happy, than normal people, and find themselves content to pass their days there.

In the Indiana Bulletin of Charities for June 1916, there is a summary of a paper by Dr. Paul E. Bowers, of the work recently introduced into the Indiana hospital for insane criminals at Michigan City. While this is spoken of as work, it is evidently play to the inmates and has been introduced into the asylum for the purpose of play.

As the experience of this institution should be helpful to others, the following paragraphs are quoted from this report:

The committee of the American Medico-Psychological Association of 1913 made the report on diversional occupation as follows: "Diversional occupation, scientifically and systematically applied, marks the standing of a hospital, and if neglected or omitted, the patients are not receiving the most modern care and treatment to which they are entitled."

It is my personal opinion that seventy-five per cent of all the patients at the Indiana Hospital for Insane Criminals can be employed seventy-five per cent of the time. The patients now look upon the opportunity of working in our shops [1] as a much coveted privilege and a very noticeable improvement has been made in the conduct of many of them to earn the chance to do and make something that is worth while.

It is sincerely hoped by the management of the hospital that we will in a short time be able to give every patient who is mentally and physically able to work an opportunity to

[1] Now let me state briefly what actually has been done in our shops since its installation, December 14, 1915. Notwithstanding the fact that the workers were insane patients, the attendants themselves without experience as to the mechanism and operation of the machines, there have been woven 2039 yards of fine linen toweling, at a cost of less than 5 cents per yard. This same material costs from 18 cents to 20 cents in the open market. In addition, 3600 pair of new socks, 100 new mattresses, 100 new pillows, 50 cushions, doormats, floormats, cloth shoes, rag rugs, hammocks, shopping bags, gloves, and shirting were manufactured. Two hundred and sixty old mattresses and 200 old pillows were renovated and 6000 pair of socks were darned. Besides this, all the repair work on hospital bedding and clothing was done.

Other diversional occupation was furnished our patients in the form of intensive gardening by careful rotation of crops. During the last three years there has been raised on a little less than an acre of pure sandy soil, the following vegetables: Onions 80,000, radishes 43,600, beans 4359 lb., peas 128 lb., lettuce 2174 lb., cucumbers 6 bu., beets 39 bu., watermelons 300, muskmelons 1700, cabbage 850 heads, turnips 1 bu., tomatoes $129\frac{1}{2}$ bu., horseradish 19 bu., celery 11,000 bunches, red peppers $1\frac{1}{2}$ bu., and Swiss chard 24 bu. This amount of vegetables was sufficient, except for potatoes, to supply the needs during the season, of both the Hospital for the Insane Criminals and the Prison Hospital, with a combined population of near 250.

Incidentally there is an economical side to this method of treatment. The products have value. That lessens the expense. Larger looms for the weaving of blankets and rag carpets will be installed as soon as possible, and then our shop will be a greater commercial asset than it is at present. It is safe to say that after all the institutional needs are supplied we can find a ready sale in the open market for the excess products.

find pleasure and relief from the ordinary irksomeness of institutional life. The experiment here has proven beyond a doubt that work treatment is valuable and necessary.

Conclusion

In conclusion it would seem that all of the institutions for children are practically boarding schools, and that there is no reason why they should be inferior as schools to Eton or Rugby in England, or Groton or Lawrenceville in this country, except the ideals which stand behind them, and the people who have been placed in charge. The school life at Eton and Rugby has been built up largely around the athletic field, and a similar organization of play in the orphan asylums, schools for the blind and the deaf, and the reformatories would go far toward securing a similar result. In all of these schools there is an abundance of time, and unless play is organized idleness always finds evil work for idle hands and evil thoughts for idle brains. Self-abuse is nearly universal and the sick rate is sure to be high. The children are lacking in initiative and do not play much unless their games are organized for them. In many of the institutions, they are much underdeveloped physically. They need the open air, and the training and joy of play. They are denied association with father and mother, brothers and sisters, and they need an intensifying and training of their social affections. To fill the aching void left by the missing parents, they need most of all the intimate friendship of and association with adults. All of these facts indicate that one of the most vital requirements for all such institutions is the organization of games and play under sympathetic men and women of high ideals.

CHAPTER VIII

PLAY IN THE COUNTRY

FORTY-THREE per cent of our farms are now held by tenants, and forty-three per cent of the owners have moved into the towns. This migration has not been due to unprofitable agriculture, for it is precisely where farming has been most profitable and farm values are highest, in Ohio, Indiana, and Illinois, that the largest percentage of tenancy exists. Just as soon as he is able, apparently, the farmer abandons his farm, and the more profitable it has been, the earlier he has been able to move.

These retiring farmers are a serious problem to the towns in which they live, because they furnish there an ultra-conservative element, who object to all modern improvements that will cost money. Farms do not rent for more than two or three per cent of their value, and the farmer who retires from a ten-thousand-dollar farm to live in the city cannot support himself according to American standards on the rent. He votes down street paving and lighting, new municipal buildings, adequate pay for teachers, and other improvements.

He makes the problem of the country in many ways. He withdraws from it at just the time when he might have assumed a position of leadership. He no longer sends his children to the rural school, and he wants a cheap teacher and a cheap school. He no longer attends or supports the rural church. He is seldom interested in the macadamizing of the country roads or other improvements. The tenant who takes the farm usually does so from year to year. He is not interested in its permanent fertility or appearance; he lets everything run down.

The retiring farmer often comes to town for the sake of his children, but the country village is probably the worst place in the world for them. The city has its art galleries and museums, its parks and playgrounds. It is a great and perennial exposition of all the world is doing. In the country the boy learns to harness and drive the horses and cultivate the crops. By the time he is fourteen, he knows a trade. But in the rural village there is little but idleness for children, and the devil always finds abundant work for idle hands to do. Although rural villages are supported entirely from the surrounding farms as a rule, it is there that we hear most about "rubes" and "hayseeds." The farm boy in the village has his mind turned away from agriculture as a pursuit.

One of the things for which the gratitude of the country is due President Roosevelt is that he appointed the Country Life Commission. Liberty Bailey of Cornell, the president of the Commission, has summed it up by saying, "The problem of the country is to develop and maintain on the American farm a type of civilization which represents fairly well our American ideals." This report has caused the introduction of courses in rural sociology into many of our normal schools and colleges of agriculture, the establishment of permanent country life commissions in several of the states, and the organization of a series of Country Life Conferences that meet each year in a number of others.

Why are the Farmers Leaving the Farms?

SPIRITUAL STARVATION

It is chiefly a case of spiritual starvation. A rounded life must have a series of aims, of which business success is only one. It must include a happy family life, a respected place in the community, and the enjoyment of various social and other forms of recreation. Business success is meaningless in itself except as it secures to men the gratification of these fundamental human desires; yet always there is a tendency for one to lose sight of the end in the pursuit of the means, and to forget essential purposes in the struggle for gain. To this blindness of pursuit the farmer has been peculiarly subject. Yet if country life is to be made attractive, it must come through the rediscovery and pursuit of these essential values, that the farmer shall no longer seek "to buy more land to raise more corn to feed more hogs to buy more land," and so on ad infinitum, but shall perceive that by this process he has land and not life at the end, and that he has been but little less dissipated than the drunkard himself.

If there is any one text that should be written over the doors of all our American homes, it is, "For what is a man profited if he shall gain the whole world and lose his own life; or what shall a man give in exchange for his life?" All through the ages the life of man has been determined by the conditions under which he was born, and even to-day there is little freedom of choice for the peasant peoples of Europe: here in America for the first time has it been given to a great people to lead a life that might satisfy the spirit; but we are bartering the gold for the tinsel; we are forgetting to live, in the pursuit of a living.

Some three years ago I spent a portion of my summer in walking through the Adirondack Mountains. The chief obstacle to my complete enjoyment of the summer was the autoists who thronged so many of the mountain highways. Often after a long climb through some steep path, one would reach a high ridge which commanded the valleys on each side, and would be overcome with the sublimity of the scene. But lo, a cloud of dust, and an auto dashes by, and another, and another at thirty miles an hour. Speak with the occupants. They have been a hundred miles to-day; they had dinner at such a hotel; they will reach such a place for supper; but of the beauty and grandeur of the mountains they had seen little; they had not had time. Perhaps the speeding autoist is typical of America. We seem as a people to be subject to the illusion that the purpose of life is to get somewhere rather than to enjoy and profit by the journey. But he who does not find his life worth while from day to day will not find it so at the end. "Write it upon thy heart," says Emerson, "to-day is the best day in all the year."

Some time ago, while on a trip to Porto Rico, I made the acquaintance of a gentleman who said that when he and his wife were married they had agreed that they would work hard and save until they were worth fifty thousand dollars. Then they would retire and enjoy life. He said they kept at work steadily without vacations until they were some sixty years of age, when they took an inventory and found that they were worth fifty thousand dollars or more. They decided to retire, but the next week his wife died, and he had taken no comfort in life since. Is not this also typical? We set some mark which we expect to reach and to begin our real lives at that time. But "our to-days and yesterdays are the blocks with which we build." We must live our lives as we go along.

The farmer is trying to get rich, but he has no great use for wealth. He can raise what he wishes to eat; he dresses very inexpensively; wealth does not confer social position in the country, nor does poverty deprive a worthy person of it. He has no great need for money, but in his pursuit of it he often neglects all the larger values of life and drives his sons and daughters from the farm. He comes home from his work at night exhausted and goes to bed, not thinking that it may be as well worth while to raise a worthy family of children, as it is a litter of pigs. He comes to church overwearied on Sunday and often goes to sleep. He has no time to take part in movements for the public welfare. He neglects his duty as a husband and father, as a Christian and a citizen, because he has given to his farm his last ounce of time and effort. Spiritually he is a beggar upon the community, leaving to others his most sacred family and social duties. This often goes on for years, and then he comes to a realization that this sort of a life is not worth living and he retires. In this he is right in his conclusion, but not in the solution that he finds for his problem.

TOO LONG HOURS

There can be little doubt but the working hours in the past have been too long on the farm, as there has often been a ten- or twelve-hour day in the fields and two or three hours more devoted to caring for the teams and doing the chores. Almost any sort of work becomes drudgery when it is carried on for too long. It leaves no time or energy for the spirit or social life. It is this, for the most part, that makes the boys and girls and the hired man dissatisfied with farm life. It is probable that the long day nearly always yields a smaller financial return than a shorter day. Forty years ago the farmer held the handles of his plow in a single furrow; to-day he is plowing largely with a gang or at least a riding plow. Forty years ago he sowed his wheat by hand; to-day he is drilling it in. Forty years ago he cut it with a cradle; to-day he cuts it with a twine binder. Forty years ago he threshed it largely with a flail; to-day he threshes it with an engine and threshing machine. From being a laborer, he has become a mechanic and a scientist. Modern farming is, according to Professor Carver of Harvard, our most learned profession. But the farmer who works fifteen hours a day will remain a day laborer still, because he has not time to acquire modern methods. He does his work wastefully because he has not taken time to plan it. He does many things that were not worth doing at all, because he has not considered; and, like we other sinners, "he leaves undone many things that he ought to have done." He does not have time to acquire the newer methods or attend farmers' institutes, or confer with his neighbors; and at present the great problem of profitable farming is the problem of better marketing rather than greater production. It is becoming increasingly difficult for the old type of farmer to make money on the farm. Bailey says, "The half holiday is coming in the country and coming fast." Let us hope for a shorter day, and a half holiday on Saturday. There is little possibility for progress either industrially or socially in the country without more time, and unless we can shorten the day we cannot hold the boys and girls and the hired man.

THE FARMER DOES NOT ENJOY HIS WORK OR THE COUNTRY

The explanation of this is largely that he is working too long hours, but not entirely so. Too long hours always detract from the enjoyment of work, but the lawyer, the doctor, and the clergyman do not on this account retire young. The farmer who continues to do his work by rule of thumb is dealing with a blind fate, but the farmer who tills his fields in the spirit of modern agriculture finds each crop, and herd of swine or cattle, a scientific experiment, no less interesting than the experiments of the laboratory, and a new joy in his work.

It is a sad fact that it seems to be the city people, not the farmers, who are enjoying the country. An appreciation of the beauty of nature should be the cornerstone of all education for farm life. The farmer who has come to this appreciation will not be content in the city; and the farmer who has not, must necessarily miss much of the culture and joy that the country has to give. Country life must have the touch of beauty to redeem it from sordidness.

THE LACK OF SOCIAL LIFE AND RECREATION

We are all social beings and most people dislike to be alone. Business, law, medicine, and most other trades and professions offer opportunities for conversation while work is being carried on, or, if they do not offer this opportunity, they at least give the sense of companionship which comes from the nearness of others. But the farmer in the field is isolated, and the farm wife is isolated in the home. In the investigations carried on by the Country Life Commission, it was this isolation at work that was most often emphasized as making farm life unattractive.

But it will be noticed from the last census that it is not only the farms that have lost in population through nearly all parts of the country, but the small towns have lost as well. One of the chief reasons for the migration to the larger cities is the recreational facilities which are offered there. Every one wants to have a good time and does not care to live where he does not. There is no lack of these opportunities in the country, but the farm population has never been trained to appreciate or utilize them.

Why are the Farm Women Dissatisfied?

TOO LONG HOURS

When any one speaks of playgrounds, we often think of the little children in the crowded slums of the city and consider that there the playground is most needed, but undoubtedly from a larger point of view the one person who needs play more than any other is the farm wife. She is working far too long hours, and her work is uninteresting and monotonous. She has almost no vacations and little social life. When the Pittsburgh Survey revealed the fact that in the great steel mills about that city one third of the workers were toiling for twelve hours a day and seven days a week, the whole country was stirred, and people said it was an outrage that anywhere people should be expected to work for such hours. There are at least a half dozen states in the Union that forbid the employment of women for more than fifty-six hours a week, but there is nothing to prevent the women from working one hundred hours a week in the farm homes. Probably they are averaging not less than ninety hours over a good share of the country. The work is unrelieved by vacations, and it is essentially uninteresting and monotonous. There is not much interest in washing the dishes to-day, and the fact that it will have to be done over for three hundred and sixty-four other days during the year, does not add to the interest. The farmer's work is out of doors where he gets the fresh air, where he can hear the song of the bird and see the distant landscape, but his wife is often nearly or quite as much closed in as the city woman. The advancing year brings to the farmer its plowing, its seedtime, and its harvest. Each day offers different duties, and all along, as he works, he realizes the profits that are to come to him from the work that he is doing. The woman's work is the same from one end of the year to the other, and it yields no direct financial return. Too often she is working fourteen hours a day for her board. It is not by accident that one finds "at rest" inscribed on so many country tombstones. In some communities where the girls have been questioned, it has been found that scarcely one of them wished to marry a farmer, and that their mothers did not wish them to. Here is surely one of the chief reasons for the townward migration.

The farm home has been the glory of our commonwealth, for out of it have come most of our strong men and many of our strong women. The life is more intimate there than it is anywhere else. The young lawyer or doctor may live in a boarding house, but a wife is a part of the necessary equipment of a farm. The wife and children of the lawyer or mechanic usually know little of the work of the husband and father. The family has few points of contact and sympathy, but farming is an enterprise in which all the family are members of the firm. They understand and take an interest in all that is undertaken. The mother is the socializing factor in all this knowledge. It is she that makes the home and the family unity. It is she that must organize the social life both of the family and of the community as well. She cannot do this unless she can have some leisure to read and visit and think, unless she has some margin of energy and time which is not devoted to household drudgery. It is said that the child learns more during the first six years of his life than he does in all the years that come afterwards. During these years, the mother is his only teacher, and to sacrifice her leisure is to sacrifice the future of the child as well. The editor of *Farm and Fireside* was speaking in northern Minnesota some time ago and urging the farmers to start a coöperative laundry in connection with their creamery. He said it would not cost them more than ten cents a week to have the family wash done in this way. A German rose in the back part of the room and said, "Vell, but vat vill mine vife do ven she don't save that ten cents." When asked how many children he had, he said, "nine." Any farmer ought to be ashamed to have a wife whose time was not worth more than ten cents a day to her family. Since the days of the pioneer, the work of the farmer has been transformed, but there has not been the same change in woman's work. The farm home contains little machinery, and the larger house, the better furniture, the more elaborate meals have all increased the farm wife's work. It is essential to the solution of all the larger problems of rural life that in some way the farm women should get more leisure and should find their lives more satisfying. This must come through the introduction of labor-saving machinery, through a more practical education, and through the better organization of the social life of the home and the community.

LACK OF LABOR-SAVING DEVICES

The sewing machine is at the present time the only laborsaving device in most farm homes, whereas there are a dozen or more such labor-saving machines on the farm. If the farm can afford a mowing machine, it may be taken as axiomatic that it can afford a windmill as well. If not a windmill, then a gasoline engine should be furnished, for running water in the house is the first requisite in the saving of labor. If there is a coöperative creamery in the neighborhood, then a coöperative laundry should be started with it, and the clothing should not be made in the home. However, the greatest consumption of time is due to inefficient methods of work. There is no money value put upon the work in the home, and there often is nothing to look forward to if it is quickly done. Consequently it is often done listlessly, and there is no attempt to study ways of economizing motions; as the result, probably fully half of the effort made is wasted in unnecessary motions of one kind or another. There is probably no other place where the efficiency movement has so great a mission at present as in housekeeping.

HAVE NOT BEEN TRAINED FOR THEIR LIFE WORK

It is difficult to see that geography and syntax have much to do with farm life, or that a knowledge of them constitutes a preparation for the work of the housewife and mother. If woman's work is to be made interesting, it must be carried up to a higher plane. It must be ennobled by love and a sense of service, and it must become a science as the farmer's has. Home sanitation and cooking and preserving are interesting to any one who is not overdriven and who understands the principles involved. A thorough training in the science of the home may do much to make its work more interesting and efficient.

During four or five months of the year the work on the farm is not hard. During this time the rural people of Denmark are carrying on their industrial and higher education. Here a great opportunity is wasted in America. Thirty or forty years ago the girls and boys were often going to the rural school during the late fall and winter until they were twenty years of age, but now they have mostly finished by fourteen. In every township at least there should be a good industrial high school which would teach during the colder months the mechanics and agriculture which are essential to the success of the farm, and the domestic economy and baby culture which are essential to the success of the home.

THE DECREASING SIZE OF THE FAMILIES IS MAKING THE COUNTRY LESS ATTRACTIVE

We are apt to think of the mother as working when she is caring for the baby, but in fact the mother with the baby is the most perfect picture of play we have, and the baby is the most successful piece of play apparatus that ever came from the hands of the Almighty. Go down on the East Side and see the women on the benches in Tompkins Square or Hamilton Fish Park on a warm afternoon. In the arms of nearly every woman is a baby. If one will sit there and watch them for an hour or two, he will be convinced that it is the necessity for recreation of the tenement mothers that is one secret of the large families on the East Side. The baby is in fact a sort of superlative doll to the mother, around which all the tenderness of life is grouped, and which with each new day becomes a new doll with a new laugh, a new cry, a new word to distinguish it from the doll of yesterday. Perhaps the saddest thing about the farm homes at the present time is the decreasing size of the families. If a child is an only child in the city, he can play with the neighbors' children, but an only child in the country has no one to play with, and consequently he becomes a little man or a little woman and not really a child at all. In the early days the families were large in the country, and the family became socially independent. There were enough for an abundance of play, and the older ones got the training that came from caring for the younger ones. The older girls were really apprentice mothers. The children kept alive the love and altruism and the spirit of joy in the lives of their parents. The families are everywhere decreasing in size in country sections, and many rural schools have to be abandoned because there are not enough children to warrant a school. It is a far sadder phenomenon for the country than it is for the city, for the city has depended on this fresh blood to maintain its decadent population; and the children have furnished all the play that has come to the farm home.

The child in the city is a luxury. He does not become self-supporting in most cases much before his majority, and nearly always, especially during his earlier years, he is a source of anxiety, as there are often no places where he can play in safety or where he can even be out of doors and establish his health without running into constant risk of life and limb. The child in the country becomes self-supporting earlier than he does anywhere else; there is an abundance of room for his play; he has around him the birds, the trees, the flowers, and the animals which are the natural environment of children everywhere; he can play by himself as a rule without danger; and he is vastly less bother than he is anywhere else. The natural things by which he is surrounded have a deep appeal to his nature and furnish a large part of his early education. The outdoor life establishes his health and stabilizes his nervous system and in every way gives him the best possible foundation for a vigorous life. The disappearance of the child from the farm home is a double tragedy, because the disappearance means the vanishing of the spirit of play and of joy from the home, and because the country at large has always depended upon these farm boys and girls to keep the stock vigorous and wholesome.

Why do the Boys and Girls go to the City?

Where the boys and girls are going to the city it is in most cases probably because the spirit that is seen on the farm is fundamentally at variance with the spirit of youth and its conception of the values of life. To youth, material prosperity is seldom an aim in itself. It wishes for fame and adventure and love, and it finds this utter devotion to material aims sordid and meaningless. Too often the time that is required leaves no margin in which to pursue the aims that are vital to it.

If a farmer is spoken to about allowing his boy to play on a baseball team, in a large number of cases he will reply that his boy does not need to play ball because he gets plenty of exercise on the farm; but play has nothing more to do with exercise than it has to do with religion. Play is the one fundamental expression of the spirit of childhood and youth. It is only in play that the boy is a real boy. Play is essentially a rudimentary organ of the soul, as Dr. Hall has said. If the tadpole's tail is cut off, the frog does not develop any hind legs; to cut off in the same way the play and adventure and romance of youth is to cut off the food supply for the later developments of the soul. The farmer is apt to look upon the romantic spirit of his daughter as foolishness, but the girl who grows up without any romance in her life may make a good hired girl or business woman, but she will always lack that delicate charm which is woman's right.

Must make the Home Life Fuller

If farm life is to be made attractive, it must be given a new spirit. Material progress must be only one of a series of aims. The hours must be shortened, and farm people must come to enjoy the country and their work. They must see in social life and play values which are not to be disregarded in the pursuit of wealth. This new spirit must come to the home, the school, and the community.

The farm homes of the past have been the glory of this country, and at their best they are so still. There is an intimacy of life and knowledge, a common participation in work, and a common appreciation of ends to be secured, such as is not found, for the most part, in other homes. But to a considerable extent, the farm home is now failing on account of the decreasing size of the families, the decreasing coöperation on the part of the children in the work and play of the home, and the decreasing social life that has come with the abundance of newspapers and magazines. The home must not forget its family life, and it must provide both within the home and the yard things that are necessary for the play of the children. Children are constantly leading the father and mother into activities that they would not otherwise have thought of, and if the home life is satisfying, the boys and girls may still be content, despite the hard work.

In passing through the country in almost any state one cannot help being impressed with the apparent materialism of the life. Generally, in the northern part of the country, the barns are better than the houses. But even though the house may be large and expensive, there are seldom any flower beds or shrubbery that indicate an appreciation of beauty. The dooryard is often littered with dilapidated machinery. Still, the play equipment that is needed is simple and easily installed. Little children always delight to play in the sand. If there are two or three little children, a sand bin will probably be used for two or three hundred hours each year. Its cost is practically nil. There should be one or two low swings suspended from the limb of a tree or from a framework erected for the purpose. There should be a playhouse or tent in the yard, because these tend to develop the imagination and assist in all the dramatizing games that the children play. A tent will enable the children to sleep out of doors during six months of the year. It can be used for week-end and other camping trips, and it serves almost equally as well for a playhouse. Such a tent can be purchased for almost any price from three dollars and a half up. Probably croquet is played more than any other game at farm homes at the present time. It is a good game to get acquainted over, is suited alike to the old and the young, the boys and the girls. It is probably the best known means of teaching honesty and sportsmanship, so far as that means a good temper and courtesy. There ought to be tennis also at every country home. We are apt to think of tennis as a city game, but it would be quite impossible to secure the land if the people of any city should seriously undertake to play. The farm has plenty of land, it has the implements if a dirt court is to be made, and there are always two people old enough to play — the farmer and his wife. I suppose it would be a serious wrench to our traditions to see them playing tennis after supper, but there are few things that would be more salutary. For the older son and daughter, it would mean life. This will seem an impractical suggestion to most, because it would appear that the farmer's work is too hard for him to appreciate such a game. The farmer is working far too long hours, but during much of the year his work is not hard physically, for more and more, in recent years, he is becoming a mechanic instead of a laborer. He gets muscle bound and stiff from his work, and almost anything that would keep him supple would add to his physical efficiency. But tennis could do far more for the farm wife and daughter than for the farmer and son. A tennis club for the neighborhood where games might be played Saturday afternoons might well be one of the best of social occasions for the young people.

Reorganize the Rural School

If this estimate of life which perceives the spiritual as well as its material values is to become general in the country, it must become a part of the training that is given by the rural school. In some way the country school must teach country people to love the country; it must help the boys to be successful in agriculture and the management of machines; it must teach the girls to be efficient housewives and mothers; it must emphasize the significance of social life, and it must teach those games which are adapted to country sections. Writing, history, syntax, geography, and at least nine tenths of the arithmetic have never had anything directly to do with success on the farm or in the farm home. These subjects are often spoken of as cultural, but they are really the dry husks of knowledge and have far less to do with spiritual growth than does the instruction which teaches the duties of the individual to the family and the community and emphasizes social relationships and an appreciation of beauty and right conduct.

There is great interest throughout this country at present in the improvement of the rural school. Certainly it needs it. More than one half of the children of the United States are still getting their education there. From it have come many of our strongest men, but they have been the superior ones who learned in spite of obstacles. To the rank and file, it has given little more than the ability to read and write and do simple sums. Its curriculum has had no relationship to the country or its problems. Its teachers have been young, untrained, and poorly paid. The building is generally unsatisfactory and the yard entirely inadequate to the play of the children. A better time is coming. We are getting larger yards and better buildings, we are introducing agriculture and domestic science. Many schools are being consolidated, and the teachers are being better trained and paid.

The Grounds of Rural Schools

The grounds of rural schools until recently, despite the fact of the low cost of land, have been wholly inadequate.

The committee of the N. E. A. on minimum requirements for rural schools placed the minimum of ground at three acres, and a recent state law in North Dakota requires at least two. Certainly a better time is upon us. Districts nearly everywhere are now getting twice as much land as they were five or ten years ago, and not infrequently they are very much larger. While at a teachers' institute in Yuma, Arizona, a short time ago, I was told by the County Superintendent that most of their new playgrounds were five acres or more in size. The same is true of the rural schools of Kern and Tulare Counties, California. It is not unknown for a ground of twenty or even forty acres to be set aside for this purpose. In the little town of Weathersfield, Ill., which is a place of about a thousand inhabitants, there is a ten-room school located on ten acres of ground which is kept under the lawn mower. There is a full-sized baseball diamond, and football field; there are three or four tennis courts, a volley ball court, a basket ball court, space for croquet, and a considerable play equipment. Besides this there are abundant trees and several beautiful flower beds. It is an inspiration to see grounds of this kind. May their tribe increase!

In some rural sections of Iowa there are a number of districts where in some way the school directors thirty or forty years ago must have had a vision of what a school ground might be. They secured two or three acres and planted maple trees around it. These trees are now seventy or eighty feet tall and the ground a delight.

In the Province of Ontario, schools which make good provision for school gardens and grounds receive extra compensation from the province, and something of that kind should be the law with us. The difficulty with many of the larger grounds is that they are not mowed, and a large ground that is not mowed cannot be used to advantage by the children. The grounds of the rural school should be fenced in order to keep out the cows, and over this fence should be some kind of a flowering vine. It should be surrounded by at least two rows of trees, and it should be kept in condition for use. Where the larger grounds have been secured for rural schools, it has often been in order that they might have gardens and conduct agricultural experiments. There is a certainly growing sentiment for a "teacherage" or teacher's house in connection with the rural school, and ofttimes for the provision of a small piece of land which can be worked partially as an experiment farm and teacher's garden. There are now some four hundred fifty of these "teacherages" in connection with rural schools of this country. More than one hundred of them are in the state of Washington. There are also many connected with rural schools in California. Two model teacherages costing $7000 each are now being erected for consolidated schools in Minnesota. The General Education Board contributed one half of this amount.

Another very interesting development in connection with some of the rural schools in California is the starting of a school forest. There is a small plot devoted to forestry in connection with many foreign schools, but I have never known of anything of this sort in connection with any school in this country until the last year. In Kern County, one rural district planted five acres of its ground to eucalyptus trees in 1912. It intends that this shall be the beginning of a picnic grove for the neighborhood, and that it shall also raise the wood for the school and furnish climbing opportunities for the children.

Recently plans have been announced for the improvement of the yard of a one-room rural school in Tulare County, California. These plans call for the planting of a row of eucalyptus trees entirely around the four-acre playground. Just inside this as an inner border there is to be a row of alternate olive and date palm trees.

When we consider the very great expense involved in the making of playgrounds for city schools, and how ugly and woebegone these grounds often appear when they are finished, it certainly seems a shame that the country should not realize its advantage in this regard, for there is no reason why the grounds of rural schools should be ugly. The city is often paying $10,000 an acre, while in the country land can usually be had for $100, and enough ground can be secured so that it is possible to save the grass.

I recently visited with Mr. Chenoweth, Superintendent of Schools of Kern County, California, a number of his rural schools and also inspected the farm and greenhouse connected with the County High School. In the greenhouse they are growing hundreds of carnations and are starting thousands of rose slips, geraniums, and grapevines to be planted over the fences of the country schools. As Mr. Chenoweth goes around from school to school, he is taking these slips with him and having them planted over the school fences. In this county also we visited a rural school that had fifteen hundred dollars' worth of steel play equipment on its grounds, and the superintendent reported that the directors responded readily to any suggestions of this kind from him. The following table shows what equipment has already been installed in the rural schools of Kern County.

SUMMARY OF PLAYGROUND EQUIPMENT OF KERN COUNTY RURAL SCHOOLS,
MARCH 1915

Name	No.	Name	No.	Name	No.
Basket Ball Courts	20	Tennis Courts	15	Traveling Rings	10
Baseball Diamonds	29	Volley Ball Courts	3	Football Grounds	4
Swings	94	Croquet Grounds	15	Handball Courts	11
Seesaws	39	Slides	8	Pole Vaulting Outfits	3
Horizontal Bars	22	Giant Strides	6	Ladders	5
Merry-go-rounds	5	Sand Boxes	13	Spring Boards	2

One of the very great problems of the rural school is how to inculcate a love of the country. The old-time country school did almost nothing in this direction, but there is now a beginning in a number of localities which may well grow into a real solution. The walking trips will contribute largely, and in a considerable number of school yards they are now raising in special places all the common wild flowers of the neighborhood, and the children are coming to recognize and love them. In many schools, also, the children are making collections and pressing all the common flowers of the neighborhood. In some schools they are keeping records of the bird migrations and of all the birds seen in their district. All of these are good and must result in a greater appreciation of nature.

In a number of counties during the last two or three years they have been holding a Country Life Day. The following is an account of Country Life Day in Jefferson County, Pennsylvania:

"A Country Life Day under the joint auspices of Jefferson County Pomona Grange and the schools was held at Brookville, October 17. The program included athletic events by pupils from the intermediate and grammar grades, the exhibit of the Boys' Clubs. Only about one half the schools observed the day. But the idea will be better understood next year, and we hope at that time to have a general observance."

Play in the Curriculum

It is difficult to put play into the curriculum of the one-room rural school for the reason that there will often be eight grades in a single room and the teacher will have twenty-five or thirty classes in a day, and it is not easily possible for her to leave part of her children to study their lessons while she goes outside with the others. However, it is entirely possible to let the small children go out to play by themselves as soon as they have their lessons, and this should always be done.

In many of the smaller towns of from six to fifteen hundred inhabitants, play, however, has been put into the program. This has come for the most part by the addition of an extra recess during the day, or perhaps two or three extra. These recesses have usually been in charge of the teacher of manual training, domestic economy, or some other special subject.

So far as it is possible to have organized play in many of the rural and town schools, it must be largely through the organization of the play of the little children by the older children, and especially the children in the high schools. It is often possible even in the one-room rural school for an older girl or boy to do something in this direction, if it is only once brought to the general consciousness that this is in itself a valuable experience for a boy or girl to have and is a real preparation for what is becoming one of our new social professions.

The Need of Better Games

Baseball is not suited to one-room rural schools because boys do not begin to play it much before they are twelve years old, and there are not enough older boys to play. School is not in session during the summer, and the hard ball stings the hands in the fall and early spring. A game that is much better adapted to the rural and city schools alike is indoor baseball, which is now played out of doors almost entirely. Children will begin to play indoor baseball by the time they are eight or nine, and the girls play nearly as much as the boys. It may be easy to play indoor baseball where it would be impossible to play the regular game. Indoor baseball also has the great advantage that men will continue to play it with pleasure long after they have begun to find the standard game overstrenuous.

Probably the best game for the rural school is volley ball. Country children are apt to be round-shouldered and flat-chested, but they must get their shoulders and head back to play volley ball. They will begin to play by the time they are eight or nine years old, and four can play the game perfectly well. Volley ball is the only team game that can be played at many of the small rural schools.

Perhaps the greatest advantage of these games is that they are almost equally adapted to the play of boys and girls. It is the girls who are suffering most at present. I have taken part in many institutes for rural teachers, and often when we have gone out to play games, we have discovered that there were almost no games that the teachers knew. The spirit of play had been so largely starved in them, that they did not at first take pleasure in games. Country women are getting far too little open-air recreation. If the women are to organize the social and recreational life of the country, the girls must learn to play and love to play while they are in school. There ought to be croquet and tennis also at every country school, because the school must be the means of introducing these into the country community.

The Consolidated School

More and more the students of rural education are coming to see in the consolidated school the solution of most of the problems of rural education. In the one-room school, the teacher has so many subjects and classes that it is impossible to give much time or thought to any one of them. It is difficult to give the special work in agriculture and domestic science that the country most requires. Perhaps the consolidated school is needed for the sake of the play and sociability of the children no less than for the reasons enumerated. In many of our one-room schools at the present time, there are not enough children to play baseball or the other typical games of American children. If any one will analyze baseball carefully and the type of mind required to play, he will find that it represents almost perfectly our American characteristics. Baseball has probably been more determining of American character than any other one thing, certainly far more so than any school subject. The boy who has never played baseball has missed a very important part of his education. The country boy has no opportunity to play with the children around the corner, and he must play at school if at all. The country child is diffident and backward because of a limited experience and acquaintance. More than any other child he needs to attend a large school.

The Play Festival and Pageant

The country school is undoubtedly the best place there is for competitive athletics. In the city schools our athletics have been subject to two serious criticisms: that there has been much rowdy play, and that it has trained a few athletic specialists and not the student body. In an interschool contest in the country, it will be almost necessary to use all the available material on the baseball and volley ball teams, and every child may well be brought into some of the contests. Country children often know only the immediate neighborhood and a narrow strip of country along the way to the neighboring town. Almost anything that takes them into another neighborhood and makes them acquainted with other children will be a valuable experience. Sportsmanship is the essential ethics of childhood, and the contest gives an opportunity for a training in sportsmanship. The country school has no loyalty, and a contest with another school is always the easiest way to develop loyalty.

The play festival idea is spreading rapidly over the country, and it would not be a surprise if by the time this book comes to print one third or one quarter of the counties in this country should be holding an annual play festival. Certainly such festivals are being held in many rural counties throughout the country. In the State of Maryland the legislature appropriated $4000 for the year 1915 in order to facilitate the holding of such a play festival in each county in the state, and the number held during the spring and summer of 1915 probably amounted to several hundred.

This is undoubtedly the easiest way to introduce the spirit of play into a country community. It will set the children to practicing all over the county, and it will give the parents also a new vision and interest that they would not otherwise have had.

Some such bill as the following would be an advantage in most states:

Be it enacted in the state of

That an appropriation, not to exceed one hundred dollars for each county in the state of   , is hereby set aside annually for the next four years, this fund to be used in the holding of an annual play festival and tournament by the elementary schools or high schools, or both, of each county in the state.

This fund to go only to those counties in which such a play festival or tournament is held, and the sum appropriated never to exceed the actual expense involved in the tournament itself.

The School Excursion

Almost anywhere that one may go in Germany, he comes upon parties of children out for a walk. There were over sixty-five hundred children who went out from Berlin with their teachers during the summer of 1913 for walks of a week or more. More than sixty-five thousand children were taken by the Wandervögel for walks of a similar duration. The number who went out for walks of a day or two would probably mount well up into the millions. There are at least five national walking associations in Germany, and there is a local walking association in nearly every town. Very many of the turnvereins go out for a walk of a week or two each year. On the school trips the children carry their cooking utensils and daily necessities in knapsacks on their backs. They buy the eggs, milk, and potatoes from the farmers and cook their meals by the wayside. They sometimes stay all night at the barracks of the soldiers, and ofttimes they sleep in the barns or on the floors of inns. But during the last three years the authorities have been taking the desks out of certain schoolrooms for the summer and putting in cots instead, so that the children walk from schoolhouse to schoolhouse and stay all night there. The estimated cost of these trips is from twelve to twenty-five cents a day. In some cases the expense is borne by the cities, in others it is borne by the children themselves. Thus far it has been the boys for the most part that have gone on these trips, but they are beginning to take the girls as well. These journeys are being promoted for several different purposes, indeed for almost as many reasons as the schools themselves. A reason that is very prominent is the development of patriotism. On these trips the children come to know at first hand the country and its products. They visit the historic battlefields, the old castles, the homes of literary men, public buildings, factories, museums, art galleries, parks, and playgrounds. They become acquainted with the country and learn to love the Fatherland and its traditions. A second reason is social. The children develop good camaraderie through these walks. They learn how to be friends under all conditions and they get a varied social experience from their contact with the people whom they meet on the way. The teacher comes to know the children and to get a hold over them that would be impossible otherwise. He teaches them to recognize the common birds and flowers and points out to them the beautiful sunsets and landscapes. One of the reasons that is most often urged is the physical one, that in this way the children spend their time in the open air, that the walking is good exercise, and that it establishes a habit that is likely to be continued. The children often take part in athletic contests with the children in the villages to which they go.

It seems remarkable that we have introduced so little of this in America, because it is fundamental to what we are trying to do in the rural school. We have three common methods of gaining information: through reading, through conversation, and through observation. The information that we gain from reading is apt to be of distant things, but the information that we gain from conversation and observation is mostly of things that are near at hand. Children do not remember well the things they read, but they seldom forget the things they observe. It may be worth while to know about the pyramids or the rivers of Africa, but this knowledge is almost sure to be dead knowledge. It does not touch our lives, and it soon disintegrates and disappears. On the other hand, the knowledge that we gain by observation is of the intimate kind that touches our lives closely and that is likely to grow from day to day. Children are not now taught to observe, and they go among things of great interest and see nothing. Emerson says there are those who will see more that is significant in a trip to the neighboring town than others will in a trip through Europe. It is entirely true. There are dozens of places within five miles of every rural school that are as interesting as anything that they will read about in their histories or geographies. Yet most of the children left to themselves do not see these places. I am convinced that children will often learn as much that they will remember in a well-planned afternoon's trip as they will in a week inside the ordinary country school. If the country is to be made attractive, the children must come to appreciate its beauty. Little children are always fond of beautiful things, and the present lack of appreciation of the beautiful, which is so characteristic of rural people, is a pure case of starvation. The child's attention is constantly turned away from the beautiful toward the practical. Walking is almost the only way to come to appreciate the beauty of the country. A large proportion of farm people are living in a world almost as unknown to them as the north pole or the dark continent. Out of nearly a hundred common birds, the children will often know not over eight or ten, recognize not over a half dozen trees or wild flowers, and know almost nothing of the habits of the wild animals of the neighborhood. They have never learned that sympathetic observation of nature which is so largely the charm of country life. All of these things the school excursion is giving to the German child and might give to the American child no less.

CREATE A SOCIAL COMMUNITY

In some way the social life of the community must be organized. From the isolated farms rural people must be brought together at frequent intervals for social life, recreation, and civic discussion.

THE RURAL CHURCH

There are a number of forces that must coöperate in the reanimation of country life. One of these is the country church. There are a number of places where a splendid beginning has already been made. But on the whole the country churches are in a decadent condition. Sixteen hundred country churches have been abandoned in the last decade in the state of Illinois alone. Most country churches at the present time are so weak in membership and have such a feeble grasp on the community that they cannot do much without rejuvenation. The country church as a rule has no resident pastor. In many communities there are two or three times as many churches as there ought to be, and rival churches are forcing the community apart rather than cementing it together. Yet almost everywhere the church is doing something to organize the social life and in some communities it is doing nearly all that needs to be done. Its oyster suppers and "donations" are in themselves valuable social occasions. The ladies' benevolent association often furnishes the only society of the farm women. But the rural church must do three things if it is to serve adequately the country community; the rival churches must federate; there must be a resident pastor; and the church must seek to minister in a social way to the whole community. If it sees this vision and follows it, there is great hope for its future. If it does not, it will probably be largely supplanted by the social center in the school. It must be said on the whole that the school has seen its vision first and already has a good start in many communities.

THE SOCIAL CENTER

The social center is much more needed in the country than in the city, and through it must come a large part of the solution of the country life problem. There has been a progressive change in country life during the last half century that has been little appreciated in most quarters. In the days of the pioneer, the farmers constituted a coöperating community. Together they put up the house of the newcomer, together they married the lovers, watched with the sick, and buried the dead. Neighbor followed neighbor with the cradle in the wheat field, and all turned out to help with the threshing. There were the quiltings and apple parings for the girls and the corn huskings for all. The common dangers and hardships cemented the community into a great brotherhood of the wilderness. With the coming of new trades the carpenter builds the houses, the nurse watches with the sick, and the undertaker lays out the dead. With the coming of the mower, the twinebinder, and the threshing machine, the farmer has become independent of the help of his neighbors and the most complete individualist the world has ever seen. The farms have become larger and the houses farther apart. There have been fewer children in the home, and everything has conspired to reduce the social life. The peasant peoples of Europe live in rural villages from which they go to their work in the morning and to which they return at night. They have the same opportunities for sociability in the evening that city dwellers have, and the women have these opportunities pretty much all the time. The American farm home is isolated. The farmer is working very hard and for long hours during six months of the year, but during the colder months he is not so busy. His days are apt to be partially occupied, but his nights at least are free. All of these things point to the social center as a large element in overcoming the isolation of the country. In pioneer days the rural school was such a center, where were held the preaching services, the singing school, the spelling down, and the debate. All of these have fallen away with the changes in country life.

P

They must be brought back and developed to meet the growing need.

The most important reason of all for the consolidated school is that it makes possible the social organization of the neighborhood. The school should have a teacher's house or "teacherage" with a demonstration farm adjoining. The principal should become the social organizer of the community. The consolidated school is usually getting a good-sized playground, often ten acres or more, and in some places there is an attempt to have a township picnic grove in connection with it. The consolidated school usually has either an auditorium or a gymnasium or both. The principal should receive an extra compensation as the director of the social center. If, now, the community will spend its Saturday afternoons at the grounds of the school in having a picnic, baseball games, and athletic contests, it will do much to revive the community life. In the winter time, the opportunity is equally good. The larger staff and facilities make possible evening classes in agriculture and domestic science for the older boys and girls. The gymnasium allows of clubs, entertainments, parties, and dances under the best of auspices. The auditorium permits of the moving picture show, the entertainment, and the public lecture, which is likely to be better attended in the country than in the city, as the Hesperia movement has shown. Moving picture machines have already been placed in many rural social centers, especially in Minnesota, California, and Wisconsin. The moving picture solves the question of attendance, and, if the films are well selected, the problem of a wholesome form of recreation at the same time.

But the most important function of the social center is

that it makes possible the organization of all the other movements for community welfare. At the present time, farmers are probably more poorly organized than any other class and there is less coöperation among them in business and public enterprises. As a result they have had relatively little influence as a class, and they have yielded to the middleman two thirds of their legitimate profits. In Rocky Ford, Colorado, they say that if they can get sixty cents for a crate of sixty canteloupes they can get on, and, if they receive seventy-five cents, they are well satisfied. Now seventy-five cents for a crate of sixty is one cent and a quarter apiece, and when twenty-five or thirty-five cents apiece is paid for these canteloupes on the dining car or in the hotel, it seems that there is a good deal of loss between the cup and the lip, and that the cost of production often has little to do with the price of consumption. For the products of the American farms in 1915 the consumers paid $13,000,000,000, of which sum the farmers received $6,000,000,000, or 46%. The farm products of Denmark are nearly all handled by coöperative selling associations, and the farmer receives on an average 92% of what the consumer pays, just twice as much as the American farmer receives. Good government, agricultural coöperation, agricultural credit, good roads, better schools, and the general welfare of the rural community are all waiting for rural people to get together somewhere to discuss their essential problems.

The idea of the social center is being rapidly extended among the rural schools of the country, and not a few of the new rural schools of two rooms or more are provided with an auditorium and moving picture machine for this purpose.

A little while ago, while riding in an automobile in an almost rainless desert in San Bernardino County, California, we came upon a building standing by itself half a mile from the nearest house. On inquiring what it was, we were told that this was a social center building which had been erected by and for the people living on the desert.

In the State of Washington during the last three or four years there have been built a considerable number of these social center buildings, but over the rest of the country the tendency has been to make use of school buildings rather than to erect separate structures.

A most interesting experiment in the way of a social center for a small community that has come to public attention is the one recently erected for the tri-cities of Lasalle, Peru, and Oglesby, Illinois. Mr. Matthiesen gave the land and $75,000, for the erection thereon in the city of LaSalle of a social center, on condition that the people of the three towns should vote an additional $25,000 to equip and maintain the center. The people promptly voted the money, and the center has been equipped with all modern appliances. It contains a good gymnasium, an indoor and outdoor swimming pool, a good theater, and a music room. There is an athletic field containing baseball and football fields, and a number of excellent tennis courts and a children's playground. The building has been used for graduation exercises by the schools, and for entertainments, and courses of lectures, for the meetings of the women's clubs of the section, and for the meetings of the northern section of the State Teachers' Association of Illinois. There is a tournament in tennis and indoor baseball in the fall, and baseball in the spring and summer. The facilities of the building and grounds have been used to nearly their full capacity all the time, and the work has been conspicuously successful from the first.

Another extremely interesting semi-rural experiment is the Scrips Playground at LaJolla, California. This is a place of some 2500 inhabitants lying thirteen miles north of the city of San Diego. The playground contains, besides a modern field house with all facilities, the equipment for every kind of game and physical exercise. A magnificent women's club building is at one edge of the grounds. A fine boarding school is at one end, a beautiful little park at another, and at the shore is a beautiful swimming beach. The playground, on a high bluff overlooking the ocean, has one of the most beautiful locations in the world. It is also one of the most expensive when all things are considered. Already a number of people have moved from San Diego to LaJolla in order to make use of its facilities, and the great problem which it should solve for the country at large is whether or not a playground can build a town.

Without question, rural teachers pretty much everywhere are taking a more active part in the play of their children, and are themselves, through the teachers' institutes and summer normals, learning many more games than they knew a few years ago. The county superintendents also are taking more interest. In Westchester County, Pennsylvania, one of the deputies of the county superintendent is giving a considerable part of his time to the organization of games and athletics. This is at least a possible solution of the organization of the work for the rural schools. The organization of the community at large is likely to be more difficult and to require the combined efforts of a number of different people and agencies.

Who is to Organize Play and Social Life in the Country?

Probably the chief reason why country life has not been attractive in the past is that no one has ever tried to make it so. The farmer has been seeking for wealth, not happiness, either for himself or his family. In the city there are parks and playgrounds to emphasize the value of recreation, and there are also commercial recreations of many forms which are offered to the people. The statistics, which seem to indicate that we are spending from three to five times as much on commercial amusements as we are on public education, show how deep a demand in human nature these must satisfy. During the first five or ten years of the play movement, most of our cities tried to run recreation systems without any one in charge, but they have finally come to the conclusion that it is impossible to do so. Probably a director of play is more needed in the country than he is in the city, because there is thus far in the country less appreciation of the value of play, and there is also less spontaneous leadership arising from the fact that the lives of rural people are isolated and leadership difficult. However, the proposition to employ a director of recreation for any township in the country would probably not secure one tenth of the necessary votes. To most farm people the proposition would seem absurd, and we must always realize that the farmer is independent and self-reliant, that institutions cannot be forced upon him from the outside, and it is not altogether easy to see just how this organization is to be brought about. However, in the organization of the recreation in the home, the mother certainly must be the leader, and she ought to have that sort of instruction in existing or extension schools which will enable her to be successful in it. The organization of play at the rural school must be in the hands of the rural teacher and the county superintendent, and they should have that training at normal schools and institutes which will enable them to do so successfully.

The social function of the rural teacher is coming more and more to be recognized, and in not a few cases she is seeing this and organizing a social center at her school and various social functions in the neighborhood.

In a small town the solution seems to lie in the employing of a person to have charge of the various social enterprises of the community. He should organize the play at the schools, the children's gardens, the Boy Scouts, and conduct walking trips, and a summer camp. If the small community can secure a man with a gift of tact and leadership for this work, it can do more through him for its young people than can be done perhaps in any other one way.

THE COUNTY SECRETARIES OF THE Y. M. AND Y. W. C. A.'S

In the ninety or more counties that now support a county secretary of the Y. M. C. A., a more or less systematic organization of athletics, Boy Scouts, walking, and camping is going on. In a number of counties an annual play festival is held which brings in a large part of the county. The county department of the Y. W. C. A. is just making a beginning, and it is to be expected that they will soon be doing a similar work for the girls. This work is surely much needed, but these organizations are at present touching so small a part of the young people even, that we cannot yet consider either or both of them as a considerable element in the solution of the larger problem.

THE COUNTY DIRECTOR OF BOYS' AND GIRLS' ACHIEVEMENT CLUBS

During the last few years there has been a remarkable development of the boys' and girls' club work throughout the United States, and upwards of a half million boys and girls are already engaged in the various activities involved. There is now a state director in every state, usually connected with the Agricultural College, and receiving a part of his pay directly through the Department of Agriculture at Washington. During the last two or three years county directors of boys' and girls' club work have been employed in a number of instances, and there is a general tendency to add certain recreational features to the industrial activities previously maintained.

A new movement for country girls and boys, known as the "Farm Boys Cavaliers" has recently been launched from the University of Minnesota. This movement, which is intended purely for farm boys and girls, is built on the ideals of chivalry but modeled closely on the Boy Scout movement. It is hoped that the farm boy may have a horse to ride. He becomes first a page, then a squire, and then a knight, in accordance with the ideals of chivalry, by acquiring skill in various farm achievements. The movement was launched in 1915 by Professor Mayne, the head of the agricultural school of the University of Minnesota. President Vincent is deeply interested and is helping in the movement, and it is hoped that it may be taken over as a regular part of the boys' and girls' club work throughout the country. If it ever becomes generally known and accepted, it has great promise for improving social conditions among country boys and girls.

THE COUNTY AGRICULTURAL SECRETARY

There are few movements that have been started in recent years that are more promising alike for rural agriculture and rural life than the movement to secure agricultural experts to advise with the farmers. Farmers as a class have failed to keep in touch with the agricultural college and experiment station and the various modern movements for scientific farming. It is only a small minority who spray their fruit or rotate their crops properly or utilize their fertilizers economically or select their seed with care; yet the application of these simple and well-known principles would probably double the profits of farming in the United States. The demonstration farms of the South have done a great work for agriculture in that section, and there is good reason to believe that the expert advice and the experimental farms that are being conducted under the direction of the agricultural secretaries will perform an equal service to the North. The agricultural secretaries are often organizing farmers' clubs with a strong social side. In North Dakota these clubs sometimes meet during the summer on Saturday afternoon at some tree claim. They have a picnic dinner. The girls have some sort of a club, the boys play baseball in an adjoining field, and the children romp about as they are inclined. In the winter time they often meet around at the houses of the members and spend an afternoon and part of an evening together. The hostess serves dinner with the help of her guests. The children have a room to themselves where they play their games. Everybody has a good time, and the farmers and the farmers' families of this community are greatly benefited by this recreation.

A PAID ORGANIZER OF PLAY

In the rural communities of Germany and Denmark a special individual is employed who is known as a *Spiele Inspector*, or Play Supervisor, whose business it is to supervise the play of the community. It may be that such an individual cannot be employed directly in America, but there is no doubt whatever of the need of such a person. At Amenia, New York, during the last four or five years, there has been given each year a notable play festival which has attracted the attention of the entire country and has carried the message of play to from five to ten thousand rural people. This has been made possible because there was at Amenia Professor Spingarn, of Columbia, who was willing to organize this occasion for that community. And there is no reason why there should not be such a play festival in thousands of rural communities throughout America, if there could be found such leadership to organize it. Wherever there is a consolidated school, the principal is the logical civic and recreation secretary for the rural community.

So far as the rural schools are concerned, the natural center for the organization of play is the office of the county superintendent. In three or four hundred counties play festivals are now being held, and this number is rapidly increasing so that it bids fair to be almost universal in the near future. In connection with very many of the county institutes, the subject of play is being presented and the teachers are being taught the games which will enable them to organize the play of their children. In a number of counties already, where the superintendent has several deputies, one of these is devoting a larger or smaller part of his time to the organization of play, and it would seem that a county play deputy might be the solution of the problem so far as the supervision of play at the rural school is concerned.

The Auto

Probably the auto has done more to take the minds of rural people from the idea of the mere making of money, than any other one thing. With the auto and good roads it is possible for the farmer and his family to attend the moving picture show or the theater, or a dance in town if they wish. They can go off twenty or thirty miles on hunting or fishing trips, or to the mountains or seashore for week ends. The auto practically places at their command all the recreation facilities that lie within forty or fifty miles of where they are living. The auto has brought good roads in its train, and many thousands of miles of macadam, asphalt, concrete, brick, and gravel roads are now being laid each year through the open country. As these roads will last many years, the work of each year is cumulative.

In most up-to-date cities at the present time it is the custom to assess the cost of laying out new parks and boulevards in part or in whole upon the adjacent property, because it is found that this property usually increases in value as much or more than the cost of the improvement. It is to be hoped that sooner or later the same plan may be carried out in regard to the building of state and county highways, for with the adoption of this method it becomes possible to make all roads good roads. A friend of mine who owns several thousand acres in the central part of Illinois tells me that, at the time the state highway was built along the side of his property, and he had an assessment of several thousand dollars to pay to cover the building of this highway, he felt it was an outrage, but that two years after the road was built he was offered $100 more an acre for the land than it was considered worth at the time the road was started. A good state highway of the kind which is being built in California, where on a basis of broken stone and concrete a smooth asphalt finish is finally laid, costs about $10,000 per mile. Within one mile of every mile of this road there will be 1280 acres of land. This land in any good section will increase at least $10 per acre in value and probably $20 or $30. An increase of $10 per acre would mean a total increase of $12,800 in the value of the property lying within a mile of the road. It is not reasonable that the entire expense of the state highway should be borne by the adjacent property, but it is reasonable that at least a part should be borne by it. If we once have a law permitting this, it solves the problem, for it is then possible to have good roads everywhere. With the great increase in automobile traffic and the building of motor trucks, each of these roads becomes nearly as valuable to the community as a new railroad or street car line. Even to-day in California, where the road system is far from complete, the automobile busses and stages are competing constantly with the railroads and are getting the majority of the traffic on distances of less than 100 miles. In many cases they are also making better time and carrying for a considerably lower rate. For instance, the distance from Bakersfield to Los Angeles is 127 miles, going over the summit of a range nearly five thousand feet in height. The railroads go around and take nine hours. The auto busses go across and take six hours. The railroads charge $10.30 for a round-trip ticket, and the autos charge $6.00. There were in 1916 four bus lines covering this road every day. On many stretches of road throughout California, the busses are now getting three fourths or more of the local trade. The coming of the auto truck is making these roads more valuable to the community every day.

Some day our country roads are going to be beautiful, and perhaps this day is not so distant as some of us might think. Changes are coming with a rapidity such as has never been known before. The Federated Women's Clubs have undertaken to place trees along the Lincoln Highway all the way from New York to San Francisco, the local clubs undertaking to furnish the trees for their own localities and to have them distinctive of the section. This will be not only in the interest of beauty but also good business, for the attractive roads will draw the tourists and increase the value of property. At the time the Royal Poincianas bloom along the military road in Porto Rico, it is thronged every day with hundreds who come out thirty miles from San Juan to see them. The cherry-blossom avenues in Japan bring out great multitudes during their blooming time.

Probably California has thus far done more to improve and beautify its highways than any other state in the Union. There are hundreds of miles of continuous asphalt running through the open country bordered with beautiful palms, oleanders, pampas grass, and other beautiful trees and shrubs. The Chamber of Commerce of Los Angeles planted out two hundred miles of rose trellises in preparation for the visitors that would come to the Panama-Pacific Exposition.

Along many of the highways of California they are now planting rows of olive trees. The olive is a beautiful tree, whether we look merely at its foliage or whether we see it full of the ripe fruit; and no one who has ever eaten a ripe olive right from the tree ever desires a second one. If all the county and state highways of California were planted with olives and lemons and cared for by the highway commission, it would seem possible that the fruit would very nearly maintain the highways, and the trees would certainly add very much to their attractiveness. But I doubt if it is necessary to plant inedible things along the highways. If there were twenty miles of almond trees, we are not to suppose that the nuts taken would be sufficient to make any appreciable difference in the crop. Moreover, the almond when in blossom is one of the most beautiful of trees, quite comparable with the Japanese cherry in gorgeousness of effect. The apricot and peach also in their blooming seasons make a riot of bloom and color that any one with a sense of beauty in his soul might well go far to see. And again if there are many miles of continuous peach trees which are to go towards the maintenance of the roads, it is doubtful if enough of them would be taken by passers-by to make much difference in the crop.

In Calhoun County, Alabama, the women's clubs of the county have undertaken to plant pecan trees along the principal highways of the county. They believe that these trees will beautify the roads, and that the profits from the nuts will defray all the expenses of the county highways.

Some four or five years ago, the University of Illinois established a department of landscape horticulture and put Wilhelm Miller, formerly editor of *Country Life*, in charge. The purpose of this department is to provide plans and to develop an interest in making the grounds of farmhouses, public schools, and public roads more beautiful. Mr. Miller's idea is that the growth of local trees, shrubs, and flowers along the highways should be encouraged. It seems likely that this idea, so auspiciously started in the great University of Illinois, will spread to other universities and will from them filter out into the community, and that our country roads may some time have a beauty of which we have but slight realization at present.

The Organization of the County

The county is an essentially unorganized political unit in our midst. It is not only unorganized, but all of its functions are endlessly repeated in various departments, and much of its work is inefficiently and very expensively done. Perhaps we shall not soon get a county manager on the plane of the city manager, but a county agricultural agent might well become such an official, and nearly every department now found in our progressive cities has already been organized in some of the counties of the United States. There is now a county park in a large part of the counties in the state of Michigan, and a law passed in the state of Texas in 1915 empowers all of the counties of that state to acquire such parks.

The most interesting county park that I have ever seen is the one acquired by Tulare County, California, in 1914. This park contains a large number of live oak trees, the largest to be found in the San Joaquin Valley. It is 160 acres in area and has a small lake in the center. There are tables provided for picnickers; there is a pavilion for dancing, and a bungalow and grounds for the person in charge are just being laid out. The quarter section cost something over

$30,000. It lies on a good automobile highway, and there is a probability of the interurban street car line going by one side of it. With the splendid automobile roads to be found everywhere in California, this park should be nearly as well used by the country people, especially on Saturdays and Sundays, as are city parks by city people.

The vast majority of the counties in the country now have a county superintendent of schools. Laws were passed in 1914 in Iowa and Kansas authorizing the establishment of county hospitals in these two states. County hospitals have been maintained for many years in California. There the law provides also that the state will furnish a visiting nurse for the rural schools of the county on request of the local authorities in the county. A considerable number of the counties now have such visiting nurses. In some of the counties of the state of Michigan there is also a visiting nurse for the rural schools. In several of the states there is now a county board of health with a county health officer. We have county courts in all counties, and in many counties there are also county probation officers. I do not know that there are anywhere at the present time county police officers or county fire departments, but it does not seem unlikely that with the improved roads and motor appliances these should come in the next few years; in any event it seems likely that nearly every department found in the city will be found also in the county government when it is fully organized.

The Need of a Survey

There has nowhere been made thus far a thorough survey or examination into the recreation facilities of any county.

Such a survey is much needed. It would be good business for every county, because any new opportunities for pleasure, such as hunting, fishing, camping, picnicking, mountain climbing, or of fine scenery, will be a real financial asset, not much less productive financially than a forest of valuable timber or a mine of copper or iron.

CHAPTER IX

EQUIPMENT AND SUPPLIES

CHILDREN have always run and jumped and climbed, thrown and fended missiles, and played games. Play is the essential spirit of childhood and uses all things as its implements. Any equipment that is furnished can never be more than an incident to it.

In German and English schools certain games are required, but there is no attempt to furnish swings, seesaws, giant strides, or similar pieces of apparatus. If we compare the training which is given by baseball with the training that is given by a swing, there is probably no one who would not say that the training by baseball is much more important. The boy who is swinging is in an unsocial activity, in which he is seeking his own pleasure to the exclusion of some other child. It creates no friendship or social spirit. It is not anywhere regarded as an accomplishment, and it does not stir the emulation or give any considerable mental stimulus. It is not an activity in which much skill can be acquired, and it is in no sense a preparation for the future. It gives very little training to the eye or the hand or the judgment, and it tends to put the intellect to sleep. It develops no grace, and even as physical training it has its limitations. On the other hand, the boy who is playing baseball is training at the same time his eye and his hand, the accuracy of the coördination of nearly every muscle of his body, an alertness of mind, quickness and accuracy of judgment, determination and courage in taking ventures and doing his best, and a spirit of friendliness and loyalty toward the other members of the team. No one would say that the attenuated training of the swing is comparable with this all-around training of the individual. Very much the same comparison might be made with any other piece of apparatus that might be chosen.

The chief value of the swing is doubtless emotional. Any one who will watch closely a child who is swinging will see that he nearly always has a happy expression. Any one who will observe himself closely will notice that swinging has a direct emotional effect. It tends to dispel the blues and make one feel cheerful. It might be a good thing if we all had a swing in our back yard where we could go to practice whenever we became downhearted.

It is the apparatus also that causes most of the criticism of the playgrounds. It leads, in an unfenced ground, to the assembling of loafers and rowdies at night. Where there has been decided objection to playgrounds, it has nearly always been due to such use of apparatus after hours. It is on the apparatus, too, that nearly all the children have been hurt who have been injured in playgrounds, and it is the apparatus which is the chief initial expense. Ofttimes its care takes so much of the director's time that he has little opportunity to organize play, and abundant apparatus always tends to suppress organized games and to make a caretaker of the director. Apparatus and organized play are the opposite poles of the play movement. Park boards have always emphasized the equipment side and have looked upon play rather as amusement than as a means of education. Boards of education have tended to emphasize the play and organization side. Equipment is worth while in playgrounds under proper conditions, and it is yielding certain advantages that cannot well be secured without it, though its chief value is probably in bringing the children to the playground in the first place.

Need of Study

The securing of appropriate equipment is usually the largest item in the expense of getting started. As the initiators of the movement usually have little knowledge of play, the equipment chosen is often unsuitable and over costly.

We need careful studies of the physical, social, emotional, and intellectual value of the different pieces of apparatus. We should know, also, which pieces and types are most popular, the chief dangers involved in their use, and the best methods of construction. It is not to be supposed that the machine companies, working down from gymnastic equipment, will be able to build play apparatus, without any pedagogy of the subject, that will meet the needs of the child. It must be remembered that play was everywhere looked upon at first as amusement, and that it is only lately that it has been perceived as the fundamental thing in education. If playground apparatus is to be also pedagogical apparatus, it should not be selected at random.

One of the things that is most needed is to establish certain standards of equipment for large and small cities, school and municipal playgrounds, including such things as the height of the swing for the small children and for the older children, of the giant stride, gymnasium frame, etc.

We have at the present time no measure of the value of

the various pieces of apparatus, or of what that value consists. We do not know what apparatus gives a definite training and what apparatus is only a decoration, an advertisement, or a mental dissipation. Psychologically the use and effect of some apparatus is similar to getting drunk. This is often the most expensive and elaborate equipment. Probably at least half of the million dollars or so that is spent each year for playground equipment is spent for equipment that is unsuitable or unnecessary. Take the simplest piece, the seesaw. Has it any value? If so, what is it? Apparently it has little physical value, little social value, no direct moral value. What value it has seems to come from a certain emotional excitement that accompanies it. It is like music, perhaps. Pedagogically we know little about it. How should it be made? How high should the frame be, how long the board? Should it have a handle? The people of the United States are probably spending fifty thousand dollars a year on seesaws. They might well afford to spend fifty thousand dollars to determine for all time whether or not the seesaw is worth while, and, if it is, what sort of a seesaw it should be. The same argument applies with yet more force to most of the other pieces of apparatus.

Just what is the value of the swing? Should swings be found in school yards or not? Nobody knows. And yet it would be fairly simple to give a series of tests upon children before and after swinging which should tell us whether the swing has a good or bad influence upon the mental capacity of the child. There are always a certain percentage of the children who are made seasick by it. How large a percentage we do not know. Over and beyond those who are made seasick there is probably a much larger percentage who are affected more or less or made sleepy. Probably any set of psychological tests would show that if a class of forty were to swing for fifteen minutes, at least twenty of them would have a lowered mental capacity at the end of the time. However, this is mere conjecture.

On the side of mere efficiency there is more need of the efficiency engineer in the play movement, probably, than anywhere in our industrial life, because our industrial plants have been erected by people who knew at least what they wanted to manufacture, and, presumably, who had some experience in the business they were engaging in; while, on the other hand, most playground systems have been laid out by those who had no clear conception of what they wanted to manufacture and had no experience in the business. There is a large percentage of the playgrounds that cannot be efficient as playgrounds without throwing considerable of their apparatus on the junk heap and resetting the rest. From the old-time swing that was hung from the limb of the apple tree and cost twenty-five cents, to the modern swing in the playgrounds which costs twenty-five dollars, there is a great difference in cost which does not correspond to an increase of value. It does not seem likely that the machine companies that are making apparatus to sell, and are naturally seeking profits, will at once devise ways of making it cheap. On the other hand, the play promoters should naturally be interested in the cheapening process.

Steel or Wooden Equipment

During the first years the equipment that was put into playgrounds nearly everywhere was of wood. But this usually was big and clumsy, and was often unsightly. It soon rotted off at the surface of the ground or just below it and became dangerous. During the last decade, wherever permanent playgrounds have been laid out, the equipment has nearly always been of steel. Steel is both more durable and more sightly than wood, and, all things considered, is probably no more expensive in the long run. However, if wooden apparatus is properly made and kept painted and is either creosoted or set in concrete blocks, and especially if the concrete is waterproofed either with oil or alum, it may be nearly as sightly and durable as the steel equipment. Georgia pine, cypress, or cedar are usually found to be the best timbers where a wooden framework is used. In steel equipment, the tendency has been to use the galvanized iron pipe, but black pipe that is kept painted is about as satisfactory as the galvanized pipe.

The Playground without Equipment

The author believes that equipment is necessary to the municipal playground, but that it is not so essential to the school playground. There is no equipment, except the apparatus for play, in the school playgrounds of Germany or England. There is none in the playgrounds of our great private schools, such as Tome, Lawrenceville, and Groton. These are without doubt the most successful playgrounds in the world. There are also municipal playgrounds which have been run for years without equipment, but it must be said in general that the attendance at these grounds is considerably less than it would have been if they had been equipped.

Who Should Make the Equipment and Supplies and Erect the Equipment

LOCAL PEOPLE

Nearly everywhere in the beginning the equipment has been made by local people. This has generally been necessary because the funds have not been adequate to purchase from the outside. This equipment has ofttimes been unsightly and not infrequently unsafe, because those who have erected it have not understood well the nature of the strains it would have to bear and have not considered much the æsthetic side. However, if there is in the local community an expert play supervisor or a skillful workman in iron and concrete, it is ofttimes possible to install a satisfactory equipment at one half what this would have cost if it had been purchased.

THE MACHINE COMPANIES

As time has gone on, the tendency has been to purchase the equipment or at least the fittings directly from the machine or equipment companies. There have been, however, many cities which have felt that they could not afford this, and there has been a general feeling that most of it was more expensive than the materials warranted. Where the selection of equipment has been left to the machine companies, it has ofttimes been unsuitable, and if the setting of it has also been in their hands, they have usually placed it in the center of the open play space where one eighth of an acre of equipment might practically destroy for play purposes two acres of ground. This method has often involved the shipping of heavy steel tubing across the country and sometimes the transportation of a gang of workmen as well. There can be little doubt but this is unwise. The steel tubing, at any rate, should be purchased of local people, and the equipment should be erected by them from designs furnished by the machine companies. This is what is recommended by Spalding. Outside of the large expense involved in purchasing equipment from the machine companies, there is also apt to be a considerable delay, as it usually takes longer to secure it from the outside than it does to have it made by people of the locality. A time limit should be put into the contract whenever outside equipment is purchased.

A SPECIAL FOUNDATION

An enormous amount of money has been given in public philanthropy during the last two or three decades in the United States. Probably more has been given during the last year and certainly during the last two years in the United States than was given by the entire world during the first eighteen Christian centuries. From twenty to fifty different playgrounds, some of which contain field houses and swimming pools of an elaborate nature, are being given to our cities each year. All credit is due to those generously giving of their millions for the welfare and happiness of children, but one cannot but regret that these same generous givers do not more often devote their means and business ability to a philanthropic business enterprise instead. If a capable manufacturer would devote a hundred thousand dollars to the manufacture of play apparatus on a four per cent basis, and would then turn back the profits of this plant into the increase of the business, it seems likely that after the enterprise were well started he might save the country as much as the original investment each year.

THE STEEL COMPANIES

In the plan of the original study of equipment for the Playground Association of America, it was intended that equipment should be standardized and that there should then be an attempt to get the steel companies to furnish the pipe of these standard lengths and the necessary fittings, so that it could be shipped directly from the factory to the city where the playground was to be erected. This was one reason that there was such strenuous opposition on the part of the machine companies to the work of this committee. The United States Steel Company is fundamentally interested in welfare work, and usually willing to please the public. They have constructed playgrounds for their employees or the children of their employees around many of their plants. It does not seem impossible that they could be persuaded to render a great public service at some small profit to themselves by cutting the steel pipe in suitable lengths for play equipment and furnishing it direct to the playground associations and commissions with several intermediate profits, which constitute four fifths of the cost, left off. If this is to be done, however, the heights of swings and other apparatus must be standardized, so that heights and sizes of pipe may be the same in the different playgrounds. It does not seem likely that the company could afford, perhaps, to take special orders of this kind at their great tubing mills, but in the case of the United States Steel Company, for instance, they might well afford to devote one mill or perhaps to erect a new mill for the special purpose of making the steel fittings and pipe for playground apparatus. If the equipment had been standardized so that a No. 1 playground equipment would consist of certain specified pieces of definite lengths with so many fittings of such a kind, it would be a simple proposition for any city to send to the factory and order a No. 1 playground equipment and have it shipped directly to them along with a detailed plan for its erection. This does not seem to offer any special difficulties, and it would save probably a half or more of the present cost of equipment. It would be one of the strongest appeals to public favor which the steel companies could make; and where the orders are running, as they are at present, into a million or more dollars a year, it should not be a source of loss to them.

THE SCHOOL CHILDREN

In a number of cities a part, and in some cities all, of the play equipment has been made in the manual training shops and erected by the children. The children should construct their own playgrounds so far as possible for three reasons: There is a very great economy in the cost. It enables children to do actual things and gives them a training in doing for others and the city. This is an essential part of their civic and manual education.

It probably is not wise in the majority of cases for school children to undertake to make the framework for swings or an outdoor gymnasium, but they can perfectly well make the running tracks and jumping pits, lay out the baseball and indoor baseball diamonds, the volley ball, basket ball, and tennis courts, make the jumping standards, and erect all of the permanent equipment. This may seem to involve responsibilities and skill which are beyond the ability of school children, and it will of course require competent supervision by a capable physical director or teacher of manual training; but under this condition it can be done fairly well. The measuring and laying out of the courts and diamonds and running tracks will be the best possible application of mathematics and mensuration such as every child should have. The use of pick and shovel, the digging of post holes, mixing of concrete, and shoveling of gravel will be good practical physical training in the open air, and when the work is finished the children will have a sense of achievement, will know how these things are done, and will be more resourceful than they would have been had they not done it. Apparently, we are passing through the age of steel to the age of concrete, and the knowledge of the making of concrete should be a part of any complete education. There are numerous schools where the concrete walks have been laid by children, in some cases by children not more than eight or ten years old, and there seems to be no reason why boys from twelve to eighteen should not be able to erect the equipment in a perfectly satisfactory way. This will mean, of course, that detailed plans for its erection must accompany the equipment, or if locally made, shall be furnished by the department of education, so that no slipshod or unsafe work may be done. We have long been lamenting that there was no legitimate work for the children to do in the cities, and this broadening out of child activities into civic enterprises should be in every way an advantage. If the children do the work they are always much more loyal to the playground and ready to protect the equipment and supplies. In the city of Gary, all the play equipment has been made by the children for some time and it seems to be quite as good as any equipment that can be purchased.

THE STATE PENITENTIARIES

Baseballs, volley balls, basket balls, etc., are essential to a playground. It is these supplies, also, which have constantly to be replaced and which in the long run are, aside from supervision, the chief source of expense. As they are for groups of children, they cannot well be furnished by the children individually. Wherever play is organized in connection with the school, the reasons for furnishing baseballs, volley balls, basket balls, etc., by the school are much more obvious than those for furnishing school books, because the books are for individual use, while the play equipment is for general use, and a sufficient amount of organized play cannot be had unless this equipment is furnished. The price of these supplies is high and in the interest of economy and the expansion of the movement there should be a strenuous effort so to cheapen the cost that they can be furnished to all children.

The making of play supplies for children would be one of the best possible employments for the convicts in the state penitentiaries. These men owe to the state some return for the depredations they have committed, and the making of these supplies would probably have a stronger appeal and secure a better response from them than almost any other articles that might be manufactured. There is at the present time the greatest difficulty in securing suitable work for convicts, and ofttimes in the articles made the rehandling and shipping of materials consume most of the profits. The contract labor system which has been in general use in the past has everywhere fallen into disrepute, as it has been shown to be the exploiting of the state and the prisoners to the advantage of certain corporations. The making of any article in any prison in competition with union labor has brought out the most strenuous opposition from labor unions everywhere, and many prison superintendents are at their wits' ends to find suitable employment for their men; yet is it absolutely essential that these men should be kept busy in order to keep them from getting morbid and unruly. The cost of a football or basket ball is nearly all labor cost. There is very little expense for the materials, and the transportation charge is also infinitesimal. In the state penitentiaries there is labor in abundance and the product can be sent by parcel post to any post office in the country for a trifle. During the last two years the states of Wisconsin and Nebraska at least have passed laws requiring that the work of the prisons shall be turned toward state and municipal ends. The making of these play supplies would meet all the needs of the situation for prisoners who cannot be placed on farms or on the roads, better than almost any other occupation that can be suggested. The labor unions probably would not object to the manufacture of baseballs, basket balls, etc., by the penitentiaries, because these are not occupations of labor unions in general, and because it would be the children of the workers who would thereby be enabled to secure the facilities for play.

Would this competition with a business already established be legitimate and likely to secure a considerable return to society? I believe so. Golf sticks and baseballs to be used by adults are on the plane of luxuries. The people who use them are able to pay for them, and there is no reason why society should be especially concerned about the price. But when it comes to the cost of equipment for the play of children, everything is on a different plane. As every one knows, who has worked among the poor, the great majority of the children are not able to purchase these supplies at the present prices, and they will not have the opportunity for play which they give unless the supplies can be furnished to them. Hence, so far as children are concerned, they are public necessities, and society is vitally concerned that the prices shall not be so high that the children cannot use them. What is the expectation of reducing the price by having them made in the penitentiaries? The price might be easily cut in two, and it might be that one fourth of the present price would still yield a fair profit. A. G. Spalding & Bros. at the present time practically dominate and monopolize the field of athletic supplies. It is impossible to say exactly what these supplies cost to manufacture; but the regular league baseball which is sold at $1.25 was furnished to their branch stores at fifty-six cents in 1910. The factory price to the corporation was said to be thirty cents, and it would be reasonable to suppose that the profit to the factory was at least five cents, making the cost of a $1.25 baseball about twenty-five cents. It is said that Spalding & Bros. furnish the baseballs gratis to the National League and have also paid down to the League five hundred thousand dollars for this privilege. The materials in the Spalding six-dollar basket ball probably cost less than one dollar. The rest is labor cost. The five-dollar Spalding javelin contains ten to fifteen cents' worth of ash and a steel point worth fifteen to twenty-five cents presumably. A similar javelin can be imported from Sweden and the duty paid for $1.20.

There are very few if any other firms in the country that so completely dominate any field as does the Spalding House dominate the field of athletic supplies. They have from thirty to forty different branch stores and their control of the field is such that dealers are practically compelled to purchase their supplies of them or of Mr. Reach who is affiliated with them if they wish to secure the supplies which they must have for their trade.

Of course the difficulty which will stare any such enterprise in the face is that at the present time the rules of all of our principal games now state that the Spalding equipment shall be used, and this has been taken so much as a thing of course by all athletic associations, that they have come to believe that a legitimate game cannot be played unless it is played with Spalding supplies. This has been a piece of sagacity on the part of Spalding & Bros. which must challenge the admiration of every one. The Spalding Athletic Library is a series of guides or rules for different American games. They are the rules followed in practically all matched contests. These guides are largely devoted to the advertisement of Spalding goods and Spalding equipment. They are inexpensively bound in paper and sell for ten cents, which would be full price if they were literary classics of this size and so bound. In all of these books of rules, which are all said to be "official," it is stated that the Spalding supplies shall be used. In the rules for Newcomb, for instance, it is stated in no less than five different places that the Spalding Official Newcomb Ball, the A. G. Spalding and Bros. Newcomb Outfit, the A. G. Spalding and Bros. Wall Post, and the Spalding Official Newcomb Score Card shall be used in all official games, and apparently no American child has a right to play an authorized game unless it is played with Spalding equipment. It will be necessary for us to have a different understanding of our responsibility to the children before it will be possible for supplies to be made by state penitentiaries and have them used. Let us hope for a time when it shall be one of the rules of play that the state-made equipment shall be used and that the games shall be played in accordance with rules authorized by the state department of education.

Undoubtedly there are certain difficulties in the way of getting a system such as has been suggested under way. The wardens of the state prisons will be only too eager to do work of this kind, as they will see at once its suitability to conditions. It might also be one of the most popular moves that any political party could make. But where are the orders to come from, and what is to be their assurance that their product will be used? Sooner or later the schools must furnish to the children the supplies for play the same as they furnish textbooks in so many states and cities. If such a provision is in operation, and there are already many cities in the United States that furnish indoor baseballs, volley balls, basket balls, and the like to the children, there should be no difficulty in the way of the penitentiaries' making a direct bargain with the cities for a certain quantity of such supplies. Or, provision might be made by the state to furnish to every city a certain amount of these supplies in proportion to its school enrollment and receive the price from the primary school fund. In any case, the state should furnish these supplies to the state industrial schools, the schools for the deaf and blind, the state orphanages, the asylums for the insane, and the other state penitentiaries, and the needs of these institutions alone would furnish a good basis for the beginning of the work. From this it might easily broaden out by putting its surplus on the market in any way that might seem most satisfactory. If the work is begun on a small scale and suitably advertised, it should be successful from the first. There should be no difficulty in getting the advertising necessary, as it will appeal to the public as one of the legitimate employments for criminals.

In this connection, the late Professor Charles R. Henderson, of the University of Chicago, American Commissioner of the International Prison Commission, in a recent letter, says: "I have your favor of September 28th and the document (this section on making of play equipment by convicts) which I took to the American Prison Association to get criticisms of competent men there. I enclose a statement of Mr. F. H. Mills which seems to cover the case in part. 'The scheme of employing convicts in the manufacture of athletic supplies is entirely feasible in the larger states provided it could be arranged to create a market that would absorb the output. The first step as stated by Mr. Curtis would be to arrange a standard Base Ball, Basket Ball, Volley Ball, etc., that would be satisfactory to the several schools and athletic associations and then somehow directing their purchase from the prisons. The conditions in each state are quite different, and no rule could be laid down for organization without full knowledge of local conditions, but the fact that all these supplies under such a system could be obtained at a very much reduced cost would soon enlarge the scope of school athletics in the public schools and make possible a much larger development of satisfactory labor for convicts.

"'If some state would make a start and give publicity to it through the American Prison Association, it would be of large usefulness in solving both the question of school athletics for poor children and the furnishing employment for the Penitentiary inmates without interference with outside labor.'"

In the State of California there has long been a law permitting the making of school furniture and any other necessary equipment by the State penitentiaries, and the authorities have just begun to manufacture play equipment.

The following bill is inserted as covering the essential features:

OUTLINE OF LAW GOVERNING THE MAKING OF PLAY EQUIPMENT BY THE STATE PENITENTIARY

Be it enacted in the state of ——— that the authorities of the state penitentiary at ——— are requested to investigate the feasibility of making the various supplies for children's play, such as baseballs, indoor baseballs, volley balls, basket balls, bats, mitts, masks, swing fittings, and other similar supplies for playground equipment, in the state penitentiary, and, if it be apparent that these supplies can be made by the prisoners so as to furnish them at a considerably lower price than that now paid, to the children of the state and still return a reasonable profit to the penitentiary, that the penitentiary is hereby instructed to secure the necessary equipment for the making of these supplies, and that these supplies shall be furnished to the following specified parties;

First, to the State Orphanage, the School for the Deaf, School for the Blind, Schools for Feeble-minded, colonies for epileptics, State Reform School for Girls, State Reform School for Boys, State Penitentiaries, and asylums for the insane, in accordance with the actual needs of these institutions.

Second: That they shall be furnished directly to the city and county school systems in this state in accordance with demand.

Third: That any supplies in excess of those required to furnish the above-mentioned institutions may be sold to any dealers within or without the state, or may be sent by parcel post to any customer.

Boy Scout Activities

CHAPTER X

THE BOY SCOUTS

For nearly a generation there has been a feeling in certain educational circles that there was need that every boy should have an opportunity to live through the race life, pursue the primitive industries and occupations, and finally come to the civilization of the twentieth century by much the same stages that the race has followed. Certain schools, as the Dewey School in Chicago, have tried to follow more or less closely the stages and processes of racial evolution in their teaching. There has been a more or less general feeling that most of the delinquency of our cities was merely the breaking out of the normal savagery which lies at the basis of the character of every normal boy, but which was finding no expression under the unnatural conditions of the city. While the first beginnings of the Boy Scouts were not due to this idea, its rapid development undoubtedly tends to strengthen the theory. It came at a time when the world was ready.

The Origin of the Order

To General Baden-Powell, the hero of Mafeking, belongs the honor of founding the Boy Scouts. But it has since taken up a series of other movements and ideals. Dan Beard had already founded in this country the order of the

Sons of Daniel Boone, and Thompson Seton had started the Woodcraft Indians. Both of these orders have been absorbed into the Scouts, and each has contributed to it an important element. Beard was seeking to glorify the pioneers and the hardy virtues of the wilderness; Seton to foster a love of nature and the out-of-doors, to get boys out of the city to practice the out-of-door arts. One of the organizers of the movement was Dr. Luther Gulick, who has been the most prominent leader in the movement for general athletics and play for adolescent boys; and its first paid secretary was John Alexander, who had formerly been Boys' Secretary of the Y. M. C. A. of Philadelphia. Thus came in the new athletics and the ideals of chivalry and honor. The ideals of the order as they now exist are a combination of the ideals of all of these movements for boys. The military ideal has remained in the form of organization, the patrol and the troop, in the uniform and the occasional drills, in the marching and signaling, but it has disappeared almost entirely from the order itself. The scouts are really citizens in uniform. They usually wear khaki suits similar to those worn by soldiers, though this is not required. They are divided into patrols of eight boys, of whom one is patrol leader. Three or more patrols constitute a troop, which is in charge of a scout master, who must be an adult. Boys from twelve years on are eligible to belong. The order is now organized in every country of the civilized world.

It seems strange that scouting, which was invented as a method of making army life more interesting, has not been more largely used there. The man who is idling away his time at one of our interior forts, in time of peace, is leading about as barren and useless a life as it is possible to lead. His training is apt to consist largely in the vices of the camp. It would seem that a training that would be of so much assistance to the soldier in time of war as scouting, should be hailed with delight by army officers, and that the new interest growing out of scouting activities might help to fill the depleted ranks.

ORGANIZING THE SCOUTS

If it be desired to organize a troop of Scouts, application must be made to the headquarters of the order which is at 200 Fifth Avenue, New York City, for permission and particulars. Mr. James E. West is the Executive Secretary of the order. The headquarters will furnish the Manual of the boy scouts at 25 cents a copy and the Scout Master's Manual for 50 cents. The person who wishes to be a scout master must be approved and duly commissioned from headquarters. The boys pay 25 cents a year in dues. The Order publishes a magazine, *Boys' Life*, which has a circulation of about 100,000 copies. It has a special committee which examines all sorts of boys' books that are submitted to them and certifies such ones as they think will be wholesome and helpful for boys. These books, whatever the original price, are sold at the uniform price of fifty cents. This office of selection should be of great assistance to parents who do not feel themselves to be expert in boys' books. The headquarters also handle the uniforms and all sorts of scouting outfits, which are furnished at a special reduced price.

IDEALS OF THE ORDER

The scouts have always been announced as a nonmilitary order, and Baden-Powell has always emphasized the fact that military drills were to be discouraged, but there is no question but the boy who has had the training of the scouts would be more resourceful and capable of taking care of himself, and more efficient as a soldier, on account of the training. Headquarters now announces that it is "not unmilitary," although military training is not its aim.

During the two years of war the boy scouts have rendered valuable services, especially in England, France, and Germany, in carrying dispatches, in watching points of communication, or for air craft, in doing the work of husbands and fathers who have gone to the war, by rendering such assistance as was possible in the homes of the absentees, and in Germany, especially, in harvesting the crops. A French scout, captured by the Germans near the Meuse, was ordered to disclose the location of a detachment of his countrymen, refused to do so, and was shot because of his persistent refusal. Baden-Powell announces that "There are no fewer than 50,000 boy scouts in Red Cross Hospital work and other public services."

The boy scouts offer a progressive training. There are three main orders. When the boy is first admitted, he becomes a tenderfoot. As he becomes more proficient in the outdoor arts required, he may become a second-class and finally a first-class scout. Lest he should now weep for more worlds to conquer, there are merit badges that may be won by gaining proficiency and passing an examination in any of the common trades and crafts or in feats of skill and prowess. As an illustration, the first seven subjects listed are: agriculture, angling, archery, architecture, arts, astronomy, and athletics. Most of these require a considerable dexterity in doing work that represents one of the great trades. It is not expected that the boy will actually master the trade, but it is expected that he will master the fundamental principles on which the trade is built. It is essentially the same sort of thing that is being given in the manual training high schools to-day, and, as the boys learned for themselves on the farm and in the shop in former times. The number of activities to choose from, however, is much larger, and the boy follows his own interest and inclination in his selections. It is well known that this skill can be most easily acquired while the muscles are plastic and the boy is still growing. Baden-Powell was led into establishing this series of badges, in the hope of increasing the industrial efficiency of the workers of England. The merit badge is of silk, a little more than an inch square, and is worn on the right sleeve. If a boy wins ten of these, he becomes a Star Scout. If he wins twenty-one, he becomes an Eagle Scout.

Perhaps the most prominent single characteristic of scouting is that it is an outdoor life. It naturally belongs in connection with the woods, mountains, and streams. It is a return to nature at a time when the love of nature and natural things is active or dormant in the heart of every boy.

At Silver Bay, in 1911, there was a large gathering of the Scouts. There were two competitions. In the first, each boy was given a stick of wood, a hatchet, a pail of water, and two matches. The contest was to see which boy could soonest bring the water to a boil. He must do everything with these materials, build his fire, support his pail, etc. The next contest was the carrying of a message. One boy was to carry a message through to the hotel, and ten other boys were set to intercept him.

If the boy scouts did nothing else than keep the boys out of doors and require the physical activities that it does, it would be worth while, because these are sure to build up the health, develop the physique, and keep the boys away from the temptations of the city.

It requires much walking to do any of the things involved in scouting, but the boys also go on long walks just as "hikes." It is to be feared that some of these trips are not sufficiently planned, and that there is often an attempt to walk too far at one time. Walking should always be incidental to going somewhere and there should seldom if ever be an effort to see how far the boys can walk in a day. Ten or fifteen miles is enough at first. Walking is almost the only way that one can come to know a country intimately.

Camping is another idea which is almost inherent in the idea of scouting. If you are to live in the woods, you must camp, as a matter of course. Camping is coming in through many new channels — boys' clubs, private schools, the Y. M. C. A., the settlements, the playgrounds; and some cities are establishing municipal camps. Most of these camps are built for the boys. The boy scout camp is the more wholesome, in that the boys must build it for themselves. The boy who has not sat around a camp fire at night and cooked his own supper over a fire that he has made, has missed one of the most appealing of experiences.

Why Has the Order Grown as It Has?

The order of the Boy Scouts of America was organized February 10, 1910. Up to the first of October 1914, four hundred thousand copies of the Scout Manual had been issued, and three hundred thousand of the Tenderfoot Badges. On the new paid basis instituted in the fall of 1913, according to which each boy pays twenty-five cents annually to headquarters and is regularly enrolled, 190,484 boys were in good standing in July 1916. It is said that there are all together more than three million Scouts.

It has been better supported by private gifts from the first than almost any other great social movement. When an idea is thus instantly seized upon, it is the presumption that it has come to fill some aching void, a need that has long been felt, even if it has not been realized. The soil in some way must have been ready, else such phenomenal growth would have been a miracle.

In fact, the order of the Boy Scouts is almost exactly what the genetic psychologists like G. Stanley Hall have been preaching for years as the great need of boys. The boy should repeat the racial history. The human brain was fashioned by countless generations of nature experiences and stimuli; the mechanism is ready to utilize their effects. The boy in his teens is in the same stage of development as was the race in the days of chivalry. The same ideals appeal to him. He wishes to do much the same things. The boy in the city has been cut off from his natural sources of inspiration and stimulation. He has languished in an unnatural environment. He has turned to vice in his idleness and become delinquent from the lack of legitimate expression for his thirst for adventure. He has often been protected and pampered and spoiled until well-nigh all the manliness has been petted out of him. Scouting is an opportunity to return to nature and original conditions, to hunt and fish, to build your own house in the woods, and sit around your own camp fire. The growth of the order shows that the boys were ready. Nearly all of the active games, which in various forms are played by the children of all climes and races, are derived from the hunt and the chase, which have been the occupations of our ancestors through nine hundred and ninety-nine thousandths of human history. The scout's life is the life itself of which games are single expressions.

The first literature of children is the fairy tale. The next is chivalry and scouting, which corresponds to the youth of the race. The coming maturity expresses itself in a love for the things that are essentially manly. The books that circulate among boys in their teens have always been such stories as the "Tales of King Arthur's Court," "The Leather Stocking Tales," the lives of Kit Carson, David Crockett, and Daniel Boone, or, it may be that the boy is buying "Diamond Dick" and "Jesse James" at the corner stand. This is what boys have been reading for generations, and now the scouts are offering them an opportunity to emulate the examples of their heroes and lead a resourceful life of adventure in the open. It is no wonder that the boys have responded. They have been waiting for this opportunity since the wilderness was cleared, the Indians subdued, and their fathers began to live the unnatural life of the cities.

Scouting as a Fundamental Education

COURAGE

An absolutely essential characteristic of the old-time scout was courage. No one without courage would brave the dangers of the life. No one without courage could live amidst its hazards. Nearly every day he was in imminent peril. He found in the stimulus of danger the incentive that was needed for most effective action. He felt a joy in conquering its difficulties. Virtue and virility alike come from the old Greek root *virtus,* which meant courage. Life once demanded it of all. It was the greatest virtue, the most estimable characteristic. As time has gone on, life has become more and more safe. Little danger is experienced in our everyday affairs, and courage must be carried up to a higher plane. We do not need to fight Indians or wild beasts, but we must fight graft and self-interest and organized capital that would oppress the weak and enslave us all. Courage is still a fundamental virtue, almost synonymous with manliness. Modern life offers too few opportunities for the training of courage, and we should welcome the scouts the more gladly on that account.

Mr. Carnegie in establishing the hero fund says the fund is not established to encourage heroism and courage, because he does not believe that courage can be created, but that it is rather a native characteristic of the individual who possesses it.

But there is every reason for thinking that courage can be developed in children just as easily as any other quality and certainly much more easily than some of the newer virtues, such as truthfulness and chastity. Courage is an old racial virtue which was once demanded of all. Under the conditions of the wilderness nearly every boy grew up to be a brave Indian fighter. Every girl developed traits which made her a fit mother of heroes. Heroic courage is a racial quality that only needs opportunity and encouragement to develop. The policemen may be corrupt, but they are rarely found wanting in time of danger. The fireman may be a man of low ideals, but he goes through smoke and fire and scales well-nigh inaccessible walls to save the life of a little child. The life savers on our coast do not hesitate to launch their little boats in any sea. It is largely the expectancy of the public and the ideals of the force that awake the courage which is really fundamental to human nature.

The scouts are getting this training. Courage is partly resourcefulness, the "being prepared" which is the motto of the order. The boy who can swim is not afraid of the water. The boy who knows the woods is not afraid of the woods. The lightning gunmen of the early West did not need much courage to get into gun quarrels with men less quick. We are not afraid of dangers that we have learned to cope with, and resourcefulness is always a large part of the cure of timidity. The Council gives an honor medal to the boy who saves a life at the risk of his own. Baden-Powell tells the following incidents: A boy stopped a runaway team in London, and there followed an epidemic of stopping runaway teams all over the empire. A boy attempted to save another from drowning but was drowned himself. He was given the Victoria Cross, and thousands of scouts took swimming lessons in order that they might be of assistance in time of need.

TRUTHFULNESS

Truthfulness is a virtue that is closely associated with courage. In general it may be said that the cowardly are always untruthful. It is one of their main defenses against strength. The strong scorn lying as a defense of the weakling. Protective coloring, which is the lowest biological form of lying, is mainly seen in the young and the frail that may easily become victims. Truthfulness is an ideal from **chivalry.**

It survives to-day in our "word of honor," "honor of a gentleman," etc. DuBois Guilbert says at Torquilstone, "Many a law, many a commandment have I broken, but my word never." The knights of Arthur's Court would soon be lodged in the penitentiary, if they went forth to-day to do the valorous deeds of his time. They were rather low-grade men in many ways, but there are two virtues that must be conceded to them, and these are courage and truthfulness. It is written in scout law: "A scout's word is to be trusted. If he were to violate his honor by telling a lie, or by cheating, or by not doing exactly a given task when trusted on his honor, he may be directed to hand over his scout badge." It is one thing to tell a boy that he must not lie, because it is wicked, and it is a very different thing to show him that it is not honorable or courageous to do it, and to show him that he belongs to an order where it is not permitted. The scout method is the one method which in history has proved conspicuously successful. It is applied to an individual in about the same state of development as the knights, and there is every reason for thinking that this method may be successful.

FRIENDSHIP

Friendship is another word for love. It is Christianity in action. The school teaches the multiplication table and the location of the cities, but it is nowhere evident that it regards the development and intensifying of friendship as important. Yet friendship makes most of the joy of life. It doubles our strength for all of its practical affairs, and is one of the surest safeguards against its temptations. It makes us public-spirited and real members of the community.

Friendship demands association, and the scouts give the opportunity, under conditions that draw the company together; for the camp fire is the supreme place for the development of intimacy, and a company who have spent evenings together within its magic circle are likely to feel differently toward each other all the rest of their lives.

KINDNESS

The scout pledges himself to do some deed of kindness every day. This is surely not a large demand to make on anyone, but, if we do not think about it, we may never get into the habit. The act, whatever it is, must be done voluntarily and on the boy's own initiative. It may be only the washing of the dishes for his mother or the picking up of a banana peeling from the sidewalk, but it must be the boy's own act. Powell says that at first the English scouts were accustomed to wear their ties outside their waistcoats until they had done their kind act. He tells the tale of one scout who remembered after he had gone to bed that he had done no kind deed that day, heard a mouse in the trap and got up and gave it to the cat. In some patrols in this country the boys are asked to report what their kind acts are. One scout master reports that he was out walking one evening when he saw a party of big boys drag a tree top across a secluded road that was much frequented by autos. As soon as these boys went away, he saw his own patrol of scouts appear and drag the tree top from the road and throw it down the embankment. They were quite unaware of his presence. In some troops they have a somewhat dramatic representation of the scout's work in this regard. For instance, in one portrayal, a thug knocks a man down with a padded stick and robs him. Others pass by and make fun of the wounded man as he lies helpless, but finally two scouts come upon the scene. They examine and bind up his bruises, make a stretcher, and carry him off. A ragged old lady enters and seems timid about crossing the street. A party of boys make fun of her, but a scout escorts her across.

DEMOCRACY

"The scout makes no distinction of classes." He receives no tips. There is no more rich and poor in a scout patrol than there is in a baseball game. You have to deliver the goods to get preferment. The leader of the patrol may be the butcher's boy, and the Mayor's son one of the members. It has been so with the scouts and pioneers of all time, "The best is like the worst." There are few distinctions other than those that come from superior achievement.

THRIFT

Before a boy may become a first-class scout he must earn and deposit at least two dollars in the bank. As a people we scarcely have a habit of saving. Many, if not most of us, are spending all that we earn from year to year and saving little or nothing for the rainy day. We hear much discussion of the high cost of living, but it is much a question whether as Hubard says we should not speak of "the cost of high living" instead. We have school savings banks in some cities, and penny provident banks in many cities, but it is not likely that one twelve-year-old boy in five has a savings account. He *must* have one if he is to be a scout, and, what is better for many idle sons of rich fathers, he must earn it himself. The

s

Jew, who starts in with a pushcart on the East Side, makes but little; but saves something, educates his children, and soon moves up town and owns the building he lives in.

The Scout Master

The scout master must be an adult. He also must be public-spirited, because he is not paid. He has a great opportunity to influence the boys, both through keeping up the standards of the order and through direct counsel and friendship. The man who goes with boys on long walks into the country, helps to build the bivouac, to prepare the meals, and sits with them around the camp fire at night, can do almost anything with a group of boys, if he is the right kind of a man.

It is difficult to organize the scouts on the playgrounds, though there are a considerable number of troops that have their drills and demonstrations there, but there are sixty-five playground systems in this country that maintain summer camps, and there is nearly always scouting in connection with these camps. The playground authorities usually have charge also of the social centers, and there are apt to be scout patrols in connection with the social centers. In many cities the supervisor of playgrounds is also the scout commissioner for the city. There are many schools where the scouts are organized by the principal of the school, who himself becomes the scout master. In some schools the boys have fitted up a special vacant room for themselves and have it decorated with all their regalia. The closer the connection between the schools and the playgrounds, the more possible do scouting activities become. Mr. West reports that there were troops of scouts in connection with six hundred and forty schools in this country in 1916.

What Shall We Do with the Scout Movement?

It would appear that scouting corresponds with a fundamental interest of boys; that it holds in solution the essential virtues of adolescence, with its thirst for manliness and achievement and heroism; that it gives health and endurance and hardihood on the physical side, companionableness on the social side, alertness and resourcefulness on the mental side, and the appropriate virtues of the period on the moral side. Every boy should have some such training. It develops manliness and virtue, where the school develops the intellect. The two are supplementary to each other. The scouts train in the old racial activities and virtues, the school in the latest acquisitions of the race.

The greatest difficulty in the way of the movement is that the scout masters are not paid, and it is difficult to get enough men to give their time freely to the work. There might be four or five times as many scouts as there are now, if the scout masters could give the necessary time to their troops. This movement is important enough to demand some of the school time. The school could well afford to give Friday afternoon in the two upper grades of the elementary school and the two first years of the high school to scouting and to the Camp Fire Girls. But we must have more men teachers. I believe that there is enough general interest in many communities already to warrant the introduction of scouting, if the conditions were favorable. Increasing emphasis on industrial work, vocational training, school excursions, and organized play are all making a similar demand for men teachers. The Boys' Club, the independent summer camp, the municipal playground, and the boys' Y. M. C. A. are growing up because, in some way, the school is failing to get a vital hold on the life of its pupils.

To put scouting into the school program would not really be so great an innovation as it may seem. It was the fact that his scouting manual had already been adopted by certain private schools in England that first led Baden-Powell to think that it might be well adapted for boys in general. Scouting activities are regularly carried on by many private and some public schools of Europe. The school excursion, or "hike," has for some time been a part of the school program in Germany. My experiences as a hunter and trapper in boyhood are almost as vivid to-day as they were then, while there is scarcely an incident from my school life that has survived in memory. This can only mean in a large way that the mind was adapted to the hunting experience, as it was not to school experiences, and that it consequently responded to them, while the school left it half asleep. Many a child grows stupid at school because the dry and to him useless knowledge that is offered cannot touch or stimulate his mind. The things that we remember are likely to be more influential in our lives than the things that we forget, and scouting may well be more educational than schooling. It is such experiences that the normal boy most craves, and it is the lack of them that is causing much of the juvenile delinquency.

One of the great difficulties in the conduct of the work of the boy scouts has been that there have been very few people who had the requisite training for scout masters. This situation is being met more or less by the introduction of courses for scout masters into the various universities and by summer courses which are being given in connection with scout camps outside of most of our largest cities. These courses are still inadequate, but they constitute a hopeful beginning.

In Columbia the work for scout masters may be taken as one of the credit courses for a degree. Professor Elsom, of the University of Wisconsin, gave a course that attracted considerable attention in the summer of 1915 and a similar course in the University of California in the summer of 1916. In the University of California there is also a course running through the entire year.

The Boy Scout as an Apprentice Citizen

The scouts are everywhere recognized as a semi-public order and are being very generally used by the various public departments and institutions to assist in their work. Some of the more common enterprises in which the scouts have taken part are the following: During the summer of 1914, boy scouts in the White Mountains built a government trail. In the state of Massachusetts they have taken a census of the condition and number of trees in the different towns. In South Orange, New Jersey, they have served as deputy wardens, reporting on the condition of trees and watching to see that no unnecessary damage is done to them. In a number of cities they have assisted in draining ponds or putting oil on stagnant water so as to get rid of mosquitoes. In Cleveland they have helped in the war on the flies and in a number of other cities they have assisted in "clean up" campaigns, have helped in the collecting and removal of rubbish, and have also given reports on the condition of alleys and other unsanitary conditions about the city. The scouts of Tacoma, Washington, have taken a bird census of the city and vicinity and kept a record of their migrations. At large public meetings and conventions, the boy scouts have generally served as guides and have often carried grips and in other ways assisted incoming guests. In connection with the inauguration of President Wilson and the G. A. R. Encampments at Gettysburg and Detroit, they were invaluable as messengers, guides, and general utility helpers. After the great fire which destroyed so much of the city of Salem, Massachusetts, they rendered invaluable assistance in collecting and distributing funds, clothing, and provisions for the relief of the sufferers.

The activities thus far carried on by the scouts serve only to suggest something very much larger which might be done and which the present activities have shown to be practicable. In nearly all European countries the young men are required to serve one or more years in the army. In this country we do not believe that this is necessary. There is, however, a kind of enlistment which is no less needed here than in Europe, now than formerly; it is an enlistment for the public welfare, to serve the state in those lines in which its real greatness consists. We are teaching civics very generally in our schools, but it is mostly book knowledge and fails to relate itself to actual conditions. A much more effective way of teaching citizenship would be to have each boy serve for a certain period of time in each of the public departments of the city. This is merely the idea of military service brought down to date in a peaceful state. There have been a sufficient number of experiments tried already to show that this is desirable.

During the years from fourteen to sixteen, when the boy begins to feel that he is a man and when the altruistic motives are first coming into prominence, every boy ought to be practically initiated into the work of the city. We have all regretted that there was no work in city homes for the boys to do, and that they were growing up without duties and without the training that comes from any form of service. If during these years they might spend one half of their time in school, and the other half in actual service in the different departments, it would be both for the good of the city and the boys. This would make each city department in a sense a part of the school system, and would require that those in charge be either master workmen who could take the boys as apprentices, or trade teachers who could give them instruction in the work to be done.

Superintendent Wirt has shown us how the schoolboys can do most of the work now required on the school buildings, for in Gary they are making nearly all of the repairs, are painting the buildings, laying out playgrounds, putting in play equipment, and similar things. In many ways this work is more difficult than that of any other city department. For instance, if the boys were required to devote a certain amount of time to the Park Department, they would in this way get valuable training in landscape gardening, the laying out of flower beds, the mowing of lawns, and even the laying of cement walks and the installing of water systems. It is also entirely feasible for boys between fourteen and sixteen to trim the trees and perform elementary tree surgery. It is not only feasible but would be very interesting for them to spray such shrubs and trees as need it, and help to exterminate destructive moths. Thus it would seem that under practical direction most of the work of the Park Department might be done by boys. It would be at the same time excellent physical, industrial, and civic training. It would also save the main cost of the maintenance of the department.

In many cities the boy scouts have rendered assistance in case of fire by helping to keep the fire lines and to protect the hose, and in some cases even in making rescues. In Pittsburgh, during the past fall, they took a prominent part in the Fire Prevention Day activities, and in fact secured the proclamation from the mayor setting aside such a day. They personally delivered letters to the various ministers about the city asking them to give notice of Fire Prevention Day from the pulpits, and on the day of the parade they assisted the police and formed a division in the procession.

To the Police Department they might render, also, a very valuable service. Many boys aspire to be policemen, and there are portions of the policeman's duty which adolescent boys could do better than the police are doing it. A considerable part of every policeman's time is always devoted to giving information and directing strangers about the city. This would be the best kind of training for boys in coming to know the city, and would give them facility and politeness in meeting strangers. In connection with conventions and other great public meetings, the scouts have already rendered this service in a number of cases. Boys might well make a survey to find out how well certain regulations are observed. They could carry notices and give instruction in regard to new regulations, and be of service in many different ways. The knowledge which they would gain would be sure to be of advantage to them later, and would probably give them a quite different attitude toward the observance of law.

In a number of cities a junior police force has been established during the last three years and the boys have proved of great assistance in running down juvenile offenders and also in locating those who were violating the laws for the protection of children. The system on the east side of New York and in the city of Oakland have attracted considerable attention, and probably similar systems have been established in a number of other cities.

To the Health Department they might be of assistance in many ways. They would enjoy the carrying on of campaigns for the extermination of mosquitoes, flies, and other insect pests, and also of sparrows and rats where these have become a nuisance. They could put up posters and give out notices, help to clean up alleys and unsanitary conditions, and be of assistance in many ways in making the city a better place to live in.

In the State of California, all the schoolbooks for the children are printed by the State and distributed to the children without cost. In the city of Gary the children regularly print the school papers, the annual report of the Superintendent, and they make many thousands of reprints of articles on the Gary system which appear in the various magazines. In view of the success of this work, which seems to be quite equal to printing done elsewhere, it does not seem impossible that the printing of textbooks, such as the law requires in California, should be done in special trade schools, by the children themselves, or if not in special schools, in connection with the Manual Training Departments in the various cities. Boys in Gary, on account of their experience in printing, are able to go into the various printing establishments and get good wages at once, and it would seem that such work would be as helpful to boys as most of the trade work offered.

They might well assist the Street Department, as they

already have done in a number of cities, by helping to keep the sidewalks clean and by giving instructions in regard to the disposal of garbage and rubbish. It would be a good thing if every boy were expected to serve one or two months on the regular street cleaning force itself, as this would give him a practical appreciation of the city's work which he might not otherwise get. There would be many boys who would regard this as unworthy labor, but it is just these boys to whom the training would be most valuable. We do not wish to train up a race of snobs, and every boy ought to have some experience with real physical labor, both for its educational value and the training in democracy which it gives.

It seems to be entirely possible, also, that nearly all the concrete work in the nature of sidewalks and curbs should be done by the children themselves. I have seen places where children in the fourth and fifth grades have laid the sidewalks around the school.

The following paragraph is from an account of the work in one of the Southern high schools, which appeared in a recent number of the *New England Journal of Education:*

In this department, the elements of concrete construction are worked out in the shop in the high school. The principles learned have recently been applied in the construction of three thousand feet of sidewalk and curb about the high school; concrete curb about the quarter-mile race track on the same field; concrete flumes and headgates for the irrigation system; headgates, feeding troughs, water tank and hitching posts for the school farm; drinking fountains for the playgrounds for each of the grade schools; flower urns and various forms of garden furniture. A large concrete silo is now being constructed on the farm, as well as the foundation and flooring for the club-house at the park. Concrete flooring and feeding devices were also put in the dairy barn at the farm.

These are only a few of many things which might be suggested for the boys to do, and other suitable tasks would be sure to appear as the work progressed. This would give a very important training to boys, for it would teach them to know the city and its various departments, they would develop a new loyalty toward it and love for it, they would be initiated into many kinds of work which would be as valuable in themselves as anything they could get in the manual training shops. Most of this work would keep them out of doors, would give them good physical training, and would be a practical minimum initiation into several different trades. It should also greatly reduce the cost of maintaining the city and enable it to do many things and to maintain a standard of beauty and excellence which under existing conditions are impossible. The idea of public service, thus wrought into habit and practice in these early years, would be the best assurance that the city could have of honest voting and generous public service during later years.

It is not necessary that a boy should become a Scout for him to undertake work of this nature. It is the sort of work that every boy ought to do, but the Scouts have given us the suggestion. The uniform in this case would be an advantage. They would be real soldiers of peace, enlisted for the public welfare.

The ideals of scouting are peculiarly the ideals of adolescence and manliness. It is to be regretted, perhaps, that the order has not thus far brought into its program something of the old initiation into manhood with its instruction in sex matters, which was and still is common amongst many if not most primitive peoples. Of these initiations, Havelock Ellis says, "Ceremonies of initiation into manhood at puberty —

involving physical and mental discipline, as well as instruction, lasting for weeks or months, and never identical for both sexes — are common among savages in all parts of the world. They nearly always involve the endurance of a certain amount of pain and hardship.

"In time, we cannot doubt, they will be revived in modern forms. At present, the spiritual initiation of youths and maidens is left to the chances of some bad incident, and usually it is of a purely cerebral character which cannot be perfectly wholesome, and is at the best, absurdly incomplete."

CHAPTER XI

THE CAMP FIRE GIRLS

FEW movements have ever seized upon the popular imagination as has the Camp Fire Girls. Woman's work in the home has always been tame and monotonous, redeemed from drudgery only by the love which gave it motive. The Camp Fire discovers in it both romance and adventure. Our schools have trained the heads of girls for the work of men. The Camp Fire promises to train the heart and hand of woman for what has always been woman's special work. The great task of the twentieth century seeems to be the developing of more intimate and loving relationships between man and man. The Camp Fire proposes to carry the loving social organization of the home into the community. Organized in the spring of 1912, it has already spread throughout the United States and in scattered groups to nearly every country of the civilized world.

There is a general resemblance between the boy scouts and the Camp Fire Girls; in fact, the order was suggested in the first place by the desire of certain girls to become Scouts. A detailed comparison of the Scout oath and law, however, does not show a close similarity with the law of the Camp Fire. The real resemblance lies deeper. The scouts were organized to give to boys a training that is essentially manly. The Camp Fire Girls were organized to give to girls a training that is essentially womanly. The boy in the teens craves manly achievement and adventure. The girl, on the other hand, desires the things that are essentially feminine and the especial adventure of women, which is romance.

The two orders have a number of activities in common. There is the same encouragement of the outdoor life and health in each order. In each there are three degrees, and one passes from the lower orders to the higher by gaining honors. In both orders these honors may be earned in athletics and a knowledge of the out-of-doors or by mastering the crafts of life for the man and the woman. Each order encourages cooking and camping and walking and friendship. Each order has its distinctive costume, oath, and law. Each has weekly meetings in charge of an adult who takes the general responsibility of guidance.

The Camp Fire Girls have certain advantages over the scouts. The scouts are seeking to promote a form of activity and of virtue that corresponds to a certain stage of human development, but which at the present belongs to history. It is a most wholesome ideal, but it is an ideal that history has left behind on account of changed conditions. It is not so with the Camp Fire Girls or better the Fireside Girls, which would really be a better name. It is no less appropriate to the present than it would have been to any time in history. It is seeking to add romance and adventure to the ordinary affairs of woman's life, and to add to her training the sense of service. The boy scouts are very much limited in their activities by living in the cities. Not so the Camp Fire Girls; they can pursue their work and win their honors

The Camp Fire Girls

nearly as well in a modern city as anywhere. Their field is as wide as the home and human relationship.

The Origin of the Order

Among all primitive peoples there is a sort of initiation into the tribe which takes place at puberty and is conducted by the old women, which corresponds closely to the Camp Fire. This is intended specifically as a preparation for marriage. It teaches the girl at that time the secret lore of the tribe, and gives her the knowledge that she will need as a woman. The Camp Fire Girls is chiefly the invention of Dr. and Mrs. Gulick, by whom it was organized March 17, 1912. Dr. Gulick is at present the president of the organization; Mrs. Gulick is at the head of the department of design which is working out the costumes, beads, banners, and general regalia of the order, and editor of the magazine, *Wahelo*. There has been no effort to secure a large membership, as, until recently, the larger the membership the larger the expense. Nevertheless, there were 60,000 Camp Fire Girls on the first of January 1914.

In the fall of 1913 the following rule was adopted:

"Annual dues shall be payable to the National office on the basis of $5.00 a year minimum fee for a Camp Fire of ten girls or less; and fifty cents a year for every additional member. For Camp Fires organized before December 1, 1913, the paying of this fee to the National office is optional. All Camp Fires organized after December 1 must pay a charter fee of $5.00 — which covers a sample outfit of Camp Fire materials — which would retail at $8.55. Six months after organization the annual dues are payable."

Most of the orders have changed over to the pay basis voluntarily. The new Camp Fires are being formed more rapidly on the new basis than they were under the old, and the order is now self-supporting.

The Purpose of the Camp Fire Girls

The purpose of the order cannot be better stated than by quotation from the constitution.

"The purpose of this corporation shall be to perpetuate the spiritual ideals of the home under the new conditions of a social community, through the organization of girls and women into units divided by age into Camp Fires and a Junior Organization.

"The organization shall endeavor to show that the common things of daily life are the chief means of beauty, romance, and adventure.

"The organization shall endeavor to aid in the formation of habits making for health and vigor, the out-of-door habit, and the out-of-door spirit.

"The organization shall endeavor to foster intimate relations between mothers and daughters by giving status and social recognition to the work of the Mother."

In his annual report the president of the organization, January 20, 1914, says:

"We are attempting to create for our times a new spirit among the girls and women for each day's work and a new program for social life — a spirit and a program that carry into the entire community the idealism, affection, devotion, and beauty which hitherto has been largely a matter within individual homes."

In an address delivered before the Central McKinley and Eastern High Schools of Washington, D. C., December 1913, he further said:

"The day when we can furnish ourselves or our children with clean adequate social relations within the home, has forever passed.

"It is not recreation and places to do things that is needed so much as it is human ties and friendships. Comradeship is a fundamental human need. It may grow through common interest in any of a hundred things — what we have always to remember is that while activities are important, the object is affection of one kind or another. That is, we are organizing people rather than activities.

"Hence, it is hopelessly inadequate merely to establish playgrounds, parks, skating rinks, and dance halls. We must create social groupings that will carry the new social spirit, and we must preserve social groups intact.

"Can you develop the geniuses who will parallel in the social world what our inventors have done in the world of steam and electricity?

"This is the task before your generation. It was our task to organize the great world of industry — to tame the forces of nature — steam — electricity — water power — harness them in great machines and drive them to do the material work of the world. This we have done fairly well — much remains to do, but even now we begin to hear of the trouble caused by 'over production.' We have taken the work of the world from human backs and have placed it upon machines. Slavery even in its figurative sense is fast going — but — we have not made friendship, comradeship, social life, romance, the common lot of all, even though it is as necessary as are food, shelter, and clothing. This was not our job. The day for community social life could only come when we had a community physical life.

"The coming generation has the material basis for this glorious new opportunity. Can you do for the affections as brilliantly as we have done for the industries? If you can, then it will be true that what there has been of love and beauty in life will prove to be but the promise of the time when human life — all of it, everyway, shall flower and fruit as it has done hitherto only in rare and isolated cases. To make this true is the supreme task and hope of human-kind."

This seems to me the largest new concept that has come into recent thought and may well prove an inspiration to every girl and every woman. Compared with it, how trivial do most women's rights programs seem, and how trivial also are the various movements for better houses or wages or safety. These are but the husks of life at best. It is not at all evident that this program is to be realized through the Camp Fire Girls, but it is certainly a splendid challenge to the spirit of woman and the age.

THE THREE DEGREES

The local lodge or organization is known as a Camp Fire. It consists of from six to twenty girls. The girls must be at least twelve years of age, but there is no upper limit of age. The girl first becomes a Wood Gatherer, which corresponds to a Tenderfoot Scout. But before she may become a Wood Gatherer, she must be able to repeat, "It is my desire to become a Camp Fire Girl and to obey the law of the Camp Fire, which is to

Seek beauty,
Give service,
Pursue knowledge,
Be trustworthy,
Hold on to health,
Glorify work,
Be happy.

This law of the Camp Fire, I will strive to follow."

When a girl becomes a Wood Gatherer, she receives a silver ring which is the distinctive badge of the order. The Camp Fire meets once a week, and once a month they have a Council Fire, at which the girls are supposed to wear their ceremonial costume, which is of galatea, and which costs about sixty cents where the girls make it themselves. The girls bind their hair so as to give them a somewhat Indian appearance when they are in full regalia. In time each girl who progresses in the order wears a string of beads which corresponds to the feathers of the Indian brave, as each bead represents an honor and must be conferred after the girls have learned the crafts involved. The arts for which girls may receive honors include all the arts of the household, cooking, sewing, caring for the baby, etc., but they also include athletics, folk dancing, walking, outdoor sleeping, and a vast number of other useful achievements. Many of them are similar to the things taught in the domestic departments of the schools. These honors have given a means for the first time, of measuring and rewarding the progress of a girl or woman in housewifely arts. As such they should be welcomed by all women.

The *New Day*[1] has the following to say about the honors:

[1] A prospectus of the Camp Fire Girls.

The everyday character of attainments for which honors are awarded are indicated by the following examples:

Cooking three common vegetables each in three ways.

Marketing one week on two dollars per person.

Taking the entire care of one room for one month, to include sweeping, dusting, washing of windows, care of flowers or plants, and what may be desirable for the attractiveness of the room.

Participate in the carrying out of a party or hike, at which there are at least as many others (either boys or girls) as there are Camp Fire Girls.

Caring for a baby for an average of an hour a day for a month.

Swimming one hundred yards.

Tramping forty miles in any ten days.

Knowing the planets and seven constellations and their stories.

Taking a dozen photographs, developing, and printing them.

Trimming a hat.

Filling a regular position for four months, earning ten dollars a week or less.

Saving ten per cent of your allowance for three months.

There are upwards of 300 of these honors which are grouped under the following heads: Health Craft, Camp Craft, Nature Lore, Home Craft, Hand Craft, Business, and Patriotism. As each girl receives honors she progresses from rank to rank.

After the girl has acquired the requisite number of honors, she may become a Fire Maker; but before she may have this honor conferred upon her, she must be able to repeat:

> "As fuel is brought to the fire,
> So I purpose to bring
> My strength,
> My ambition,
> My heart's desire,
> My joy,
> And my sorrow
> To the fire

Of human kind;
For I will tend,
As my fathers have tended
And my fathers' Fathers
Since time began,
The fire that is called
The love of man for man,
The love of man for God."

Before a girl can pass to the third degree and become a Torch Bearer, she must have trained at least three other girls in some of the lower honors, and she must herself have become proficient in a large number of the arts of the home and of the out-of-doors. It is at the present time the best assurance that we have anywhere that the girl has acquired the arts that every woman should know before marriage, that she knows how to cook and sew and care for the baby, and has imbibed something of the spirit that makes a real home.

THE BLUE BIRDS

The Camp Fire Girls must be twelve years old, but as there are many younger girls who have sought admission, a junior order has been formed for them. These younger girls, from six to twelve years of age, are known as Blue Birds. This order has not been formed in fact for their benefit, but in order to establish the big sisterly relation for the older girls, that they may have a definite form of service open to them in conducting games and entertainments for these little girls. There is a special manual for the Blue Birds. Each guardian is allowed to have one camp fire and one nest of Blue Birds, though she will use her older girls for the most part in managing the activities of the little girls.

THE GUARDIANS

The great difficulty for the movement is to secure as guardians of the Camp Fire, women who can and are willing to give their time and who have the ability to lead girls and to secure progress. However, the difficulty is not as great as it is for the scouts, because there are more women who can take the time than there are men on an average, and because women have a stronger feeling for social service. In a half dozen years, after the present Camp Fire Girls have graduated from the order, it should be easier to secure competent guardians. Normal training for Camp Fire Guardians is already being given at certain normal schools and universities, and, as Dr. Gulick says:

"The key to future success and permanency lies in the character and equipment of the women who take up the work as guardians. Short courses should be established in our leading colleges, normal schools, summer camps, and summer schools.

"The Camp Fire offers to the average college graduate the best opportunity there is of fitting herself and her college equipment into her own home community, but to do this she must become familiar with the work while at college."

ORGANIZING CAMP FIRES

The Headquarters of the Camp Fire organization is at Fourth Ave. and Thirty-second Street, New York City. The organization issues an excellent manual for twenty-five cents that contains the information that is needed by those who wish to organize. There is also a very attractive Camp Fire Magazine known as *Wahelo*.

Camp Fires cannot well be organized on the playgrounds themselves, but there is an excellent opportunity for them at the summer camp, if there is one, and at the social center of the school. The great trouble of so many boys' and girls' clubs is that they have no purpose. The Camp Fire is a girls' club with a definite purpose. It has every advantage that the ordinary club has, with the added advantage that it gives a definite social training, and then, too, it has its ritual, its regalia, and council fires to add to the variety and spice of the meetings. Poetry, romance, and a sense of service are wrought into the ritual and ceremonies of the Camp Fire in such a way that a girl can scarcely fail to imbibe some of it. Life will surely be more beautiful and significant to most of the girls, on account of the order. Everywhere it has met with the enthusiastic support of the mothers, because it inclines the girls to be more helpful in the home and gives them a new interest in home duties.

The Scope of the Movement

The Camp Fire Girls are already organized in every state of the Union, and in Canada, Japan, Siam, the West Indies, Panama, and in Scotland. Under the circumstances, it seems certain that the Camp Fire will soon become a really world movement and, while it will never be as spectacular, will be really as common as the scouts.

The Training of the Camp Fire

On the whole, the training of the Camp Fire is the most fundamental training that is anywhere being given to girls. Cube root and partial payments have little to do with the life of woman, but household tasks and the care of children have much. Too often our girls are coming up to marriage and motherhood without any real preparation, almost entirely uninstructed and uninspired in the things that are to be their life work. The Camp Fire is giving this vital training.

Much of woman's work has always been uninteresting and monotonous. The work of to-day is a repetition of the work of yesterday and a prophecy of the work of to-morrow. It is the sort of work that makes for narrow-mindedness and gossip. It has no apparent incentive and it is not measured or directly rewarded. It seems to have none of those elements of romance which all girls crave. Surely the thing that we all need most is to find our adventure and romance, not in Castles in Spain, but in our daily duties, and the order that can find poetry in washing dishes deserves all support from women.

The age that is coming in is a social age. It has a new spirit of service, of brotherhood, and human responsibility. The education that will really prepare us to live in the twentieth century must train this sense of service. This training will not come from the study of scholastic subjects, but will come almost entirely, if it comes at all, through early learning to do things for others. The older daughter was once her mother's chief assistant in the industries of the home, but changing conditions have made this less true during the last half century. The Camp Fire through giving the girl a new and romantic interest in the home and its duties is bringing in a more wholesome relationship between mothers and daughters, and the mother once more becomes the teacher and the expert in something that the daughter wishes to learn. The organization of the Blue Birds extends this helpful relationship to the younger sisters and makes the Camp Fire Girl an apprentice mother as well, which every adolescent girl ought to be. A girl has no more right to be married without knowing how to manage a home and care for children than a young man has who has no trade or profession and no means of supporting a family. The Camp Fire offers a method of extending this spirit of service to the community. It is one of the most promising social inventions thus far seen for creating a sense of service among the young people. There are, however, about five million girls of Camp Fire age in this country who ought to have this training. There are 60,000 Camp Fire Girls. It does not seem likely that for a good many years to come, at least, it will be possible to get enough guardians to furnish Camp Fires to a considerable proportion of the girls. When some of the present Girls have graduated into maturity or matrimony, this should be easier, but it seems very doubtful if it can ever be met by volunteer help. It would doubtless be better if this could be quite apart from the schools and the guardians might all be volunteers. Whether or not this is possible, there can be little doubt but that the things that the Camp Fire is encouraging are more vital to woman's life and success than the things that she is learning in the school, and we can but ask ourselves why the school should not give this training in preference to much that it is now giving. Certainly, it is one of the very best activities for all social centers and all summer camps, but it is well worth Friday afternoons at least from the school time for the older girls. The girls are all interested in matrimony and a preparation for its duties during the teens, and they would be sure to welcome it, provided their teachers were of a kind with whom they cared to have relations of personal intimacy. It is a question that is vital to all education just now whether it must train only in the fads and frills, such as the three R's have always been for women, or whether it may also undertake a training that prepares directly for wifehood, motherhood, the making of the home, and the service of the community. The Schools for Mothers are one of the most promising educational movements of Europe at the present time. The Camp Fire Girls were, on January 1, 1914, organized in connection with eighty playgrounds and four hundred and fifty-two schools in this country.

A Civic Enlistment

For the last fifteen or twenty years in Germany they have been discussing the idea of requiring all of the girls to serve in connection with the hospitals, kindergartens, nurseries, and other public institutions in the same way that the boys are required to serve in the army. There are probably not as many opportunities for the useful employment of girls in social and public enterprises in the city as there are of such employment for boys; but they certainly could serve with advantage in the nurseries, kindergartens, playgrounds, hospitals, clinics, milk stations, and in considerable of the relief work. They could also be of assistance and would enjoy much of the landscape gardening in the parks. Doubtless there is some work in connection with most of the city departments that is feasible for them. If women are to be citizens and voters and take the same part in public life that men have been taking in the past, it is very desirable that before their maturity they should have some practical acquaintanceship with the mechanism of the city government. If they are to be members of the city household, they ought also to be initiated into the city housekeeping.

It does not seem impossible also that a large part of the organization of the play of the children on the public playground should be placed in the hands of high school girls. In the city of Gary many of the high school girls and boys do apprentice work of this kind on the playgrounds and in the gymnasiums, and for this work they receive advanced standing in the School of Physical Education of Chicago. Experience of this kind would be in the nature of a direct preparation for those who wish to undertake either playground work or teaching in later years, and it would often be the very best thing possible for the girls' health. Probably the girl who had some experience in organizing the games of younger children during her high school period under the direction of a trained supervisor would be a more successful play director a little later, than she would be if she waited until she were twenty-five and had already finished a normal school, before she began to take part in activities of this sort. But even if the girl did not contemplate becoming either a teacher or a playground director, her experience in playing with and organizing the games of little children would be of great advantage to her later, as a mother. In fact, the kind of social training which she would receive in this way would be valuable to her in every relationship of life. The Blue Birds are already offering to the Camp Fire girls an opportunity of this sort, but there are not as many of these as there should be.

THE GIRL SCOUTS

The Camp Fire Girls were organized because it was found that there were many girls who wished to become scouts and were actually undertaking to do the work intended for boys. Recently there has been formed an order of the Girl Scouts which has headquarters at 17 West 42d St., with Mr. Montague Gammon as chief executive. Its oath and manual are modeled closely after the manual of the Boy Scouts, and it is proposing for girls very similar activities. It is generally organized in the municipal playgrounds of Philadelphia in preference to the Camp Fire Girls. In a number of places the girls have become Scouts rather than Camp Fire Girls because of the lesser expenditure involved. There are now about ten thousand Girl Scouts in this country.

CHAPTER XII

THE RECREATION SURVEY

Before a doctor treats his patient he must diagnose the case. Before a tailor makes the suit of clothes, he must measure his customer. It seems reasonably evident likewise that, if a play system is to fit a city, it must be built upon a study of the city's needs. A system that is less than this cannot well be better than a custom-made suit and may be no more appropriate than the dress of a five-year-old girl would be for a boy of twelve.

If a tailor is to make a suit of clothes, there are certain definite measurements which he takes, because he has found these dimensions are essential in order that he may produce a fit. In recreation surveys, no such definite and fixed measurements have yet been agreed upon. Authorities differ as to what it is desirable to know about a city before the playground system is cut out. People also disagree as to how much time should be spent on making such a survey, and some are of the opinion that they already know all that is necessary. But it would be a moderate statement to say that the tailor could cut out a suit of clothes quite as well by looking at his customer, as to say that any man could plan an appropriate play system for a city, without first making a study of the conditions that the playgrounds must satisfy.

The Survey a New Business and Social Method

Ever since the Pittsburgh Survey was made by the Russell Sage Foundation, it has been the accepted doctrine that every large undertaking should be preceded by a careful study of the conditions. There is now a Bureau of Surveys under the Russell Sage Foundation. The vice commissions in the different cities nearly always base their recommendations on a rather careful study of their problem. Since the study of Gulick and Ayres in New York, the educational survey has been the proper thing. The agricultural colleges are attempting to carry on agricultural surveys in all the states, and in general the survey may be said to be the orthodox beginning of any well-considered project. Stated in its simplest terms, it is an attempt to find out what the problem is before its solution is undertaken. As such it is a requirement of the commonest of common sense. The first recreation survey made in this country was made by the author in Washington, for the Playground and Recreation Association of America, but since that time such surveys have been undertaken in many cities.

What the Survey Should Discover

In connection with the schools, the survey should discover the area, equipment, and condition of all school grounds; the number of hours per week devoted to play and physical training in each grade of the elementary and high school; the number of physical trainers employed; (In Gary, the physical trainers represent one fourth of the entire teaching force and they should probably never represent less than one tenth in any city system.) the number of gymnasiums, the number of swimming pools; the number of tennis courts, basket ball courts, baseball fields, football fields, and running tracks; the number of books on play in school libraries.

For the city at large, the survey should seek to find the number and ages of the children, their present activities in their leisure time, and the effects of these activities as shown in their physical and social development, the present play facilities, and the possible sites that might be secured in acquiring a system of recreation grounds. In securing the number and ages of the children, the school registration, or, better, the school census, serves as a fairly satisfactory guide. The present activities of the children and young people will have to be a matter of personal study, and for the effects of these conditions, physical tests and the records of the juvenile court may be taken. Play authorities disagree as to just how far it is desirable to go in the investigation of the details of each of these items, but there is little disagreement that the survey should include them.

THE AGES OF THE CHILDREN AND YOUNG PEOPLE

It is necessary to know not only how many children a play system is to accommodate, but also their approximate ages; as entirely different facilities will need to be provided for the young men and women from those furnished to the small children, and the working boys and girls will have to be provided for at night. As has been said, the school census, which records every person in the city under twenty-one, serves as a fairly good guide, both to the number and ages of the children.

It may be supposed that the proportion of children to adults is pretty much the same in the different parts of the city, and that the most crowded part is the place where the playgrounds are most needed, but this is frequently not the case. The younger families with the smaller children tend to gravitate toward the suburbs where rents are cheaper and there is more room for the little people. The old and wealthy parts of cities will be found to contain few children. Permanent colonies of foreigners are apt to have a high percentage of children, while a transient colony has very few.

HOW THE YOUNG PEOPLE ARE SPENDING THEIR LEISURE TIME

Having found the numbers and ages of the young people, the next subject of inquiry should be how they are spending their leisure time. The problem naturally divides itself into three parts. What are the little children doing? What are the school children doing after school and on Saturdays and Sundays, and what are the working boys and girls doing in their leisure? There are no records that will help much in securing this information, but the information is easily secured. The investigator need only go about the city where the children are and put down on a pad of paper what each is doing. The activities are easily classified, and the records are easily made. The results are sure to be interesting. There is no phase of the work which more strikingly illustrates the need of the survey than the opinion of adults in this regard. The people who object to supporting playgrounds usually call themselves practical people, but it is wonderful how unpractical and almost feeble-minded their suggestions look when confronted with the facts. In a town of northern Illinois, a number of people said that they did not believe in furnishing playgrounds for the children because the children ought to work. But in a number of trips over the city, I was not able to find a single child that was working, outside of a few boys who were carrying papers. It was evidently not a case of play or work, but a question of play or idleness. Again a number said, "Playgrounds are not needed in this city; the children can play in —— Pasture." Observation showed a large pasture well within the city. It had a high barbed-wire fence around it, and never at any time did I find a child there.

In the city of Houston, Texas, there were a number of people who felt that playgrounds were not needed because "there were plenty of places where the children could play." In two trips about the city in the time after school, in the observation of 123 children, the first night I found 3 were riding bicycles, 5 were running errands, 4 were chasing each other, 70 were loitering up and down the street, and 40 were loafing or playing listlessly in front of their houses. A second evening, I was able to locate 229 children; of these, 1 was studying, 5 were reading, 2 were looking at pictures, 2 were caring for babies, 4 were going errands, 7 were carrying papers, 1 was watering the lawn, 2 were swinging, 3 were playing with pet rabbits, 5 were playing at keeping house, 2 were rollerskating, 9 were bicycling, 4 were playing catch, 46 were playing ball (as a result of organized contests going on in a nearby school yard), 40 were strolling on the street, and 90 were loafing. Thus 131 out of the 229 were doing nothing of advantage to any one, and the baseball, which was found only in this section, was apparently directly due to a series of school contests which were going on in a neighboring school yard every evening.

THE NEED OF THE EVENING PLAYGROUND

Should playgrounds be lighted for use at night? There are three kinds of information that are of prime importance to the solution of this problem. What proportion of the young people are working during the day, so that they cannot use the playgrounds then? Is the ground shaded enough and cool enough so that the children will enjoy using it by day, and what are the children at present doing in the evenings? Here the question comes largely to a study of the poolrooms, dance halls, moving-picture shows, pleasure parks, ice-cream counters, saloons, etc.

THE NEED OF THE SUNDAY PLAYGROUND

One of the acute questions of the play world is whether or not the playground is to be open on Sunday. The information that is needed is, first, the nature of the community in which it is placed. If it is in the midst of a colony of orthodox Jews or Seventh Day Adventists, Sunday will be the day when the community itself will most desire to use the playground. In communities where the inhabitants are largely recent immigrants from the continent of Europe, the same will be true. Nearly all the great athletic events and play festivals in Germany take place on Sunday afternoon. On the other hand, if the playground is in the midst of an orthodox Protestant community, it probably will be unwise to open the playgrounds and ball fields on Sunday forenoon at least. But, after all, the really conclusive answer to the social desirability of having the playgrounds and ball fields open on Sunday is what the young people are doing on Sunday under present conditions. What do the police records for Monday morning show?

WHAT ARE THE YOUNG PEOPLE DOING IN THE SUMMER VACATIONS?

It would be very interesting to know how many parents take their children out of the city for a longer or shorter period during the summer and why they do it. Every such trip takes out of the city much money, and often spends the savings of a year. It is desirable that children should know the country and spend a good deal of time there. But conditions are seldom wholesome for them around summer resorts. It is surely bad business policy for a city to drive its people to the resorts for their recreation, because it has failed to make proper provision for it at home. It is probable that more money goes out of most cities for this reason every summer than it would cost to maintain a very expensive system of public recreation. These figures are not easy to secure, but in any typical school it is not hard to find how many weeks were spent out of town in the aggregate, and the total for the city can be estimated from this. Even if the expense of these weeks of absence is very moderately estimated, the amount of money thus taken out of the city will be found to reach an enormous total.

RESULTS OF THE LACK OF PROPER PLAY FACILITIES.

We have no satisfactory measure or statement of the results of inadequate play facilities upon children. It is probably the lack of these statistics that has made the play movement go more slowly than some other social movements have done. The results must be recorded on the physical, intellectual, and social side. The only study that has thus far yielded much that is definite was the study in Chicago, which seemed to show a decrease of nearly 50 per cent in juvenile delinquency. It is not at all impossible, although it would take time and money, to get a measure of the physical results of these conditions.

The year following the introduction of organized play into the curriculum of the schools of Prosheim, Germany, the number of days' absence on account of sickness was reduced nearly one half. Our school hygiene departments ought to be required to show for every city the absences due to sickness. This is, of course, a direct measure of the things that they are supposed to promote, and is the only way of estimating the need of and the efficiency of the department. These would be also the facts which would be most useful to the play promoters.

There can be no question but that the development of motor skill and grace comes largely through play. It is doubtful if one ever gets a buoyant, elastic step and sprightly carriage by any other means. The peasant peoples of Europe, whose physical development has come mostly from work or formal gymnastics, have often seemed like awkwardness personified. But neither awkwardness, grace, nor motor skill are easily measured, and it is well-nigh impossible to secure statistics of grace.

On the side of physical development, it should not be so difficult, as we have three methods of measurement. The one is by direct anthropometric and dynamometer tests of physical development and strength, a second by the test of the Public School Athletic League, and the third by pedometer records of activity. We are getting a series of anthropometric records from a number of cities now, and we already have standards fairly well worked out for height and weight for the different ages and races. It seems to be fairly well determined that exercise and food are the two external factors which condition growth. We have no careful and full dynamometer records of the strength of school children. These would require time, but would be very valuable, as they would give a direct measure of the effects of the child's daily life in terms of strength. The test of the Public School Athletic League is more easily tried and is an advantage in itself. The first test is for boys under thirteen to jump 5 feet, 9 inches standing, chin a bar four times, and run a 60-yard dash in 8 seconds. In Washington we tried this test in all the playgrounds, but did not find a boy who could do the three things. After four summers of organized play we tried the test again. There were five hundred boys who did the three things. There were more than two thousand boys who could do one or two of the three things. Doubtless the same progressive development has taken place in other cities. As the result of a careful investigation in Germany of those passing a creditable physical examination on entrance to the German army, the numbers varied in the different cities from 28 per cent in Berlin to 72 per cent in Mulheim. This was in almost direct ratio to the play facilities that were available in these cities.

Probably the most valuable test that could be secured, however, would be a pedometer record of activity. I am myself convinced that in closely built up cities that make no provision for play, the average activity of the children is two or three miles a day less than it is in the cities that make ample provision. This opinion is based on a brief pedometer study which I made in Worcester, Mass., several years ago, and on my observation of children in all parts of the country. It was the listlessness of the play in Washington that led us to organize the contests there. It is probable that the daily activity of the children during the warmer months in the South is two or three miles a day less than it is in the North; and that when the nervous system has become habituated in childhood to the daily development of a small amount of energy, it will be difficult to greatly increase this rate later in life. In other words, if the child does not have an opportunity for energetic play, his later life will not be as energetic as it might otherwise have been. This is, of course, the same principle of development through training that lies at the basis of all education. Joseph Lee has said the same thing in another form when he said, "The child without the playground is father to the man without a job." If pedometer records should show that the average activity of the children of one city is nine miles a day and that the average activity of the children of the second city is only six miles a day, we may safely infer that the children of the second city will show only a little more than two thirds of the physical development of the children of the first city, that they probably will not be quite as tall or heavy, and that the number of absences from school, on account of sickness, will be considerably greater. Also it is true that when the boys and girls of the second city grow up they will not be as energetic as the children of the first city. No body of citizens would be willing to have it said that all of these things were happening in their city because they had failed to make provision for the proper play of the children. Hence if this data could be secured from enough cities to fix a standard, it would solve the question of play propaganda.

The Study of the Existing Play Facilities

The play problem of any city is naturally divided into three parts, corresponding to the ages of the young people. These three parts are: play for the little children who have not yet entered school, play for the school children, and play for adolescents. The three corresponding types of playgrounds are: the dooryard, the school ground, and the park, athletic field, and municipal playground by day and the social center and municipal gymnasium at night for the adolescents. A study which will determine the actual needs must cover the yards of the house, their size and condition, the size, condition, and use of the school yards, and the presence of athletic fields, swimming pools, etc., in the parks, social centers, and the schools.

SIZE AND CONDITION OF THE DOORYARDS

Parents will often say that they do not believe in playgrounds, as the children ought to play at home. However, it will be found, in most cases, that there is no provision for the children's play at home, and that the front yard is inhabited by flower beds and the back yard by ash cans. Probably not more than one or two per cent of city dooryards contain any considerable equipment for the play of the children. It will often be found that a lot two hundred feet deep will not bring any more than a lot one hundred feet deep, showing how little value parents put on play opportunities. Many city blocks are so small that when a good-sized house is put back a reasonable distance from the street there is almost no space in the rear. When the blocks are only an acre and a half to two acres in size, it may be taken for granted that there can be little play in the dooryards, unless the lots are very wide or all the residents will turn their back space into a common for the children. It will be found, in general, that almost no children are playing in the yards of the houses where the blocks are so small. On the other hand, where the blocks are three or more acres in size and are kept in reasonably good condition, these yards often offer an excellent place for the play of the little children. The children who are under six have all their time for play. Their health is largely dependent on their being much in the open air. They cannot go far by themselves. Every yard should provide the necessary equipment.

If the yards of the houses, then, are adequate, it will mean two things of importance for the play system of the city. It will mean that the city in that section is scattered and that there will not be a large child population per acre. It will mean also that little if any public provision needs to be made for the children less than six years of age.

The survey should indicate the approximate size of the blocks, the width of the parking line in front, and the size and condition of the back yard; also whether or not there is any equipment for the play of the children, although, in general, it can be taken for granted that there is none. The back yard is the proper place for the sand bin, the slide, the seesaw, and the swing, but if the parents will not provide these for the little children, it is best for the community to furnish them in the playground. It must be remembered that the dooryard in general can provide for the play of the little children only, and affects the problem of play for the children of school age very little. There can never be vigorous games, such as the older ones should play, in the dooryard. Doubtless this survey of the dooryards seems formidable, but in actual fact a mere stroll through the neighborhood with eyes open and pencil in hand will reveal most that needs to be known.

THE SIZE AND CONDITION OF THE SCHOOL GROUNDS

In some cities the schools themselves furnish fairly adequate space for the play of school children, but, in not a few cases, this space is entirely unutilized. No new playground should ever be purchased until it has been determined that there is no city-owned property that is already available, and the school yards should naturally be investigated first. Where the school yards are an acre or more in extent, it would be folly to purchase other small grounds for play. It is a good thing to get a mechanical drawing of each school yard. This can often be done by the upper classes as a lesson in mechanical drawing. It will be as valuable a lesson as they could possibly have, as it will deal with actual conditions, and will appeal to the children as useful. The drawings should indicate directions, distances, the size of areas, presence of trees or shade, nature of surface, presence of fences and the like, also the condition of the yard and whether or not there is any play apparatus in it, the number of children in the school, and the number of square feet of playground for every child. I secured such a set of drawings of the Washington school yards when I first went there. We used them constantly, and the superintendent sometimes sent down to borrow them. These figures show at once whether any further play facilities are needed in that section. By adding all these areas and registrations together, it is possible to find the average number of square feet per pupil furnished by the school yards of the city, though here it is necessary to avoid the vitiation of the results from adding in large outlying tracts in connection with new schools with small registration. In some cities such a study will show such a gross deficiency that it will be good campaign material for immediate enlargement of the school yards or the provision of other playgrounds. In general it may be said that every school should have at least one block of ground, if the blocks are less than four acres in size. There should be not less than one hundred square feet of playground for each child connected with the school.

Wherever the school grounds are reasonably adequate, the play of the school children belongs there, and the plan need make very slender provision for their play outside, except that it must furnish a place for swimming, wading, baseball, and tennis for the older children.

If, for any reason, it is impossible to get the mechanical drawing of the school yards, the estimate of the superintendent of schools may be taken as to the size and suitability of the yard for play, and the registration of the school may be put in by the school clerk.

The condition of the school grounds is of importance, as a large part of them are in wretched condition. Often they have never even been leveled off since the cellar was dug. Ashes will often be found strewn about the yard as well as brickbats, stones, paper, etc. The ground is frequently gullied out by the rains and obstructed by the projecting roots of trees. If all the schools of the country should be dismissed early this afternoon, and the older boys set with hoes, rakes, and shovels to putting the ground into condition, probably 25 per cent of them at least would be improved 100 per cent thereby.

VACANT LOTS

To most people, who have not thought much about it, a playground is a place to play, and there is no problem if there are vacant lots available. These people have almost completely misunderstood the play movement and its meaning, for it has not grown chiefly out of the congestion of our cities but rather out of the new social conditions and the new psychology. The vacant lot makes little difference in the need of playgrounds, but it makes great difference in the possibility of securing them. The vacant lots do not belong to the city, and the child is usually a trespasser and often a nuisance there. They will soon be built up in any growing city, if they are not speedily purchased. In a study of available sites in Washington in 1908 there were found 113 sites large enough for playgrounds. Sixteen of these were built upon the next year, showing that six more years at the same rate would put an adequate playground system almost beyond the reach of the District. The vacant lot does not attract the small children or the girls, who need the play facilities more than the boys do. If anyone will keep track of the attendance of any particular vacant lot he may choose, he will find that it will average less than one per cent of the school registration from the neighborhood. Such a ground is used by the big boys for baseball in the spring and football in the fall, but it will be found that a large proportion of the games break up in a quarrel or dispute. It will be found also that a great deal of the language would not be allowed to go through the mails. The presence of such vacant lots in the neighborhood makes little difference in the attendance at organized playgrounds.

CONDITION OF THE STREETS

Most people imagine that, if the playgrounds are provided, it is going to keep the children off the streets, and in fact it does to a large extent. All of the children who are on the playground are off the streets, and most of them would probably have been there if there had been no playgrounds. But the street is so much more accessible that the children will probably always play there, if the street is suitable, more than they do in the playgrounds. There is nothing inherently demoralizing in street play. It is the play in the alleys and stables and lumber yards that is apt to be harmful. If a street is little traveled, fairly wide, asphalted, and reasonably well shaded and cleaned, it serves for much play, and the playgrounds for such a section do not need to be as large as they do in a section where it is paved with cobblestones, unshaded, and left in a filthy condition, or as they would if it were much frequented by automobiles.

PARKS AND THEIR FACILITIES FOR BASEBALL AND TENNIS

One objection that was usually made by some member of Congress to the playground appropriation for the District was that there were so many parks that the playgrounds were not needed, but anyone who knows much about the small circles and triangles of Washington must know that while they answer more or less for romping or horseplay, they are not adapted to games. The same things can be said of any of the small ornamental parks of our cities. In the larger parks there generally are facilities for sports and games, and, if there are adequate baseball diamonds, tennis courts, and swimming places, these with ample school yards may provide for all the play needs of the city. It should be the policy to locate tennis grounds, ball fields, and swimming places within about a mile of each section if possible, and in general these should be along car lines, as the older young people use these facilities and can often afford to pay car fare. All of these available sites should be summed up and listed before new facilities are purchased by the city.

SWIMMING FACILITIES

All available natural facilities for swimming should also be listed, and, if possible, the statistics of drowning from swimming in these places should be secured.

When all of these data have been obtained, it should be possible to tell the need of the playgrounds and approximately where they should be located and what facilities they should contain. If the yards are large, there will need to be little provision for the small children, and the playgrounds will not need to be so large because there will be fewer children within a given radius. If the school playgrounds are large, there need not be much provision for the ordinary play of the school children, and the problem will mainly be to reach the working boys and girls and the young men and women, but there should be provision also for tennis, baseball, and swimming for the older school children, unless the school also has space for these games. If the streets are asphalted and well paved, the children will have much of their play there, and the playgrounds need not be as large as would be necessary in a section where the streets are paved with cobblestones so that they cannot be used for play.

DANCE HALLS, POOLROOMS, AND SALOONS

These have no direct relationship to the playground, but the playground will be a new and effective rival of all of these institutions, especially if it is open at night and really suitable to the social enjoyment of the young men and women.

If a city shows a surplus of such institutions, this may be the best possible reason for opening public gymnasia, reading rooms, swimming pools, and public dances. It is certainly an abundant reason for asking that all the play facilities of the city should be open at night as well as by day.

THE LOCATION OF POSSIBLE PLAYGROUND SITES

All the studies that have been made of playground attendance indicate that the maximum range of playground effectiveness is not more than one half mile, but that the younger children do not go regularly much over a quarter of a mile. This would indicate that there should be at least as many playgrounds as the city has square miles of territory. This does not imply, however, that so many playgrounds need to be purchased unless the schools are practically without grounds. Where the school grounds are large enough to use, these should always be taken into consideration, and it may be that all the outside playgrounds that will be needed will be ones which have a range of a mile — which is fairly true of baseball fields, tennis courts, and swimming pools. This would be one for each four square miles of the city's surface, but the location of car lines should always be considered in selecting these sites. It is generally wiser to enlarge the existing school grounds, whenever this can be done at a reasonable price, than it is to purchase separate grounds.

In the actual selection of sites, the first thing to determine is the availability of present property belonging to the city. It is seldom possible to take a park for play purposes, because the people who live around it object, and because there are none too many parks in our cities now. There is, however, in most cities some public property that has been forgotten, and in some cities there is much such property. This property is difficult to find, because it is seldom listed in any one place. It may be land that was purchased earlier for stables, waterworks, schools, hospitals, or other purposes, or it may be land that has reverted to the city for the nonpayment of taxes or for other reasons. The tax-exemption sheets were the only ones that showed the public and semi-public property that might possibly be used in Washington.

In the older cities there are often a number of cemeteries that have been abandoned for burial places, and frequently all the bodies have been removed. We found in Washington that thirteen cemeteries had been abandoned during the last thirty years. Nearly all the cemeteries that are well within the city will be given up sooner or later. London has secured more than sixty of these for playgrounds during the last forty years, and it is said that there are five hundred others that will soon be taken for this purpose. The cemetery sites, in general, will have to be purchased, but they can usually be had much more cheaply than any other similar pieces of property. A large number of these have been secured in American cities during the last decade. One is reminded of the request of Mayor Johnson, of Cleveland, that they should bury him where the children might play over his grave.

There are many who doubtless think this a desecration. But we feel very differently about it now from what we did a few years ago. Most millionaries would be ashamed to invest a considerable proportion of their fortune in a mausoleum, and more and more our wealthy men are erecting tombstones in the shape of libraries, fountains, and similar public gifts. From the nature of the case it is not less fitting that children should play over the graves of the dead than that flowers should grow there, and it must be remembered that in any case the graves have generally been vacated, the tombstones destroyed, and all traces that might serve to identify the graves removed. It will be found also that these neglected graveyards soon become a tangle of luxuriant vegetation, which is likely to become the worst sort of a resort for drinking and vice, so that they are often the chief "hang-outs" of gangs of tramps and loafers, and the place of seclusion sought by immoral boys and girls. A careful study will also generally find a constant usurpation, at least in the South, by the surrounding property owners and tenants, so that the size of these neglected cemeteries is likely to grow less and less from decade to decade.

Nearly or quite all reservoirs that are located within the cities must be abandoned or covered. They are subject to all sorts of defilement, and the land is really too valuable to be devoted to such use. These old reservoirs, with their sloping sides, make a natural athletic field and stadium. Pittsburgh and Baltimore have each secured one for a playground. The city of Reading, Pennsylvania, has covered one of them for a rink for the roller skaters.

The low places around a city can often be filled in so as to remove a nuisance and make a splendid pleasure ground very cheaply. There is an enormous amount of waste material that is being produced by every city every year. In a hundred years, the waste of New York City would probably make solid land of New York harbor, if it were all deposited there. Several years ago sixty-five acres were built on Rikers Island from ashes alone in a single year. If a city would develop beforehand some plan for the depositing of the ashes, dirt from cellars, and streets excavated, cans, bottles, and other solid waste, it could fill in valleys, ponds, and lakes, make embankments, and build mountains at will. A few years ago I climbed a high hill, with a good observatory on top, in the outskirts of Leipzig, which I was informed was built in this way. It was covered with grass and flowers and even had some good-sized trees. The children of many of our prairie cities would appreciate such an artificial slide and playground. Chicago has been very successful in building Grant Park from waste materials, and the new Chicago Plan calls for a series of outlying islands and lagoons that are to be largely constructed in this way. Outlying islands protect a harbor from storms and add greatly to its scenic attractiveness. They furnish the most delightful and accessible pleasure grounds that a city can have. Many cities might develop a series of islands in this way without its costing them a cent. Belle Isle Park, Detroit, is an example of how attractive an island park may become. A large part of the parks and playgrounds of Boston have been made by filling in the ponds and marshes. The hydraulic dredge works so cheaply it may often be possible at a reasonable cost to make a harbor, suppress a mosquito marsh, and build a splendid park and playground at the same time.

It is well then to put in from the city plat-books or insurance maps all of the sites within the city that are large enough for playgrounds.

x

SLUM SITES

It is not strictly necessary that the site selected should be vacant. Mulberry Bend and Seward Park Playgrounds on the East Side of New York were made by demolishing slums. There is often a section of a city in a most unsanitary and unsavory condition, where existing conditions are a grave menace to health and morals. Sometimes this property is so cheap that it will cost little more than if the ground were vacant. The construction of a park and playground will, in nearly every case, cause a great increase in the value of the surrounding property as well.

OUTLYING SITES

Everywhere to-day we are lamenting that our unplanned cities have not left sufficient space for public purposes. The condition of the centers of such cities as New York and Chicago is well-nigh incurable, but not so the suburbs. No new section should be allowed to come in without setting aside at least one tenth of its area for parks and playgrounds, and, in the outer edge of growing cities, as soon as possible, a chain of small parks and playgrounds, encircling the city at intervals of not more than a mile should be secured. These may be used as ball fields for the present and developed into playgrounds or parks as the city needs them.

When all the possibilities have been located, these should be put in on a school or outline map of the city and preferably in different colors, so that one can see at a glance the nature of the areas indicated. After we had prepared such a map for Washington, we found that there were several sites that belonged to the city that we could secure at once without purchase, but our ideas changed greatly as to which sites were desirable. We found that some that we had hoped to secure were too near to others that we already had, while other sections were fairly well covered by large school yards and that still others were in sections where there were few children. The city that spends $100,000 on playground sites without first making a study of needs and resources probably wastes, on an average, about half of the money.

What Sort of Sites Should be Chosen?

Here park boards often make a serious mistake. A piece of hilly and uneven ground may do very well for a park, but play requires ground that is nearly level, and it is likely to cost more to level a plot of uneven ground than it would to purchase a piece of level ground in the first place.

A ravine may be a delightful place for walks and drives and shady benches. It may be a delightful place for children to stroll by themselves or in groups, but it will be almost valueless for an organized playground. Similarly, if there are no school grounds of importance, it may be worth while to purchase a plot of land not more than an acre in size, but such an area will not be worth while if the school sites in the neighborhood are of similar size. Where a playground is selected for such a city and mostly for the use of the young people, it should be not less than five acres in area, and twenty would be a great deal better. Twenty acres has been taken by the South Park Board as the standard for its future purchases. In a ground of this size, there is room for a field house, a swimming pool, athletic fields, ball fields, tennis courts, etc.

Where Should a Playground be Located?

It may seem that this topic has already been covered, but it has not in actual fact. Perhaps it may be clearer if we point out some places where playgrounds should not be located. In general they should not be located on the edge of a settled section or on a point of land. If a playground draws from a territory one half mile in radius, all of which is inhabited, there will naturally be four times the attendance that there will be if it draws from a quadrant of such circle only, or twice the attendance that it would have if there were a built-up section on one side only. The playground is essentially a neighborhood affair, and it should be located in the midst of a neighborhood so far as possible.

A playground should not be so located that the children will have to cross the railroad tracks or a boulevard that is much frequented by automobiles, or a street that is congested by traffic. This should be evident, but is often disregarded.

A playground site should be in the midst of a homogeneous population. Sections of the city often have to be regarded as separate entities, because the people from these different sections live to themselves and do not mingle with the people of adjacent sections. Children will not go from a well-to-do section into a slum to attend a playground, or *vice versa*. Children often will not go from an Irish section into a Jewish section, and so forth. All of these considerations must be held in mind. In the South the playgrounds for white and colored children must be absolutely distinct. A white playground on the edge of a colored section will draw only from the white side, and while it may be in the midst of a densely settled section, it might as well be on the edge of the city. There is always a likelihood of race conflicts on these playgrounds that are so situated. Such a playground may be the best way to overcome race antagonism and probably will be in the long run, if the two races are races that might possibly mingle, but it will be sure to reduce the attendance at first.

What Sort of Playgrounds?

If the dooryards are providing for the little children, then the playgrounds need not make much provision for them. If the school grounds are providing for the school children, then the municipal ground need only reach the older people. If there are many working boys and girls, perhaps the playground that will be most needed will be the evening playground, which suggests the social center, the public gymnasium, the swimming pool, the municipal dance hall, and the like, and by day, baseball, tennis, and swimming.

The Making of Surveys a Proper Function of a Playground Association

It will be seen that the making of such a survey as has been indicated, if done thoroughly, will involve a considerable expenditure of time and some money. There has been an attempt to indicate a maximum and minimum survey, but nothing should prevent a systematic examination of the size of the school yards and registration of the schools, the location and extent of existing property belonging to the city, and the making of a map which will show these things as well as all the pieces of property which might be purchased or borrowed for recreation purposes. If half-mile circles are drawn around these proposed sites and the school registrations from within the circle are examined, a good idea of the probable attendance at the playground can be obtained. The making of such a survey is a piece of work that belongs logically to a playground association. Associations cannot hope to maintain a playground system. All that can well be expected of them is to demonstrate the need and help the city to begin right.

Many surveys have been made and many city plans drawn which have afterwards been put away in pigeonholes and have had no considerable effect upon developments in the city. In order that a survey may be effective, it is necessary that its results shall be made known to the people of the city. It should be followed at once by some public exhibition and demonstration in which the facts discovered shall be shown in graphic form so that the superiorities and deficiencies of the city shall be apparent at a glance. The facts should be fully reviewed in the papers and commented upon editorially, but, after all, an effective educational campaign is much like the political campaign and demands much the same kind of tactics in public speeches and newspaper comment.

In connection with such a campaign, also, the interest of the public library should always be enlisted, and it should publish in the papers and put on special shelves whatever books and magazines it has dealing with play and recreation.

CHAPTER XIII

WHAT IS THE COST?

Cost to the City

If a man buys a glass of whisky for ten cents and drinks it, he knows that he is worth at least ten cents less than he was before; but if he buys a house or a piece of land for a thousand dollars, he will be worth less or more than he was, in proportion as he has made a good or a poor bargain. It seems absurd that we should confuse expenditures so very different as these two, but much of the current discussion of taxes fails to discriminate between them. There was a time when taxes were levied to secure the personal gratification of the king, who was not expected to render any service in return; taxes were like the drink of whisky that is bought for some one else. But to-day in a democracy the whole tax is supposed to come back to the people. It is either an investment or communal pay for services rendered.

Boards of trade in the different cities are generally working for a low tax rate, with the feeling that a city with a low rate must be an economical city to live in. Yet a glance over the items of any city budget shows that a low tax rate may well mean that the city will be an expensive city to live in. One of the largest items in the budget is the school tax. If we should drop the public schools, the tax would be largely reduced, but it would cost the taxpayers more to send their children to private schools than the previous school tax had been. If a city were to continue to reduce its tax rate by dropping successively its police, its street lighting and cleaning, its fire protection, etc., thus requiring these services to be paid for by the citizens individually, again the taxes would be less, but the city would be a more expensive place of residence, and the value of property would be greatly depreciated. An enormous number of things that were formerly paid for by people individually are now borne in the city budget. Probably all of these have been secured more cheaply through the city than they were by the individuals. They have also greatly improved conditions and increased the value of property. Not only does the tax in a well-governed city represent a cheap communal price for common necessities, but in all social matters the value of our own purchase is increased by every person who participates and is able to share with us in the benefits. Many taxes are not only good bargains in themselves, but they make other and larger expenditures unnecessary, as where the purification of the water supply and sanitary precautions prevent an epidemic. The important question in regard to the tax rate of any city is not how high or low it is, but "What is the city getting for it?" We should avoid always the high rate that spells incompetency and corruption, but we should avoid no less the low rate that represents the standards of the eighteenth century rather than the twentieth. It may well happen that as our municipal governments become more honest and efficient we shall intrust to them the purchase of more and more of our common necessities, and that the tax will become high in proportion as the government is efficient and economical. Such an increasing tax rate will mean almost inevitably a general rise in the standard of living and the value of property, and at the same time the city may well become cheaper and cheaper as a place of residence.

I have never yet heard of a man who boasted of the small amount that he furnished his wife to maintain the house, for it is well recognized that she will not be able to furnish the same comforts for five hundred dollars that she could for a thousand, or for a thousand that she could for two thousand. There is no reason why a city should boast of a low tax rate, for it almost inevitably means that the city is not being properly maintained. Under the same or similar conditions one city can surely not secure for ten thousand dollars an equally good government, or furnish the same utilities that are found in a city that is spending twenty thousand dollars a year. Health and morality in a large way are purchasable if a city is willing to spend the money that is necessary; but it is just these things that are always neglected by a city that is striving for a low tax rate.

If we endeavor in this way to estimate what the playgrounds are costing the cities, or what an adequate system would cost, we shall find that the ultimate expense to the city and the people may have no direct relationship to the playground appropriation. By an adequate system of playgrounds I mean a system that would reach every child, and that is open all the year round. We are now spending about $10,000,000 a year, or ten cents per capita, on public recreation. An adequate system which would really reach the people of the country would cost us $100,000,000 a year, or one dollar per capita.

PREVENTION OF ACCIDENTS

A part of the cost of maintaining the playgrounds may properly be credited to the improving of the streets. If posts or bowlders were fixed in the thoroughfares at intervals, it would be possible to steer around them without much nervous strain, but it is very difficult to steer around a playing child, because it is impossible to calculate his motions. If we run into a post, we do not injure anything but the vehicle, but if we run over a child, we may crush out a human life. Children are the greatest obstruction there is to traffic in many crowded quarters. They are putting themselves, their parents, shopmen, and all motormen, drivers, and chauffeurs under a nervous strain, which we may not realize at the time, but which will surely be recorded in drink and dissipation, in lessened capacity for work, in lessened enjoyment of life, in nervous breakdowns, and, in the next generation, in degeneracy. A friend once told me that after driving an automobile through the East Side for an hour after the schools had closed, he was scarcely able to stand, so great had been the nervous strain. The first year that the school playgrounds were opened in New York, parents came to me on two or three different occasions and said something like this: " This is the best thing the Board of Education has ever done. Before, we never took any comfort during the summer, because we were always looking out of the windows to see if the children were safe in the street. Now we send them over to the playground, and we don't worry." The street department could very nearly afford to maintain the playgrounds for the improvement of the streets.

The public street or highway is not only an avenue for commerce, but is becoming increasingly in these days of the auto a means of recreation, and the improvement of the street is usually more than paid for by the increased value of the adjoining property. In Kansas City some fifteen years ago a very ideal system of parks and boulevards was started by Mr. Kissler. The entire cost of this system was assessed against the adjacent property, the assessment decreasing with distance from the improvement. There was the bitterest opposition in the beginning, but it was soon found that the property adjacent to these parks and boulevards had increased from one hundred to four hundred per cent in value, and since that time there have been petitions from all parts of the city for an extension of the parks and boulevards, although it is understood that the entire expense will be borne by the property of the neighborhood. This seems to be a direct measure of the increase of the value of property with its increase in attractiveness for residence purposes.

There are two main elements in the growth of a city or the development of any section of country. These are the opportunities which it offers for business or the making of money on the one hand, and the advantages which it has as a place of residence on the other. The former reason is more apt to appeal to the man of the household: the latter to the women and children. The schools and playgrounds are very large elements in determining the advantages of any particular city as a place of residence for a family in which there are small children.

What is the value of public recreation to the city? California is the answer. Probably not one half of those who are living in California are making as much money there as they did in the places from which they came, but they like the climate in California, they like its parks and beaches, its automobile roads, its theaters and picture shows, and even if they do not get rich they prefer to live where they enjoy themselves to making more money in less pleasant surroundings.

THE VALUE OF THE LAND

If cities are free to sell or exchange the land they acquire, within a growing city, almost any purchase of land at a reasonable price will be a good investment, because the city can borrow the money at a low rate of interest, it will not need to pay taxes, and it thus secures to itself the unearned increment in the value that comes from the growth of the city. For the money spent for playgrounds, the city will have the land which will be worth as much as the money.

SOCIAL INSURANCE

A part of the money that is spent on the maintenance of playgrounds may properly be put down as social insurance. There is a growing feeling of discontent among the workers of the world, a feeling that the worker has not had his just share of the product, that present conditions of poverty, low standards of living, and long hours of labor that mean nothing to the spirit are unnecessary and unjust. The worker not only feels that he has not had his share, but he is developing and enlisting leaders for his cause, and he is feeling a new sense of power. We are sitting on the lid of an industrial volcano, that might in almost any decade rend our commercial world in sunder and bring forth destructive strikes, anarchy, or French Revolutions. The reasons for discontent are not industrial alone. The focus of the whole matter is the difficulty under existing circumstances of leading a life that is worth living. Neither the work of the father in the factory, nor the life of the mother in the tenement, nor the play of the children on the street is satisfying to the spirit, and there has been no provision for public recreation or for a satisfying use of leisure that might feed these growing hungers. When the people of Rome grew discontented, she built the Circus Maximus and the Colosseum, and offered free spectacles to all. When Cuba rebelled, Spain built municipal theaters in Porto Rico. Doubtless a playground that can furnish safety and exercise and health and fun to the children, and a family resort in the evening, can do much to improve conditions and to quiet discontent. Perhaps the capitalists could afford to maintain the playgrounds for this reason alone.

A few years ago the Board of Trade of the city of Little Rock was seeking to promote the establishment of factories for the city. They sent a representative to Detroit to secure workers for these factories. He was empowered to offer the men fifty cents a day more than they were receiving in Detroit, but many of them were unwilling to come. He said that the first question they asked him was, what can we do on Saturday afternoons and Sundays? Here our children have good schools and playgrounds, we have a good time when we are not at work. We do not care to go where we shall not enjoy ourselves even if we do get more pay.

CITY ADVERTISING

A part of the playground cost may properly be credited to city advertising and the developing of civic loyalty. Most western cities have a large or small fund for the purpose.

There are, however, two important conditions affecting sales; the one is the making known to the prospective purchaser that you have the article; the other is having something worth buying when he comes. Commercial bodies may advertise their city as much as they choose, but, if it is undesirable as a place of residence and business, not many people will come or remain after they have come. The desirability of a city as a place of residence for the family is largely determined by the conditions surrounding children in that city. We have been singularly blind in this regard in the past, but we have an awakened conscience and perception in the matter, and better conditions are being increasingly demanded.

Wherever any considerable number of people come to appreciate any new development, this is inevitably expressed sooner or later in the value of property. It will soon be as difficult to sell a house in a city that makes no provision for public recreation as it would be in one that had no public schools. Denver seems to have realized this, and nearly every issue of the "City of Denver," which is purely a booster magazine, contains a section devoted to the playgrounds. Whenever I am locating with my family in any city for a longer or shorter period, its nearness to some available play space for the children is always a large element in the selection of any particular house, and this will shortly be true of many others.

The most effective advertising that a city can have is for the people who visit it and its own citizens, when away, to speak a good word for it. What is the value to a city of the reputation of being a progressive city? There is no answer, of course, but such a reputation is probably worth as much to a city as it is to an individual. There are now more than twenty times as many cities in the United States maintaining playgrounds as there were eight years ago, and the same rapid growth has taken place throughout the civilized world. It is no longer a question in regard to any particular city as to whether or not it will maintain playgrounds for its children, but only as to when it will make a beginning. Under these circumstances, the city's place as progressive or reactionary is largely determined by the time at which it takes up the movement.

What is it worth to a city to gain the loyalty of its children? Why should the children be loyal to any city? The reader may say, because the city is giving them an education at a very great expense to itself. It is true that the city gives the children the public schools, but it is also true that they do not always appreciate very highly this opportunity, and that the school often seems to them a hard taskmaster. The school appears to them an institution furnished by adults on account of their own desires; but the playground is something which the children desire for themselves. Anyone who has had charge in the schoolroom and on the playground knows that he gets a very different reaction in the two places. In the opportunity for play, children feel that they are receiving what they want.

KEEPING THE PEOPLE IN THE CITY

Cities are often willing to expend many thousands of dollars in money and to build great convention halls to get conventions to come to them. San Francisco raised seventeen millions of dollars for the Panama Exposition. Is it not worth as much to a city to get its own people to remain in town as it is to get other people to come there? In a city of a hundred thousand people, there are probably at least ten thousand people who go out of town for two months each summer. If they spend on an average in railroad fares, board, room, etc., five dollars a week, this would amount to fifty thousand dollars a week, or four hundred thousand dollars in eight weeks, that is taken out of the city. Certainly a large part of those who leave town for the summer do so on account of the children. If the city were made pleasanter and more wholesome for them, not so many families would leave the city. Of those who do go to the country, many would not remain away so long. Children have been known to refuse to go on fresh-air excursions, saying that they would rather stay and play in the playgrounds, and occasionally children who have gone away for six weeks have come back after a week in order that they might play on the baseball team or take part in some contest. Certainly the reasons for a child going to the country if he lives near a good playground are much less urgent than they would be if the playground were not there. Of the eighty thousand weeks that we have estimated as spent out of the city, at least ten per cent, or eight thousand weeks, would be saved to the city by furnishing an adequate system of public recreation. At five dollars a week, eight thousand weeks would represent forty thousand dollars saved to the city. The average city of one hundred thousand inhabitants is probably spending less than twenty thousand dollars on its playgrounds.

The opportunity for recreation which the city offers is nearly always a determining factor in the city's growth. All over the country rural communities and small villages are decreasing in population while the great cities are growing; and an inquiry nearly always shows that it is the lack of recreation and social life in the small places that leads to the townward migration. Almost any talk with country boys or girls reveals the same condition. They are out for a good time and they want to go where there is an opportunity for it. Playgrounds, parks, theaters, and various recreation resorts in the cities are powerful lodestones for rural and village dwellers, and the development of adequate recreation facilities is one of the most effective ways of stimulating the growth of the city.

This argument applies with special force to all forms of recreation for adults. Grown-ups are ofttimes singularly blind to the needs of children, but they always appreciate an opportunity for a good time themselves. This means that sooner or later all cities must take over and maintain the moving picture shows, dance halls, and social centers, from pure self-defense. The commercial dance halls are the hunting ground of the prostitute and the procurer and are often the cause of the delinquency of our boys and girls. In the defense of public morality, the city may well take over and manage its dance halls. The social center in the school is already a public institution with most of these features. The business men must realize that anything that organizes the social life and intensifies it tends to make the city more attractive, that every new friendship formed is a tie which binds people to the locality, and that in proportion as this life is intimate will the present residents be unwilling to leave and others will be drawn within its borders. This influence, of course, cannot entirely overcome business conditions or bring people to or keep them in cities where there is no work for them to do; but, other things being equal, it will be one of the strongest forces toward the growth of the city. Where one city in a locality makes such provision, other cities will be compelled to do so for self-protection.

If the country and small towns would keep their population, they also must provide that their people enjoy the life within their boundaries.

Two or three years ago I became interested in the social center development in Barnes County, North Dakota, and talked with a number of people who had helped to initiate the movement. They said that at the time they organized their farmers' clubs and social meetings more than one half of all the land in that district was for sale, but that now there was no land for sale. The farmers had made friends, had become attached to the locality, and did not wish to leave. The social organization had nearly doubled the value of the property.

The town of four or five thousand inhabitants may well make as good provision in the way of moving pictures, playgrounds, social centers, and similar facilities as the large city, and it will surely find it good business to do so. It is almost impossible in the large cities to furnish adequate opportunities for baseball, football, and tennis, but these can be furnished at comparatively slight cost by the small towns. Anything which knits together the social life forms a web in which the individual is held. It twines about him threads which he must strain or break if he is to go elsewhere, and each will be like stretched cord to bring him back if he has gone away. And in actual fact much of our surplus beyond what is required for the actual necessities of life goes to some form of recreation, and no city can afford to drive its people to get their recreation in other cities or resorts because it has failed to make suitable provision. Hundreds of millions of dollars are spent each year in the resorts of Europe, Florida, California, and New Jersey, which would undoubtedly have been saved to local cities if they had made better provision for the recreation of their people.

The last census gives Chicago 2,185,283 people. It is spending about five hundred thousand dollars a year on its playgrounds. These figures mean that for a system of playgrounds, open all the year round, Chicago is paying less than twenty-five cents per capita, the price of a half-afternoon spent in a cheap, and probably demoralizing, vaudeville show. What have those centers done for Chicago? They have Americanized grown immigrants more effectively than any other agency. They have given foreigners a loyalty to their adopted country that they did not have before. They have brought the people together and created a community sense. They have reduced by twenty-eight per cent the number of juvenile arrests in their neighborhood, and they have increased by thirty-two per cent the successful dealing with the children placed on probation. There are probably several thousands of people who come to Chicago every year in order to see its playgrounds, or who remain over longer than they intended in order to do so. How many thousands or hundreds of thousands of dollars this represents, it is hard to say. It doubtless keeps in the city more money than its cost of maintenance. Jane Addams has said that the city is saving in the expense of delinquency alone more than this cost.

THE COST OF CRIME

It is not likely that many who have led a life of rectitude up to eighteen or twenty enter upon a life of crime after that.

Probably ninety-five per cent of all adult delinquents were juvenile delinquents also, though they may never have been arrested. In an article in the *American Journal of Sociology* for September 1914, Mr. A. W. Trawick states: "Mr. Eugene Smith in 1900 estimated the number of persons who lived wholly or in part by theft, forgery, embezzlement, and similar offenses at 250,000 in the United States, and placed their annual income by misappropriation at $1600 each, or a total of $400,000,000." . . . And again: "The United States, according to figures generally accepted by students of the problem of crime, pays annually for police, criminal courts, prisons, jails, and like institutions, the sum of $200,000,000, which, added to the $400,000,000 abstracted by thieves, burglars, and embezzlers, makes a total of $600,000,000 annually paid for crime." . . . "Reformatories, schools of correction, and houses of refuge being a part of the educational institutions are not included." This vast sum does not include either the loss of productive energy due to the fact that the criminal class do not produce. It does not include the expense of locks, vaults, and safety devices. It does not even consider the loss of time that comes from taking precautions or the many things that we do not do or do at nervous expense on account of the haunting fear of the criminal.

If we could stop the production of juvenile delinquents, we should probably stop at least ninety per cent of the crime of adults. If we may trust the Chicago statistics as to the effect of the playgrounds on juvenile delinquency, we might expect an adequate and well-administered system of playgrounds to prevent or cure about fifty per cent of the juvenile delinquency, and so to save the country about three hundred millions of dollars annually in the cost of crime, a rather tidy sum, which would maintain all the playgrounds in the country for thirty years. But, if we suppose that the playgrounds would only reduce delinquency and crime by ten per cent, this would still amount to sixty millions of dollars, enough to maintain our existing playgrounds for six years. When we consider, also, the indirect expenses of crime, this estimate seems moderate.

Throughout the civilized world during the last few years there has come a general demand that industries should bear the expense of the injuries which they cause, and compensate their workmen or the families of their workmen for all injuries suffered, either through accident or through the unhealthful conditions which they have furnished. The result has been that the great machine shops have begun to protect their buzz saws and dangerous machinery so as to prevent accidents which apparently had heretofore caused them little concern. There can be little doubt but that the city's responsibility for the welfare of its citizens is at least as great as the responsibility of the factory to its workmen, and that the city is morally responsible for the delinquency and the ruined lives which result from slum conditions and its neglect of the social welfare. It is not likely that there will ever be a law which will hold cities legally responsible for the devastation of human life which comes from this neglect, but if such a law should ever be enacted, cities would find their neglect of fundamental social needs more costly than any conceivable provision for the public welfare might be.

THE COST OF PREPAREDNESS

Congress, during the years 1916 and 1917, has appropriated several billion dollars for preparedness, but has thus far never seemed to take into consideration the fact, which is generally admitted by all authorities, that the physical and social condition of the man behind the gun is at least half the problem. Germany, for a generation, has emphasized play and physical training and the maintenance of good physical condition as almost a religious duty for every good German, in order that he might be ready in case of war.

Not only is it necessary that those who are going to war should be able to carry a gun and the necessary supplies, to make long marches without undue exhaustion, and to bear the privation of the trenches and exposure to winter storms, but the loyalty of the citizen and his willingness to sacrifice himself for the country is crucial to success. The boy generally feels more grateful for the playground than he does for the school, and, if we are to spend five hundred million dollars on preparedness, two or three hundred millions of it should go toward building up the physique, health, and loyalty of the coming generation.

Cost to the Individual

Our present average tax rate is said to be $15.82 per capita. If this is multiplied by one hundred millions, we shall have a total direct tax of one billion, five hundred eighty-two million dollars for the country. Add to this our various indirect taxes for the national government, and we shall have two billions and a half a year in taxation. According to the best statistics that the Playground and Recreation Association of America was able to gather from the cities, they spent during the year 1914 approximately eight million dollars on playgrounds. These statistics are incomplete, as a considerable number of expenditures are not reported, but the total is probably less than ten millions. This is only two fifths of one per cent of two and a half billions. Or, to apply it to the individual, out of a total annual tax of twenty-five dollars he is spending only about ten cents on public recreation. Now recreation is the most essentially social and communal activity of which we have any knowledge. We can work by ourselves, or study by ourselves, but we cannot play by ourselves. We are spending at least five dollars per capita on commercial amusements of very doubtful value.

It remains to consider the direct effect of playground expenditures upon the private expenses of the individual. How far will this increase of taxes be compensated by decreased personal expenses? Of course, this question cannot be answered with any definiteness. It will vary with the individual and the section of the city. But it may be worth considering that the fees from one merry-go-round would support two playgrounds, and that the playground is much the cheapest institution we have. If the city does not provide the playground, the parents must provide more toys and apparatus to amuse the children. It costs less than half as much to maintain a playground for a child as it would to purchase a doll or a doll carriage for a little girl, or an express wagon for a boy. Yet no one can imagine that these toys have at all the same value for children that the opportunity for vigorous play has, and we spend sums with the greatest unconcern for candy, ice cream, and theater tickets for them, which are in the aggregate many times what would be required to maintain an adequate system of playgrounds. If there are no playgrounds, we will also take them on more excursions and to more places of amusement.

In a number of cities, playgrounds have been started at which a charge of from fifty cents to a dollar a week for each child has been made. These playgrounds have often proved popular. At the World's Fair in St. Louis and at the World's Fair in San Francisco there were playgrounds in which children might be placed for a small fee. They were generally crowded. We do not wish to encourage mothers to neglect their children or prompt any movement that will make the relationship between parent and child less intimate, but it is often a great relief to the mother if she can send her small children where they can play in safety during the time that she is doing her morning or afternoon work, and it is very much better for the children to have vigorous exercise outdoors than it is to be moping about or getting into mischief in the house. In many homes a nurse girl is employed to take care of the children simply as a relief to the mother. If there were a well-directed playground in the neighborhood, children might be sent there at times and the nurse girl would not be so necessary.

In the recent Child Welfare Exhibition in Kansas City, it was shown that commercial amusements (dance halls, pool rooms, theaters, and an excursion boat on the river) were costing the people of the city more than five millions of dollars annually. Kansas City is a city of 248,000 inhabitants, and an expenditure of five millions means twenty dollars per capita. If Kansas City is typical of the country, we as a people are spending about two billions on commercial amusements annually. The Board of Public Welfare for Kansas City estimates that twenty-five per cent of these amusements are vicious in their influence. It will be noticed that Kansas City is spending for these questionable pleasures eighty times as much per capita as Chicago is spending for its playground system. If one quarter of the amount that is now spent for commercial amusements were saved through facilities furnished by the city, which is a modest estimate, probably less than the actual saving, this would be five dollars per capita, five times as much as the adequate system that we have outlined would cost. It is also twenty times as much as Chicago and fifty times as much as the country at large is spending on public recreation.

SAVING FROM THE TUBERCULOSIS BILL

It is estimated that from six to seven thousand school children die each year from tuberculosis. Almost all of these deaths would be prevented if these children were having the proper amount of open-air play. At the International Meeting on School Hygiene which was held in Buffalo in August 1913, it was estimated by our foremost authority that there were one million tuberculous school children in this country.

In the tests that were made on the school children of Baltimore, it was found that fifty per cent in the first grade and ninety-three per cent in the eighth grade reacted to the tuberculin test. Most of these children did not have consumption, but they were carriers of the disease, and it is generally conceded that the ranks of the adult consumptive are constantly replenished from them. At the Panama Pacific Exposition in the charts of the Anti-Tuberculosis Society, it was estimated that the annual cost of tuberculosis to the people of this country was $2,300,000,000. If we could give to every child an abundant life in the open air and strengthen his lungs by vigorous outdoor play, we should save a large part of this annual loss from consumption, which is sufficient to maintain all the playgrounds in the country for 230 years.

But it is not the tubercular children alone who would be benefited by the provision for open-air play, but all the children would be strengthened, and probably at least as many deaths from other diseases would be prevented as those from tuberculosis. Besides the deaths from disease, the playgrounds would save a considerable percentage of the deaths from street accidents and drownings from swimming in dangerous places.

If we should say that an adequate system of playgrounds and play that would reach every child would save this country twelve thousand lives, each year a little more than a twentieth of one per cent of the school population, this would seem to be a moderate estimate. If we consider these children are worth to the country a thousand dollars apiece, which would not be much of a temptation to their parents, we should again save the tidy sum of twelve millions of dollars a year.

It is usually estimated that for every death there are seven or eight people who are sick. Every one realizes that vigorous health is dependent to a considerable degree on the amount of time we spend in the open air and upon our getting enough exercise to keep the body in healthful condition. The person who lives a vigorous outdoor life and takes care of himself is almost immune from many of the troubles which prostrate the weakly child and adult.

There are more than twenty million children of public school age in the United States. If we estimate the annual doctor's bill of these children at only one dollar per capita, or $20,000,000 — and this is of course a great underestimate — we shall see that a reduction in the doctor's bill of one third would very nearly maintain all the playgrounds.

The person who develops a vigorous physique in childhood will live longer than the one who grows up imperfectly developed and puny. In some cases this may amount to fifty or sixty years; in some cases it will be only a few months; in some cases there will be no gain. It would seem likely that an adequate physical development for all children would add at least one year to the length of human life. There are about twenty millions of children enrolled in the public schools. Considering the parochial schools and the children not in school, there must be more than twenty millions of children between the ages of five and fifteen in this country. If an adequate playground system can add a year to the productive activity of twenty millions of people, this would mean twenty million years of work. If we value these years at only five hundred dollars apiece, this would be ten billions of dollars. If we credit each of the school years with one tenth of this amount, this would be a saving of a billion dollars a year. All through the lives of these twenty millions of people there would be an increased efficiency due to better health and a good physique. This should add to productive efficiency another increment at least as great as the other. To be conservative, we will throw this in with the doctors' bills and the loss of lives, and estimate the total saving through physical training and a developed vital resistance at a billion dollars a year.

INCREASING STRENGTH AND EFFICIENCY OF LIFE

At the time the playgrounds were opened in Washington, D.C., an athletic test for the Standard Button of the Public

School Athletic League of New York City was given. None of the children were able to pass. After four summers of organized play we tried the test again; more than five hundred children passed the three requirements, and more than two thousand children passed one or two of them.

Each year the average accomplishment in all the athletic contests was considerably better than it was the year before. Perhaps there is no one thing that is more determining of human happiness and human efficiency than the health and vitality that we carry with us into life. The person who is strong and well can work long hours without breaking down. His active years are longer, and all through his life he retains a cheerfulness of spirit which makes him a better companion and citizen than a person who is constantly suffering from overwork or ill health.

THE RIVAL OF THE SALOON

Public recreation is the most effective rival of the saloon that has thus far been discovered. In the homes of the poor there are no adequate provisions for sociability. The young man does not care to receive his friends in the kitchen or the bedroom, and, ofttimes, the house furnishes no other opportunity. Under the circumstances, it is no wonder that he sees them in the saloon instead. He often wishes to belong to a club, but the only clubroom that seems within his means is generally in connection with the saloon. He wishes to have a party or give a dance; the only hall available is the saloon dance hall, and in all cases the saloon expects that the hall will be paid for by the drinks that are ordered. If the city furnishes a play system with social center features, there is always a place to go to until ten o'clock every night that is physically more attractive than the saloon. There are well-lighted rooms where clubs can meet for nothing and where intoxicants cannot be had. If a party of young men wish to give a dance, there is often an opportunity. If they prefer to have gymnastics or swimming in the evening, the field house furnishes the gymnasium and the swimming pool and the physical director to see that it is worth while. If they wish to have athletics during the day, the playground furnishes the athletic field. The playground keeps the boy out of the saloon by giving him a more attractive place to go and by giving him other thoughts to absorb his mind. The personal standards and touch of the directors influence him more or less, and he soon learns that if he would excel in athletics which are apt to be his greatest interest, he must abstain from drink. Despite the temperance agitation all over the country, the per capita consumption of malt, spiritous, and distilled liquors has doubled during the last thirty years. Our drink bill now amounts to about two billion dollars per annum. There are scarcely any who would claim that any positive advantage came to the drinker or society from this enormous expenditure. At the International Congress on Alcoholism, which was held in London in July 1909, it was estimated (from a series of tests in typesetting in which a moderate portion of wine was given the workers, and where it was found that the quantity and quality of the work depreciated about ten per cent), on the basis of a population of eighty-three millions, that the loss in productive capacity in this country through drink amounted to one billion, one hundred and fifty millions a year. According to the life insurance companies, drink reduces the longevity of the habitual drinker by about twenty-five per cent. The mortality of infants of habitual drinkers during the first year is three times that of non-drinkers.

Drink is the cause more or less directly of at least half of the crime, of very many industrial accidents, of much of the poverty that robs the next generation, and of the industrial inefficiency that leads to unemployment and low standards of living. It is filling our almshouses, hospitals, jails, orphan asylums, insane asylums, and institutions for the defective and feeble-minded. By a very conservative estimate, this indirect cost must be at least as great as the direct cost. We will be conservative again and suppose that it is only two billions. If an adequate playground system saved only ten per cent of this (it would probably save twenty-five per cent), this would still be two hundred millions of dollars annually, enough to maintain our present system of playgrounds for twenty years, or the adequate system that we have been considering, for two years.

SAVING FROM THE TOBACCO BILL

The boy who attends the playgrounds is obliged to discontinue smoking for the time at least. He soon learns that he cannot succeed in athletics if he smokes, because it injures his lung capacity. The sentiment created in the playground is against it. Our tobacco bill is nine hundred millions annually. If one tenth of this were saved, this would amount to ninety millions of dollars a year.

THE VALUE OF THE SUMMER VACATION

There are probably four or five millions of children in this country whose summer vacation is wasted. The evil habits and associations formed in idleness under bad conditions fully offset any advantage that may be derived from the play and the vigorous exercise in the open air. What is the value of the summer vacation to the child? Supposedly it is worth as much as that much school, else why have the vacation? We do not set a money value on the time that the child spends in school, but we refuse to allow him to leave school early to go to work, because we believe that by so doing he is robbing his future, and the total achievement of his life will be really less with these early years given to labor than it would if he had spent them in school; which means, in the last analysis, that the child's time spent in school is worth just as much to him there as it is in his life work later. The preparation is necessary and he gains that preparation as rapidly at ten, perhaps, as he would at forty. To take a simpler illustration. A young man spends four years in a medical school and afterwards practices for thirty-six years, earning $160,000. What was the value of the four years in the medical school? In a sense it is $160,000, as everything has depended on the preparation, but more truly we may say the forty years has brought a return of $160,000; no year has been more important than any other; these four years of preparation were worth four thousand dollars a year to the student. Four million summer vacations will represent approximately fifty millions of weeks. If we estimate these weeks to be worth only five dollars a week, they will represent, if wasted, a loss of possible wealth of $250,000,000; but if we estimate that these weeks, with increasing wages everywhere, are worth ten dollars a week, then the loss will be five hundred millions of dollars.

It may be said that this chapter deals exclusively with

fictitious statistics, which must be admitted. From the very nature of the case actual statistics are impossible at present. No two persons would estimate alike, probably, the saving in the drink bill, tobacco bill, juvenile delinquency, tuberculosis, and other forms of sickness, or the private expenditures which would be made unnecessary through an adequate system of playgrounds. These savings would be different in different cities and in the same city in accordance as the system developed was efficiently or inefficiently managed. But it is believed that the figures which have been given are so conservative that it is well nigh impossible that the actual saving involved should not be at least as great as the necessary expense, and it might well be ten or twenty times as great. But in any case the values that are involved are so vital to the welfare of the community that if it were a pure extra expense, no community can afford to withhold the funds that are necessary.

Down in his heart every one knows that what we are really after is not money, but happiness, and that the wealth that does not bring increased comfort and enjoyment of life is not worth while. Gold eagles to Robinson Crusoe would be no better than the pebbles on the beach.

Public recreation is good business, yielding its own financial return; but happiness after all is what we are after, and we do not need to be paid for having a good time. It is in our leisure time and in our opportunities for sociability and the forming of friendships that most of this happiness finds expression.

When we speak of the public schools, we are accustomed to admit that they are costly, but to say that the expense is justified by the results, that an educated citizen is more valuable to the state and the city than an uneducated one, and education is necessary to the welfare and perpetuity of the state. We may give exactly the same argument with quite as much force for the playground. The playground develops the physique, gives robust health, and forms social habits. The children learn to coöperate and compete, to act together for common ends; they acquire loyalty and social feeling through group games. And these are no less important to the welfare of the state than arithmetic or geography.

If we choose to compare the grounds on which recreation and education may each lay claim to public expenditures, several notable differences and similarities may be observed. Education is held to be necessary to the welfare of the state, but Kidd has shown us that the survival of countries is not determined primarily by intellectual standards but by social and moral standards. It is in their leisure time and pleasures that people mostly fall into vice. Private schools probably cost two or three times as much as public schools, but commercial recreation costs from ten to one hundred times as much as public recreation. Education often requires seclusion and thought, but recreation is social and communal from its very nature. We do not care to play alone. It is often said that education is necessary, but play is a luxury. Neither education nor recreation is necessary to existence, as is proved by history, but both education and recreation are necessary to the larger life of the spirit. Play is the most democratic activity we know. The poor do not spend money for education, but they all spend a considerable amount for pleasure. We are not to suppose that the people of Kansas City are all rich. A large part of the five millions comes from very poor people. If the people of a city are going to have recreation at any cost, as is evident, and the city can furnish it much more cheaply than the people can secure it for themselves; if amusements privately conducted often lead to vice and crime, while public recreation may be made elevating in character, the wisdom of the city's furnishing these facilities seems evident.

In our discussion of this subject thus far, we have considered the playground as a purely economic factor; the value of the joy of childhood, of a normal child's experience, of the difference in the product of the playground and the penitentiary, has not weighed one grain in the scale. Nevertheless we all realize that the question we have considered is not primarily economic, and that within bounds of a reasonable expense, the economic aspects can scarcely claim the right to consideration. What is the value of the life of a child? What is it worth to save a man from drowning, or a woman from a burning building? What is the value of the manhood of the boy or the virtue of the girl? We do not consider finances in questions like these. Play is the central thing about the child. What is the value of the joy and forgetfulness, and comradeship of childish play? It is impiety to ask the question.

Whenever the project of maintaining a system of public recreation is brought before a city, there are always many who say: "We cannot afford it." We have seen that this view does not bear investigation. But quite apart from the economy of public recreation over private recreation, the situation has something to say to our chivalry and our sense of justice. We are spending two billions a year on drink, nine hundred millions on tobacco, and a billion or more on commercial amusements. At least three billions of this may be charged to the personal gratification of us adults. For the most part it will not leave us wiser or more efficient. We are spending somewhat less than ten millions, one third of one per cent of this amount on facilities that mean to the child at the same time a joyous childhood, a normal life, physical development, and health. The price of a theater ticket at a moderately good performance would provide a playground to a child for the entire summer. We afford the ticket, but we often say we cannot afford the playground. An adequate system of public recreation would probably cost a hundred millions a year. It would very likely save a thousand millions from other expenses. But even if it effected no saving and gave no valuable training, if we can afford to spend three billions a year on drink and tobacco, we cannot well refuse a paltry hundred millions for the promotion of health and happiness and efficiency.

INDEX

Numbers refer to pages

Accidents, legal responsibility for, 49; prevention of, 314.
Age grouping in playgrounds, 31, 32.
Agricultural secretary, 217.
Apartment houses, playgrounds on, 141.
Apparatus, for school yards, 50; need for study of value of, 228; standardized, 234; *vs.* organized play, 227; *see* Equipment.
Apprenticeship, on playgrounds, 60.
Asylum, New York Orphan, 151.
Asylums, orphan, 146.
Athletics, class, 39; for industrial schools, 168; interest in, 48; track, 77; *see* Games, Sports, Tournaments, Track, *etc.*
Automobile, 125, 219.

Badge test, Public School Athletic League, 292, 332.
Band concerts, 112.
Baseball, 36, 98, 99, 201, 202; indoor, 38, 42, 50, 175, 201, 212; in industrial schools, 168; in vacant lots, 300; space for, 38, 98.
Basket ball, 37, 50, 168.
Blind, equipment for, 154; games for, 154; gymnastics for, 158; play for, 153; schools for, 160; social recreation for, 159; villages for, 160.
Blue Birds, Camp Fire, 277.
Boulevards, 105.
Bowls, for insane, 175.
Boys' and girls' clubs, 216.
Boys' Club, Columbia Park, of San Francisco, 53.
Boy Scouts, 54, 168, 245; as citizens, 248, 261; growth of, 250; ideals of, 247, 267; organizing of, 248; origin of, 245; purpose of, 259; relation to the schools, 259; training afforded by, 248, 252.
Braucher, H. S., 17.

Camp, school, 54; summer, 73, 170.
Camp Fire Girls, "Blue Birds" of, 277; Guardians of, 278; number of, 281; organization of, 278; origin of, 271; purpose of, 272; service of, 276; social value of, 281; three degrees of, 274.
Camping, 250; *see* Camp.
Celebrations, 112; special, 113; *see* Festivals.
Cemeteries, abandoned, used for playgrounds, 303.
Chicago, park playgrounds of, lessons from, 66; cost of, 323; *see* South Park, West Park.
Childhood, play needs of, 96; Montessori Houses of, 136.
Children, in the country, 190; study of activities of, 288.
Children's gardens, 66; extra compensation for, 196.
Child work, disappearance of, 3; modern conditions of, 5.
City, advertising, 317, 321; attraction of, for country children, 191; keeping people in the, 319; waste in building playgrounds, 305.
Civic duties, of Boy Scouts, 248, 261; of girls in Gary schools, 283.
Civic enlistment, 282.
Class athletics, 39; *see* Rural schools.
Clubs, boys', 53; boys' and girls', 216; farmers', 217; rural, 216; women's, 12, 70, 71, 221.
Color scheme in playgrounds, 86.
Columbia Park Boys' Club, 53.

341

Concerts, band, 112.
Concrete construction, by children, 236; in Southern high schools, 266.
Concrete playground, at N. Y. Orphan Asylum, 150; value of, for blind, 155.
Congestion, effect of, on children, 6.
Consolidated schools, 202, 210; homes for teachers of, 197, 210; *see* Rural schools.
Control in park playgrounds, 67.
Conventions, public, 319.
Country Life, Commission, 179; Day, 199.
County, agricultural secretary, 217; organization, 223.
Courage, as Scout ideal, 252.
Courses for playground workers, 22, 51, 56, 58, 60.
Court playgrounds, 131, 137, 239, 295.
Crime, 290; cost of, 323; increase of, 8.
Criminal Insane, Indiana Hospital for, occupations at, 176.
Croquet, 175, 199, 202.
Curriculum, play in, 200.

Dance halls, municipal, 108, 321; how to survey, 302.
Dancing on street, 120.
Deaf, colonies for, 162; schools for, play in, 161.
Defectives, colonies for, 165; schools for, play in, 162.
Delinquents, colonies for, 172; director for, 169; schools for adults, 171; boys, 166; girls, 170.
Democracy, as Scout ideal, 257.
Director, cost of house for, 72; at Los Angeles, 22, 51; for reform school, 169; of play, 55, 76, 144, 218; of recreation, 115; training for, 22, 51, 56, 58, 60.
Dodge ball, 70.
Dooryard, as playground, 131, 169; size of, 295.
Drink, cost of, saved by playgrounds, 334.
Drudgery, 187.

Efficiency, in play, 30; in use of playgrounds, 33; need of, 230.
Equipment, 13, 47, 97, 132, 210, 226, 230; cost of, 239; for blind, 154; injury by, 48; making of, 232; model law governing making of by penitentiary inmates, 243; standardizing of, 228, 234; the playground without, 231; *see* Apparatus.
Erie, Pa., Home for the Friendless in, 152.
Evening playgrounds, need of, 290; value of, 66.
Excursions, 204.
Experimental play schools, at universities, 40.

Family, decreasing size of, 189.
Farm, homes, 192; spiritual starvation on, 180; women, drudgery of, 187.
Farmers' clubs, 217; value of play for, 164.
Feeble-minded, colonies for, 163; games for, 164; institutions for, 162.
Feeble-mindedness caused by drink, 334.
Festivals, municipal, 112; rural, 15, 203; *see* Celebrations, Pageants.
Field events; *see* Track.
Field houses, Chicago, 64; Los Angeles, 72; Philadelphia, 71.
Fire prevention, 264.
Football, 37, 77; for blind, 156, 264; in vacant lots, 105, 299; space for, 100.
Forestry, in schools, 197.
Four-term school, 52.
Friendship, as Scout ideal, 255; in play, 31.

Games, 79; characteristics of good, 36; for blind, 154; for feeble-minded, 164; for insane, 175; for rural home, 193; for rural school, 200, 201; in municipal playgrounds, 85; need of better, 36, 201; space for, 38, 98, 100; Spalding rules for, 240; street, 119.
Gardens, children's, 66; extra compensation for, 196.
Gary, play movement in schools of, 19, 34; repairs by boys of, 263; schools of, described, 40; training for playground workers at, 60, 283; work done at, 265; *see* Wirt.
Gary schools, of New York City, 41; *see* Wirt.
Germs on street, 121.
Girard College, 156.
Girl Scouts, 284.
Girls, clubs for, 216; needs of, 45; reformatories for, 170.

Good roads, beautifying of, 219; cost of, 220; maintenance of, 222.
Groos, Karl, 1.
Grounds, condition of, 297; of rural schools, 195; school, 45, 231.
Guardians, Camp Fire, 278.
Gulick, Dr. Luther, 15, 17, 39, 130, 246, 271.
Gymnastics, for blind, 158.

Hall, G. Stanley, 251.
Handball, 49.
Health, resulting from play, 292, 337.
Henderson, Prof. Chas. R., on supply making in prisons, 242.
Home life, 186.
Homes, farm, 192.
Horizontal ladder, 50.
Hospitals for insane, play in, 175; play for, 173.
Hours of labor, shortening of, 29; women's, on farm, 187.
Houses, for teachers of rural schools, 197; of Childhood, 136.

Idleness, effect of, 8.
Indoor baseball, 38, 42, 50, 201, 212; space for, 38, 98.
Industrial schools, play in, 166.
Insane, bowls for, 105, 175; Indiana state Hospital for, 176; play in institutions for, 175.
Institutions, for blind, 153; for criminals, 171; for deaf, 161; for delinquents, 166; for feeble-minded, 162; for insane, 175; for orphans, 146; for sick, 176; play in, 146.

Johnson, Alexander, on play, 164.
Junior, police, 264; Republic, 168.
Juvenile, court, 170; delinquency, one cause of, 260.

Kindergarten playgrounds, 131, 137, 239, 295.
Kindness, as Scout ideal, 256.

Labor, hours of, 29; on farm, 182; women's, 187.
Labor unions, 232.
Lajolla, Cal., Scrips Playground at, 213.

Landscape effects *vs.* recreational use, 104; *see* Good Roads.
Lasalle, 212.
Laundry, hindrance to play, 144.
Lee, Joseph, 16, 17, 18, 98, 119, 294.
Leisure time, children's, 51; how used, 288; preparation for, 35.
Length of life, effect of play on, 331.
Los Angeles, playgrounds of, 71.
Lots, vacant, 105; football in, 299; how to survey, for play, 299; use of, 136.

McKeever, Prof. William, 18, 60.
Model laws, playground, text, 23; equipment-making in prisons, 243.
Model playgrounds, in training workers, 58.
Monotony, 88.
Montessori, Madame, 136.
Mountains, 94.
Moving pictures, 109, 210, 321; for deaf, 161; for insane, 175; in rural schools, 210.
Municipal, dance halls, 108; festivals, 113; forests, 94; skating rinks, 108; social centers, 106; swimming pools, 107; universities, 60.
Municipal playgrounds, 13, 62; administration of, 86; necessity of, 79; attendance at, 82; equipment for, 231; of Chicago, 63; of Philadelphia, 69; politics in, 84; race problem in, 84.
Music, for feeble-minded children, 165; for insane, 175; on roofs, 139.

National parks, free lectures on, 28.
Nerve strain, in city streets, 118; in modern factories, 5.
Normal schools, place for development of play, 58.

Oakland, Cal., recreational system of, 75.
Open-air play, 42.
Organized play, effect of, on school attendance, 42; in Philadelphia municipal playground, 61; recent experiments in, 39; *vs.* apparatus, 227.
Orphan Asylum, the New York, 151.
Orphan asylums, 146.
Outlying grounds; *see* Vacant lots, Sites.

Overbrook, Pa., Institution for the Blind at, 159.

Pageants, 114, 202; *see* Festivals.
Park, facilities for baseball and tennis in, 300; lawns, 95, 101; *see* Good roads.
Parks, national, 28; public, 95, 103.
Pedometer, record of activity by, 293.
Penal colony, 172.
Penitentiaries, model law governing supply making in, 243; play equipment for, 237; play in, 171.
Philadelphia, municipal playgrounds of, 69.
Physical training, age of, 44; girls' need of, 45; schools of, giving courses on play, 57; state commissioner of, 29.
Picnic grounds, municipal, 105; rural, 223.
Picnics, 98; *see* Walking trips.
Play, at high schools and colleges, 43; at lowest ebb, 3; at rural schools, 200; at school, 30; closing streets for, 127; courses in, normal, 22, 48; courses in, university, 58, 60; director of, 55, 76, 144, 218; economic value of, 331, 317; equipment, for blind, 154; *see also* Blind; facilities for, lack of, 291; facilities, how to survey, 295; festivals, 203; for blind, 153; for deaf, 161; for criminals, 166; for defectives, 162; for delinquents, 166; for feeble-minded, 184; for hospitals, 173; for insane, 175; for institutions, 146; for sanitariums, 173; friendship in, 31; grouping in, 30; health resulting from, 292; how to survey for, 293; in dooryards, 19, 131, 169; in institutions for, *see* Play, for ———; in school curriculum, 34, 200; in schools for, *see* Play, for, ———; in schools of Gary, 41; instinct of, 1; new need of, 28; normal curriculum of, 21; on streets, 117, 128; organization of, 81, 213, 214; organized, 2, 39, 69; organized, in rural schools, 200; outside of playgrounds, 87; preparedness and, 293; physiological and social needs of, 6; public control of, 22; rebirth of spirit of, 21; separation of the sexes in, 30, 177; social grouping promoted by, 42; social needs of, 6; Sunday, 51, 100, 290; three principles of, 30; time allotted to, *see* Time;

value of, to blind, 159; deaf, 161; feeble-minded, 164; *see* Games, Sports, Names of various games *and also* Playgrounds.
Playground and Recreation Association of America, 12, 15, 326.
Playground associations, 12; function of, 309.
Playground directors, 55, 76, 115, 144, 169, 218; house of, 72; training courses for, 22, 51, 56, 58, 60.
Playground law, model, text, 23; New York, 25.
Playgrounds, administration of, 86; apartment house, 141; apprenticeship on, 60; as city advertising, 317; as social insurance, 316; at Lajolla, Cal., 213; attendance at, 31, 82; automobiles and, 125; beautifying of, 75, 85; concrete, value of, for blind, 155; conduct of, 83; cost of, Chicago, 323, to city, 311, to individual, 326; court, 131, 137, 239, 295; directors of, *see* Director; dooryard, *see* Court; education in, 122; equipment, erected by children, 235; evening, need of, 166, 290; germs in, 121; how to survey for, 293; in city blocks, 20; municipal, 62; physical results of, 292, 332; prevent accidents, 314; public building, 140; radius of influence of, 308; roof, 138; saving effected by, 334; school roof, 139; sites, 302, 308; streets as, 117; Sunday, need of, 51, 100, 290; surfaces for, 70, 124, 150, 155, 236, 266; training for workers of, 56, *see* Director; tree-planting on, 126; Union Settlement, 135; use of vacant lots for, 136; value of, for blind, 155; to city, 317, 336; without equipment, 23; workers, training for, *see* Director.
Play schools, experimental, at universities, 40.
Politics in municipal playgrounds, 78.
Pools, swimming, 102, 103, 106, 107; wading, 97.
Preparedness, and play, 11, 29, 293; cost of, 325.
Prevention of accidents, 314.
Promenade, 144.

Public buildings, 140.
Public conventions, 319.
Public recreation, facilities for, 92; in parks, 95; rival of saloons, 332; value of, to city, 315; *see* Social Centers, Pools, Skating, Dancing, Moving Pictures, *etc.*
Public Schools Athletic League, N. Y. City, 39.

Race problem in playgrounds, 84.
Recesses, 39.
Recreation, a determining factor in city growth, 320; director of, 115; facilities for, 93; financial value of, 27, 225, 335; lack of, in country, 184; need for, 27; public, *see* Public; survey, 255; subjects of inquiry in, *see* Survey; therapeutic value of, 173; value of, 315.
Reformatories, directors for, 169; for boys, 166; for girls, 170.
Reform schools, *see* Reformatories.
Reservoirs, abandoned, used for playgrounds, 304.
Responsibility, legal, for accidents, 49.
Riis, Jacob, 15.
Roads, beautifying of, 219; cost of, 220; maintenance of, 222.
Roofs, for playgrounds, 138; of apartment houses, 141; of public buildings, 140; of schools, 139; promenades, 144.
Roosevelt, Theodore, 15, 148, 179.
Rowing, 78, 104.
Rural church, 207.
Rural school, beautifying of, 195; games for, 201; moving pictures in, 210; need for reorganization of, 194; play at, 201; play equipment in, 199; teacher, social function of, 215; *see. also* Consolidated school.
Russell Sage Foundation, reports on playgrounds, 57.

Salary of play director, 76.
Saloon, doomed, 28; how to survey, 302; rivaled by recreation, 332.
Sand bins, 96, 132.
Sanitariums, play for, 173.
School, consolidated, 202, 210; for blind, 160; for deaf, 161; for delinquents, 166; four-term, 52; industrial, 166; normal, 58; play, 40; reform, 166; roofs of, 139; rural, 194, 195, 199, 201, 210; summer, 58.
School, camp, 54; day, length of, 33; excursions, 204; *see* Walking; grounds, condition of, 47; grounds, how to survey, 297; improving of, 45; size of, 23, 46, 210; rural, 195.
Scouts, Boy, *see* Boy Scouts.
Scout Master, *see* Boy Scouts.
Scouting, *see* Boy Scouts.
Seesaw, value of, 229.
Segregation, of blind, 160; of deaf, 160; of defectives, 165.
Sex, in playgrounds, 30, 177.
Skating, 103; rinks, 108.
Social center, 54, 106, 111, 208, 321; equipment for, 212; rural, economic value of, 211.
Social community, in rural districts, agencies in creation of, 207; in rural church, 207; in social center, 208.
Social groups, in play, 273; promoted by play, 42.
Social insurance by playgrounds, 316.
Social welfare, 9.
South Park, Chicago, 63.
Space, for sports, *see* Names of sports, *also* Play *and* Playground.
Sport, ideals of, value in reformatories, 170.
Sports, water, 93; *see* Athletics, Play.
Stadium, 115.
State, penitentiaries, 171, 243; roads, social value of, 220.
Statistics, of play, 21; on savings effected by playgrounds, 336.
Streets, closing for play, 127; condition of, 300; dancing on, 120; education of, 122; games on, 119; germs on, 121; play on, 117, 127; surface of, 70, 124, 150, 155, 236, 266; trees on, 126.
Summer camp, *see* Camp, Camping.
Summer school, *see* School.
Summer vacation, 51; how used, 291.
Sunday, play, 51, 100, 290; use of, 288, 290.
Supplies, *see* Equipment.
Surfacing, 70, 124, 150, 155, 236, 266.
Survey, recreation, general method, 285; California, 27; made by universities, 18; need of, 224; Washington, 16, 286.

Index

Swimming, facilities for, how to survey, 301; see Pool.
Swing, 226; value of, 227, 229.

Tax rate, 313, 326.
Team, spirit in play, 31; work, develops loyalty, 168.
Tenancy of farms, 178.
Tenement playground, 131, 133.
Tennis, 50, 101, 188, 196; for insane, 175; space for, 100.
Tests for results of play, 291.
Theater, municipal, 110.
Thrift, as Scout ideal, 257.
Time allotted for play, after school, 50; all year, 71; for girls, 45; for elementary schools, 44; in Gary schools, 41; in high schools and colleges, 43; in model law, 23, 25; in playgrounds, 68, 118; in South Park playgrounds, 63; in work and play schools, 40; necessary, 30; use of playgrounds, 33; Saturday and Sunday, 51; Summer, 51.
Tournaments, 51, 77, 83.
Toys, 327.
Track, 77; for blind, 157; see Athletics, etc.
Training, afforded by, Boy Scouts, 248, 252; Camp Fire Girls, 279; for playground workers, see Director.
Tuberculosis, cost of, 329.

Union Settlement playground, 135.
United States Steel Corporation, 234.

Vacant lots, 105, 136; how to survey, 299.
Vacation, summer, 51; how used, 291; value of, 334.
Value, of baseball, 226; of Boy Scouts, 248, 252; of Camp Fire Girls, 281; of play, 155, 317, 336; of playground apparatus, 228; of playgrounds, 66, 155, 337; of public recreation, 315, 336; of winter sports in playgrounds, 67.
Volley ball, 37, 38, 42, 50, 201; for insane, 175.

Wading pools, 97.
Walking trips, 52, 87, 199, 204, 207, 250, 260; for blind, 158.
Waste, city, 305.
Water sports, 93.
West, James E., 247.
West Park, Chicago, 66.
Wirt, Supt. William, 35, 41, 263; see Gary schools.
Women at play, 76; drudgery of farm, 185, 188.
Women's clubs, 12, 76, 77, 221.
Work, 4, 5; change in methods of, 183; disappearance of child, 3; long hours of, 184; of city departments, done by boys, 263; of women's clubs, see Clubs; of women on farms, 185, 188.
Work and play schools, at Oakland, Cal., Los Angeles, and Boston, 40.
Workers, playground, training for, 22, 51, 56, 58, 60; see Director.
Y. M. C. A., rural, 215; clubs, 216.
Y. W. C. A., rural clubs, 215.

Printed in the United States of America.